ECHOES OF WAR

ECHOES OF WAR

A Thousand Years of Military History in Popular Culture

Michael C.C. Adams

THE UNIVERSITY PRESS OF KENTUCKY

Publication of this volume was made possible in part
by a grant from the National Endowment for the Humanities.

Editorial and Sales Offices: The University Press of Kentucky
663 South Limestone Street, Lexington, Kentucky 40508–4008

06 05 04 03 02   5 4 3 2 1

CIP data available from the Library of Congress.
ISBN 0-8131-2240-6

This book is printed on acid-free recycled paper meeting
the requirements of the American National Standard
for Permanence of Paper for Printed Library Materials.

Manufactured in the United States of America

For All Our Children

Contents

Illustrations and Maps

Illustrations

Maps

Preface

Citizens Who Quest (For Knowledge)

A lthough it is often said that Americans don't appreciate history, there is actually a large popular interest in the past. Attendance at museums is healthy; historical reenactments draw thousands of weekend spectators; works of popular history sell well; The History Channel, The Learning Channel, PBS, and A&E bring us a variety of documentaries and historical dramas; Hollywood finds that movies based on historical events not only continue to draw audiences, but can be box office blockbusters.

Many academic historians are dismayed rather than comforted by what they see, however. They feel that too much in the popular arena is distorted, inadequate, shallow, and misleading, actually detracting from the serious appreciation of history as a study of important events and themes in human development. They have a point. Reenactors can accurately reproduce uniforms, equipment, the surface form and structure of past events, but a reenactment of, say, the bloodiest day in American history, at Antietam, September 1862, done without real terror, mutilations, dysentery, stench, and weeping, inevitably lacks reality. Some museums have the feel of play parks rather than centers of learning. The quality of historical programming on television varies widely, and commercial film willfully sacrifices historical authenticity for broad audience appeal.

Some popular history supports conventional beliefs at the expense of serious analysis. Many Civil War books, still among our best-selling historical product lines, tend to retell the well-worn but politically inoffensive and commercially successful tales of values-neutral military engagements rather than probing the tough and potentially divisive questions of what the war was about and what it did to Americans of

Historical reenactments draw thousands of spectators.
Knights joust three times daily during the annual Renais-
sance festivities in Harveysburg, Ohio. Courtesy of the Ohio
Renaissance Festival, Harveysburg, Ohio.

different regions, classes, genders, and races. It can be charged that we
have reached an almost absurd level of detail in trying to turn the war into
a diverting board game (Company A of Regiment B in the fourth hour of
the third day at Gettysburg).

   True as all this may be, it overlooks the fact that, from the historian's
point of view, all engagement with the past is positive. That there is so
much of it gives grounds for optimism. Living history, if an incomplete
realization of the past, at least stimulates the historical imagination
through visual images, as does film, no matter how shallow it can be in

Cartoonist Steve Benson suggests one possible result of Disney's interest in history. Steve Benson reprinted by permission of United Feature Syndicate, Inc.

other ways. When, in the 1990s, Disney proposed developing a Civil War theme park in northern Virginia, many historians and conservationists objected. Yet we should not oppose Disney getting further into the history business if this ignites enthusiasm for the past, as Disney and MGM films did for youth in the 1950s. If too much history designed for the mass market is indiscriminate, playing on popular fashion, failing to provoke and challenge, it is partly the fault of professional historians for not getting into the mix and presenting better alternatives, rather than sighing and turning away.

I believe that many lay readers want to be discriminating and nuanced in their understanding of history; they simply have neither the time nor the tools and training to differentiate always between the many versions of history that are pitched at them. Those of us whose work entails spending our days thinking about the past have an obligation to be guides through this forest of historical material, providing signposts and road markers where we can to help our fellow time travelers choose satisfying and sustaining paths. The challenge is an exciting and pleasurable one.

———•◦•———

In this book, I hope to help in a modest way those interested in history to develop patterns of insight about the past which might help them assimilate what they later learn. I want to look at one of the most popular fields of history, the study of war, to see how it has been treated in mainstream culture and how we can begin to categorize or join together elements of the vast amount of material with which we are deluged, so that we can better make sense of the mass. I shall also suggest by example ways of analyzing critically the various versions of the past presented to us.

The book is arranged in six chapters, each of which takes a significant past era of military history and suggests some important reasons why we recur to particular characteristics of that time, significant military and social factors then, that have resonance for us also. For example, chapter 1 considers the rise of the mounted knight. He dominated military and social life in the medieval period and so we remember him as an important historical figure of that time. But he also has contemporary meaning for us as a potential symbol of strong character and nobility of motive. The bowman, a common soldier, was important in the later Middle Ages, as he helped to bring down the knight. He is remembered as a military figure, yet he also works for us as a symbol of the underdog fighting unjust privilege, a concept synonymous with the name Robin Hood.

When we move out of the medieval into the Early Modern period, the struggle of parliamentary bodies to limit the authority of the central state becomes a dominant theme in the English-speaking world. The contest was inextricably linked to control of the developing armed forces and to the nature of military organization, as soldiers were a key tool for government intervention in the lives of subjects. Coincidentally, this time period encompassed the settlement and growth of British North America, so that events had a profound effect in molding how Americans thought about government. Chapter 2 proposes that memory of the era in some sectors of popular culture has left a pervasive distrust of central government and the professional soldier in a police role; hence the private militias' image of a New World Order using mercenary troops to threaten our liberties.

Americans in the Colonial and Early National periods often had great faith in the amateur and were skeptical of the trained professional as opposed to the ordinary person armed with common sense. The notion survives today in, for example, the election of school boards and lay governing bodies of universities. In military terms, the idea meant faith in the utility of the citizen bearing arms versus the regular soldier, a view that seemed to be borne out by military events taking place between the French and Indian War of 1755–1763 and the 1836 Texan War of Independence, when gifted amateurs appeared to beat the best professional armies on the continent. Chapter 3 suggests that this view was largely myth, but a myth that has had profound lasting consequences on American ideas, such as those regarding private gun ownership.

For many centuries, the professional soldier was seen as a mercenary or paid hireling, little better than an assassin. After the decline of the knight and the break-up of Christendom with the Protestant Reformation, war itself was stigmatized as a pestilence. A clear change of view becomes apparent in the early Victorian period of the mid-nineteenth century, our fourth era of military history. The common soldier of this time came to be held up as a symbol of duty and sacrifice, engaging in war as a healthy antidote to the materialism and self-centeredness of peace. The changed view was a side effect of the Industrial Revolution, which generated wealth at such an unprecedented level that people feared for the moral corruption of society. Two incidents reflect the positive view of the soldier, the 1854 Charge of the Light Brigade and the 1863 attack upon Fort Wagner. Today, there remains an afterglow of the Victorian mindset in the belief that public service of some kind, such as in the military, is inherently good for youth, and in the more widespread idea that a war brings us together in a spirit of national unity and rededication to fundamental values.

As chapter 4 suggests, by the latter part of the nineteenth century, the figure of the soldier in battle was freighted with symbolic meaning, often as a model of character. But chapter 5 argues that, as cultural needs changed in the twentieth century, the earlier figure of manliness came to carry different and more negative symbolic values as our societal emphases changed. George Armstrong Custer's Seventh Cavalry in the West and Theodore Roosevelt's Rough Riders in Cuba were first seen as symbols of the "white man's burden" to carry civilization to the world on the point of a saber. After the end of imperialism in the twentieth century and a greater understanding of what expansionism had done to native peoples, a sense of remorse led the troopers to be recast as examples of unfairness to non-white peoples. At the start of the twenty-first century, a further symbolic use was seen, particularly in the Little Bighorn battle, as illustrating the opportunities and dangers posed by an era of rapid technological change. Thus, these legendary soldiers continue to be bearers of cultural burdens.

Since the Civil War and the closing of the West, the United States has no longer been a battleground, and most Americans are innocent of the face of battle. The final chapter looks at what this has meant for the veterans who often feel somewhat out of place in society. It also considers how innocence shapes the way many in society perceive war and how their perceptions affect the methods by which military actions can be conducted. I conclude that many people do not fully grasp the nature of modern war and that they need to be well educated in the broadest sense about this most costly of human activities. Thus, society benefits from the many citizens engaged by the study of war and the increasing number of professional historians who participate in public discussions of war.

———◆———

Grouping and analyzing material under major headings, joining themes together, goes some way toward organizing and making collective sense of the mass of military history floating about in popular culture. Other themes could be chosen for each era, but I hope that I have isolated some important ones that make evident the reasons why certain events and issues from past wars are with us in memory today, the functions they continue to serve, and the ways they can be analyzed in order to perceive their military and cultural significance. In this guided tour through a thousand years of history some guiding principles of methodology will be demonstrated in practical application throughout the text, and they may be of later use in helping the reader individually choose and evaluate books, films, and reenactments relating to our military past.

First, although they may at times seem random, chaotic, even bizarre, most artifacts of war that appear in popular culture probably deserve to be there, either because of intrinsic military significance or because they help people to articulate ideas and values of importance to them. Thus, although Custer may not have been the greatest Indian fighter, he quickly became a cultural icon because of other factors. Andrew Jackson, who was an important military leader, also served as a pivotal symbol for his age.

Second, historical interpretations of people and events are not static, but are in constant evolution. How we view the past will be affected by such factors as race, class, gender, national origin, and political persuasion. Each generation as a whole will also have overarching concerns that lead to the reinterpretation of the past in the light of current shared values and goals. The Charge of the Light Brigade was seen in the 1850s as a sublime triumph of self-sacrifice coming up from the ranks, while in the very different political climate of the 1960s it appeared as the epitome of blind stupidity inflicted from the top down. The bottom line is that history is not "just the facts, ma'am," but an evolving dialogue over how the facts should be interpreted. By analyzing this dialogue, we hold up a mirror to what most concerns us as a culture at any given time.

Realizing that what we often assume to be the facts of history are actually hypotheses built on facts and subject to modification or even refutation can be downright frightening at first. Yet, as we get used to this concept, we start to see history as a great detective work in which we are the sleuths dedicated to separating fact from interpretation and weighing the importance of both. Or historical investigation can be compared to an archaeological dig in which books, movies, poems, and songs are our artifacts. Take as an instance the common availability through VHS and DVD of nearly a century of film. This means that in our own homes we can examine, as in a time machine, how successive generations have seen an event such as the Battle of Agincourt or the Alamo. Each cassette may be viewed as an archaeological artifact from a specific chronological layering, revealing what a particular age did with the event. The same thing can be done with books, once you have ascertained the date of publication and figured out the author's school of thought or viewpoint.

We have said that what remains in popular culture mostly deserves to be there. But this doesn't mean that it represents the total of what has passed in history or what might have been remembered. For example, we remember Little Bighorn, but we rarely recall the Fetterman massacre, another Plains Indian victory. Cultural, like individual, memory is selective and tends over time to simplify the complexity of events into a digestible and satisfying pattern. To be remembered, an event must have historical or symbolic significance for a society. Yet it also seems important for an able artist, poet, or other powerful communicator to pick up and popularize the meaning of a happening; otherwise it may never leave obscurity. With modern communications, the artist can create an instant legend. Traditionally, myths seem to have developed slowly, over centuries. For example, the stories of King Arthur and his knights are assumed to have been elaborated over a great period from a simple beginning. Now, however, an event like My Lai can enter the household vocabulary overnight and might stay in our cultural inventory as a usable myth. Thus, we should get used to looking at even comparatively recent events, such as World War II, as having legendary dimensions, in this case the shining "Good War" myth.

At the same time that some events are becoming legendary, others will leave public memory if they lose their symbolic usefulness and have no intrinsic military significance to sustain them. Some previously famous encounters are now forgotten. Thus, there is a regular traffic between the dark attic and well-lit parlor of our cultural memory. Sometimes, a happening that is lying neglected in the attic of our minds will be dusted off and brought into the light if it again fulfills a purpose in our imaginative lives. The 1836 Battle of the Alamo, which had been notorious at the time and was then forgotten, popped up again in the Cold War of the 1950s when it appeared to have renewed moral meaning for America. The July 1863 attack on Fort Wagner by the black Fifty-fourth Massachusetts regiment was initially memorialized by leading artists, then lost to public view, only to resurface when racial equality became an issue in the late twentieth century.

The coupling of racial and military issues leads to a further observation, which is that events in war and in peacetime are not isolated from each other but powerfully interractive. A society's character affects how it acts in battle. By the same token, what happens in war modifies how a culture thinks and behaves in peacetime. War and society are integrated; they do not occupy separate spheres. A good example would be the Vietnam War: how we fought it was shaped by dominant traits in our politics and society at that time; what happened in Vietnam helped to frame America's public discourse for the next two decades. Thus, we should never expect military history to be free from politics; instead, we should seek to understand how interpretations of events are affected by politics.

Finally, because we all need a useable past and we all have different values, we will not all have an identical interest in the same historical events any more than we subscribe to the same points of view about the past. Although we can speak of a single popular culture, it also has many subgroups, composed of people with different interests in and reasons for exploring the past. For example, there are adolescents who play with dragons in medieval dungeons; African Americans in search of a prideful past; beleaguered white males who seek affirmation in frontier military legends; the middle-class audience, both male and female, for *Masterpiece Theatre* British Empire costume dramas; and the concerned citizens who wonder if our claims for the efficacy and humanity of strategic bombing as practiced in Yugoslavia are accurate. This variety has somewhat influenced my choice of topics, which is meant in part to show the large range of different interests in our military past.

These, then, are my observations or guiding principles regarding history. Our collective understanding of history is constantly evolving and is not simply a fixed statement of fact. If we study how history is viewed in our culture, we will have an intimate window not only into the past, but into ourselves. War, as part of our past and present, does not happen outside the normal cultural perimeters of a society, but plays an active role in the internal ongoing life and development of a people. A society's character and values will determine its approach to war, and the battlefield will in turn help to shape the culture's future definition of itself. An event may become part of our mythology at first partly because it got some form of special artistic attention, but to remain alive in memory it must fulfill a viable symbolic purpose; otherwise it will drop into darkness. Thus, what a culture remembers about war may appear random but the memories actually help the society to define itself purposefully through the form of useable myths. Different past events will appeal to different segments of society as offering moral parables and lessons of value for that particular group. Overarching all, each generation will broadly reinterpret the past according to its needs.

My experience has been that the study of history has very serious purposes, yet it is also a source of great pleasure—fun, in short. I intend that we shall have fun as we join together in exploring some past battles and military fashions that have struck me as worth sharing more widely as a result of my time travels to that past that is always a vital part of our developing present.

Finally, a word about my intellectual debts. This book is the result of many years of studying, teaching, and thinking about the role of military history in popular culture. It would be impossible to retrace and acknowledge the development of each detail of thought about a thousand years of history. At the end of the book, I have tried to suggest some major intellectual influences on me that I believe will also be of value to the reader. Here, I would like simply to note the profound effect on me of two works by great authors: Edmund Wilson's *Patriotic Gore: Studies in the Literature of the American Civil War* (1962), an exemplary model of the extended essay style of writing; and James Burke's *Connections* (1978), a brilliant study in the relevance of history to the world we live in, which made me determined to work on showing how the elements of war and society are joined together. Although he has died, I remain enormously grateful to Marcus Cunliffe for sharing with me his nuanced way of viewing history; he still influences my work. Former President Leon E. Boothe and the governing body of Northern Kentucky University made me a Regents Professor with support for my research. President James C. Votruba, Provost Rogers W. Redding, Dean of Arts and Sciences Gail W. Wells, and former Chair of History Robert C. Vitz encouraged the scholarly endeavor on which this book is based and joined with the Faculty Senate in recommending a sabbatical leave, during which much of the text was written. Dennis Hall, a fine scholar of popular culture, read and made valuable comments upon the manuscript. Finally, my wife, Susan, continues to be my closest friend and colleague, listening to and commenting on all of my ideas.

ONE

✢

Knights on Horseback

In this chapter, we shall consider the rise and fall of medieval knight-hood as a viable military-political order. Our discussion will be illus-trated through the examination of three battles, all of them important in the history of the knight. They are Hastings (1066), Agincourt (1415), and Bosworth (1485). We shall also offer some explanations for why the image of the knight and the ideals of chivalry continued to exercise a fascination for modern people, and helped frame their identities, even down to our own technological age.

Although knighthood as a dominant military institution was waning by 1500, its images continue to live in our everyday culture, largely but not entirely through the entertainment media. William Shakespeare's his-torical plays, evoking the best and worst of chivalry, find new perform-ers and new interpretations in each generation: Kenneth Branagh revived *Henry V* (about Agincourt) in 1989 and Ian McKellen adapted *Richard III* (about Bosworth) in 1995. The man who did most to memorialize knighthood as it was passing into history, Sir Thomas Malory, has had many disciples eager to keep alive the legends of King Arthur and the Knights of the Round Table. Recent film examples include John Boorman's *Excalibur* (1981), Jerry Zucker's *First Knight* (1995), and Steve Barron's *Merlin* (1998). In Frank Herbert's 1965 sci-fi classic *Dune*, although we visit technologically advanced cultures with atomic weapons, they also fight with swords and lances; their leaders are counts, dukes, and even a "troubadour-warrior." We might include here also the *Star Wars* sequence, which is in part a high-tech retelling of the Arthurian legends, with George Lucas in the role of graphics bard. The Jedi Knights are a variation upon the fellowship of the Round Table, with Obi-Wan Kenobi as King Arthur, Yoda as Merlin, and Darth Vader as Mordred, the Black Knight. Luke

Skywalker is the virginal noviciate on his first and most pure knight's quest and Princess Leia poses as the classical damsel in distress. In Boba Fett we have the mercenary soldier of the Middle Ages, complete with a twelfth-century helmet. As for Han Solo, he is the cowboy of western legend, who in turn was the modern inheritor of the knight errant's mantle. And the Ewoks are a somewhat whimsical evocation of Robin Hood and his merry men.

This brings us to the longbowmen, who ranked below the knight in the military hierarchy but also helped to unseat him. They, too, stay in our historical imagination. Recent film depictions include *Robin and Marian* (1976), *Robin Hood: Prince of Thieves* (1991), and simply *Robin Hood* (1973, 1991). That other common soldier of the Middle Ages, the pikeman, likewise gets a positive backward glance in Mel Gibson's popular 1995 offering, *Braveheart*. Gibson, an Australian, plays Wallace as a twentieth-century freedom fighter. Although the characterization of Wallace is inaccurate, it was true that the cavalry of King Edward I of England was unseated by ordinary Scots footmen with long spears in the battles described.

The manifestations of popular fascination with knighthood go on. Football players are "knights of the gridiron"; Marine Corps ads perennially cast recruits as (white) knights; members of the heavy metal group Iron Maiden once posed dressed as medieval warriors enjoying a boar's head feast in the mead hall; New Age singer Enya dreams of dwelling in marble halls surrounded by vassals and serfs; and young people play medieval fantasy computer games such as Dungeons & Dragons or Ultima, between reruns of the cult movie *Monty Python and the Holy Grail* (1975).

In places where the chivalry never trod, like California, we have weddings in medieval attire, and annual Renaissance festivals, from Maine to Alaska. The Pennsylvania Renaissance Faire, held at Cornwall, is fairly typical, promising "400 years of fun for the entire family!" with attractions such as a petting zoo and "roasted turkey legges," dished out by "flirtatious serving wenches." Shaking one's head is easy: turkeys were hardly known in England before Jamestown and wenching is a sexist concept today. But the occasion also includes some solid historical references: there is a joust with couched lances, and the field of encounter is called Bosworth, both important to our understanding of knighthood's rise and decline. In fact, our popular culture is resonant with important

The popular fascination with chivalry. Visitors enjoy a day with knights and their ladies in Bosworth Field. Brochure for the 1997 Elizabethan Time, courtesy of the Pennsylvania Renaissance Faire.

images of the medieval military world. What we need to do is provide a sound historical context for understanding how these images fit together.

A good place to start is the 1066 Battle of Hastings, which cemented the military and social power of the mounted soldier or knight. The battle was brought into popular focus by science historian James Burke in his television series and 1978 book, *Connections*. In these he suggests that Hastings taught medieval soldiers what they thought was a profound lesson for centuries to come: the winning power of the couched lance delivered at a mounted gallop.

Hastings was fought between rival contenders for the throne of England, which became vacant at New Year's of 1066. One claimant was Duke William of Normandy, a duchy in France. The duke said that the late king, Edward the Confessor, had promised him the throne in 1065. His rival, Harold Godwin, Earl of Wessex, a landholding in the south of England, said that the dying king had willed the state to him and he was crowned accordingly. A contested kingship was a grave matter in a period when monarchs were the political and military heads of state; on them rested the stability and prosperity of the kingdom.

William determined on an invasion of England and got the pope to bless his cause as a holy crusade, a powerful morale boost. He landed on the south coast at the end of September and established a beachhead at Hastings. Harold moved south from London to confront him, and the two armies met north of Hastings on the morning of October 14, 1066. They shared some characteristics. The better-off soldiers in each army wore a steel cap with a nasal piece to protect the face, a coat of chain mail or overlapping metal scales sewn onto leather, and a long, kite-shaped shield.

But there were also fundamental differences. The Saxon or English army usually fought entirely on foot. At the heart of this force were the housecarls or household troops, professional soldiers who rode to battle on ponies but then dismounted to wield terrible two-handed axes capable of cutting through man and horse. Also professional but of lesser status were light troops armed with bows and slings. The army's numbers were augmented by the *fyrd,* an early version of the militia, in which all able-bodied free men of a local district were expected to turn out in an emergency to protect their towns and farms. The training and the equipment of the *fyrd* were patchy, some having no more than staffs or pitchforks, so that the discipline and fighting quality of this auxiliary force were uneven.

Across the lines, Duke William's army was entirely professional and comprised three arms. At the lowest level of prestige were the archers and slingers. Next in rank came heavily-armored foot men-at-arms. These might be knights who had lost their mounts or ambitious soldiers aspiring to be knights through gain in battle. At the apex of the military structure were the knights, dressed much like the armored foot, but horsed and carrying a lance. Cavalry were considered the vital arm in Normandy.

Because he commanded a more disciplined, flexible force of foot and horse, William had more options available to him, and he took the offensive. Harold, with an uneven foot force, had to cling to the defensive. To make his situation more difficult, he had less than a month earlier defeated a Viking invasion force at Stamford Bridge near York in the north and had come south in such haste that many of his professional light troops could not keep up and were absent now. Harold chose a good defensive position on Senlac Hill, a low ridge dropping off sharply on both ends, forcing an uphill frontal assault, with woods behind to impede mounted pursuit if there should be a defeat. Here the Saxons waited behind a wall made of shields. Harold had about two thousand housecarls gathered around his standard, with up to five thousand of the *fyrd,* while William mustered some six thousand men, of whom about a third were cavalry.

William began the battle just after 9 A.M., sending both light and heavy foot up the hill. They were driven off, so William launched the pride of his army, the mounted knights. Seeing the enemy elite approaching, the housecarls moved to the front ranks and a vicious encounter followed at the shield wall. A contingent of Bretons on William's left panicked and fled, almost precipitating a Norman debacle. But many *fyrd,* ill-disciplined and ignorant of war, broke ranks and pursued the fleeing Bretons. William, seizing advantage from the near-disaster, surrounded the wretched yokels and butchered them.

The brutal battle continued all day, with William launching repeated assaults on the Saxon line. At least once again he staged a planned retreat to lure more of the inexperienced militiamen into a trap. As evening neared, William gambled on an all-out assault to win a victory before night. A barrage of arrows caused confusion in the tired Saxon lines and the armored troops broke the shield wall, the knights riding through to strike down Harold by his dragon standard. With the king dead, the English left the field, the housecarls turning to fight when the Normans pressed too close. Although pockets of Saxon resistance continued for several years, the heart went out of the English. Some said that Harold's death was a sign of God's displeasure at his defiance of the pope. William was crowned King of England on Christmas Day, 1066.

The Norman Conquest had profound ramifications for the history of warfare and for English, European, and American history. The Normans who now ruled England also held lands in France and steadily extended their influence, finally claiming title to both realms. So that, while Hastings linked England and France, the battle fostered an increasingly hostile relationship and lasting enmity. In the great age of European expansion that came with the modern period, this struggle became worldwide, and included rival claims to vast territories in America. In 1763 Britain finally wrested Canada from France. The French got revenge fifteen years later by helping American rebels win their independence from Britain. The enmity smolders today in parts of Canada.

In a domestic cultural context, the Conquest not only displaced the Saxon ruling class but made French a language of England. Thus, the English tongue, already enriched by Celtic, Latin, Greek, and Anglo-Saxon influences, was further enhanced by French idioms and words, such as *county* for a shire, and *ville* for a burgh. Less positive in its impact was a downgrading in the status of women. For the culture that triumphed in 1066 was dominated by male, military values.

The primary source of wealth and power at this time was landholding. In a cash or capital short economy, land, held as an estate or *feu*, was leased in return for services rendered. Hence this was not a *capital*ist but a *feu*dal system. Norman landholding was much more aggressively tied to military obligation than in Saxon England, where the landholding aristocracy and the army were not synonymous. Consequently, in England, a man (or warrior) did not necessarily have to be the head of an estate, a widow might be able to retain title as her lord's vassal or *mann,* a generic Saxon term meaning a person. Similarly, women might hold office as king's counsellors or as high church officials, female church officers being able to hear the confessions of their sisters. This changed after Hastings. William divided England into knights' *feus,* each capable of sustaining a knight in his defensive castle, along with his retinue. By this method, he could count on five thousand armored cavalry. But it left no major role for women; a *mann* was now a man-at-arms. Women also lost status in the church, seen by Normans as the spiritual battalion of God's army on Earth and therefore inherently masculine; women were enjoined to subordination and to silence.

The knight's *feu* was crucial because of how the Normans interpreted their victory at Hastings, which became an axiomatic illustration of correct deployment in a universally-accepted medieval military orthodoxy. Thus, the battle served to underpin a way of looking at war and society that lasted for centuries. In retrospect, we can see many reasons for Harold's defeat at Hastings. His forces were tired, incomplete, and partly made up of amateurs. He fought under the morale-sapping shadow of a papal ban. William had won at the end of the day by launching an all-out combined-arms attack, featuring cavalry and both heavy and light foot, including archers. But, in the memory of the knights who dominated the military and society, and thus were in a position to mold how the battle was remembered, their prowess alone had been crucial.

They were experimenting at this time with a new method of mounted attack. Traditionally, the lance or spear had been carried overhand by a horseman, who either threw the missile like a javelin or stabbed down at the opponent with the lance after riding up close and almost stopping the horse. The latter was dangerous, as the proximity to the enemy meant that the foot soldier could make use of his weapons to hurt horse and knight in this close-quarters exchange. But the new cavalry tactic coming into use at Hastings gave much more power to the horseman: instead of carrying the lance overhead to jab down with it, he couched it under his right arm, gripped against his side, pointing at the enemy, and then ran his horse full tilt at his victim, making maximum use of the horse's collision speed to ram the lance home in the opponent's breast. The knights were convinced that this offensive tactic was an unimpeachable winner.

To be remembered in popular culture, an event has to be important either for its tangible results, its symbolic value, or both. But it also has to have positive exposure; it must become the theme of talented artists, writers, or other interpreters of the happening. Some events that should be remembered are forgotten because nobody made their greater meaning clear and memorable in words or paints. In the case of Hastings, we have two remarkable products, both of which sharply reflect the knights' worldview. The first is the Bayeux Tapestry, a 231–foot-long, 20–inch-wide woven pictorial representation of the battle, sponsored in 1067 by Bishop Odo of Bayeux, William's half-brother. Only a rich man could afford such a memorial and so it has an aristocratic bias. Odo himself is shown fighting in the field under the papal banner, clearly illustrating the masculine warrior character of the Norman church. But, most importantly, the tapestry showcases the temporal knights, featuring their use of both the old overhead and the new underarm lance attacks. Light footmen are depicted occasionally, bowmen and slingers, but to suggest their lack of social status and military significance, they are drawn midget size and often appear only in the borders, as footnotes to the magnificent feats of the cavalry.

The second artwork is *The Song of Roland*, an epic poem recounting

Hastings as it was remembered. Norman knights, holding the lance in both the overarm and underarm (couched) positions, attack the Saxon shield wall. A bowman appears in miniature to suggest his inferior social status. Panel from the Bayeux Tapestry, courtesy of the City of Bayeux, France.

the last stand against the Saracens made by Count Roland of Brittany, a knight of the Frankish king Charlemagne. Although written about the Battle of Roncevaux in 778, the eleventh-century *Roland* is contemporary with Hastings and thus reflects the military thought of the later period, specifically that of the Norman-French knights who paid for the poem to be sung by the great fire in the main hall. It is said that William's minstrel, Taillefer, may have recited the poem before battle was joined at Hastings. The common soldiers, bowmen and such, do not appear at all in the poem, only the knights. And they are obsessed with the collision power of the couched lance, which is repeated in scene after scene. Here is Roland killing a Saracen at full gallop in stanza 93 of the 1957 Dorothy L. Sayers version of the poem:

> His blow he launches with all his mightiest effort;
> The shield he shatters, and the hauberk [mail coat] he rendeth,
> He splits the breast and shatters in the breast-bone,
> Through the man's back drives out the backbone bended,
> And soul and all forth on the spear-point fetches.

We see the faith in a blow that could at once fetch out spine and soul. Hearts, livers, and lungs, split by couched lances, litter the text, some put there by Archbishop Turpin, a companion of Roland and the representative militant churchman of Norman society, the fictional equivalent of Odo.

This is an aristocratic male world. Common people appear not at all and upper-class women enter only as a chorus line to applaud male fighting prowess, or as the spoils of war, along with captured lands and arms. Thus, a Saracen lord, encouraging his men to battle, cries in stanza 245: "I'll give you women, noble and fair of hue / Honors and fiefs and lands I'll give to you." After Charlemagne has avenged Roland's death, he carries off the enemy queen to be his concubine. In this warrior world, the obligations of man to man matter most; the loyalty of a vassal or *feu* holder to his lord, and of knight to knight as comrades in arms. Treachery between men is the worst crime, for it destabilizes the military and social orders, and it is punished brutally: Ganelon, the man who betrays Roland into an ambush, is pulled apart by wild horses. We shall return later to the theme of betrayal as a weakness of the feudal system.

A key consequence of building the military structure around the mounted knight was having to gear the economy to support the massive outlay entailed. The knight, his mounts, and retinue—the squire to dress him in armor, the blacksmith to mend his gear and shoe his steeds, the stable hands, and other servants— were expensive to maintain. Horse and rider had to be progressively cased in more and more metal to protect against equally dangerous mounted opponents. This also meant that progressively bigger, stronger horses had to be bred to carry the increased weight and still achieve a gallop. Even with progressive improvements in medieval farm implements and land usage methods, which increased crop yield, a large portion of society's productive effort was siphoned into the upkeep of the knight and his entourage; hence William's division of England into knights' *feus*.

———◆———

For centuries, the knight dominated the society, the art, the politics, the very imagination of Europe. A rich body of literature developed around the deeds and character of the soldier class. Steadily, the crudity of warrior culture was rubbed off and manners became more polished. An etiquette of conduct, the code of chivalry, was developed to refine the violence of the warrior caste and confine it within humane limits that would work for the good of society. The knight, at least in theory, became an exemplar of honorable and magnanimous behavior. Castles, no longer just barracks, became more comfortable. By the late thirteenth century, private rooms were heated by separate fireplaces and chimneys, allowing for more intimacy in relationships; this led to the development of a special genre of literature dealing with courtly love, the romantic love between knights and ladies. Although women remained subordinate to men and served in many ways as objects, even if of desire, their status improved and some achieved real power in a society not quite so rigidly military. To the knight in his solid stone home, surrounded by admiring retainers, the power of this order must have appeared to be divinely blessed and earmarked to last for eternity.

Yet the factors leading to knighthood's decline were already in place. The ultimate difficulty with this aristocratic military ordering of society was not only that it was expensive; it was also exclusive and self-absorbed, even myopic, and consequently blind to objectionable realities, which made it difficult to acknowledge and address weaknesses within the system. These faults would eventually destroy the hegemony of the mounted knight. The seeds of decay were there from the start.

To begin with, there was no guarantee that the family's firstborn male, the one who would inherit the *feu* or estate in return for military service, would want to be a soldier or would be particularly good at it. With the lapse of time, some knightly families ceased to produce good warriors. As hostile incursions became less frequent, as society became more ordered and consequently more prosperous, many knights became more country gentlemen than warriors, devoted to farming and civil pursuits. Such knights began to use some of their surplus income from rents and produce to pay a fine or fee to avoid military service. The fine could be used by the overlord to hire a substitute. The arrangement worked for the lord or king because he could then hire a professional, someone whose life was devoted to soldiering and who could be assumed to be competent and reliable, so long as the wages or booty kept flowing.

As commerce grew, a thriving urban middle class arose, merchants and bankers prepared to give the crown cash in return for privileges and political rights, including legislative seats. This money, too, could be used to hire professionals, called mercenaries. The trend, clear by the thirteenth century, was very important by the fourteenth century.

Mercenaries could be mounted men-at-arms, aspiring to be captains or even knights. The professionalization of the armies allowed for some social mobility within the ranks. Thus a French knight, Jean de Bueil, began his career by stealing laundry to make himself a padded military coat, then goats to pay for a horse, and really began his rise when he stole an enemy captain's cow. However, many mercenaries were common foot soldiers, carrying either pike, longbow, or crossbow. Pikemen, carrying a twelve to sixteen foot pole with a steel spearpoint, sometimes also fitted with an axe or hammerhead, had been in medieval armies for a long time. But it was their use in large, well-drilled units that gave them the discipline and cohesion to defeat mounted knights. Such prowess was achieved by the Swiss, whose disciplined phalanxes of pikemen massacred Burgundian chivalry at Grandson in 1476. Duke Charles of Burgundy, viewing the world through an upper-class prism, had ignored warnings that these common footmen would prove "hard churls" to beat. Scots pikemen had slaughtered English knights at Bannockburn in 1314. Contrary to the somewhat whimsical and romantic portrait in *Braveheart,* these were not lightly-clad Celtic farm workers in blue Pictish war paint (which had died out of use centuries before) but steel-capped and mail- or leather-vested heavy infantry. What the movie did get right was that they were not noble, and, like many other warriors before and since, they taunted their enemies before battle with rude gestures, intended to provoke fear or, even better, thoughtless anger that could lead to fatal tactical errors.

To break up these formations of Scots pikemen, as much as to unseat French knights, the English turned to longbowmen, who used a six-foot yew longbow and a three-foot or "clothyard" arrow. This bow, a large and more powerful evolution of those used at Hastings, was in widespread use by the mid-thirteenth century and by 1285 its practice was made compulsory in the English militia. A good bowman could launch nine arrows per minute, with a carrying range of about 275 yards. A French chronicler said that English arrows were like hail and obscured the sun; another compared them to snow falling. The English bowfire was said to be so rapid that when the French showed their backsides as a taunt, their breeches were nailed to them with arrows. Such, for example, happened at Caen in 1346.

Despite its awesome firepower, the longbow had two potential deficits, one military and one political. Militarily, the bow could kill lightly-armed footmen and horses but its penetrating power against armor was only certain at close range. The archer drove a pointed stake into the ground forward of his position so that he had some measure of protec-

English longbowmen in action. A French soldier, who has exposed his buttocks to taunt the English, finds his bowels feathered with a clothyard shaft. By permission of the British Library, manuscript number: COTT.JUL.E.IV Art 6 f20v.

tion should his arrows fail to unseat the charging knight. Politically, the bow caused upper-class concern because it put a cheap, easily-made weapon in the hands of the lower orders, an asset to outlaws and even rebels. It is not coincidence that the legendary Robin Hood, who may well have been based on a real outlaw operating in Yorkshire at the start of the fourteenth century, was an expert bowman, the terror of those establishment figures, the sheriff and the tax collector. The bow was a potentially subversive weapon in the hands of the underdog and so it is appropriate that Morgan Freeman, a man of color, from a traditionally repressed ethnic group, should play Robin's lieutenant in the recent *Robin Hood: Prince of Thieves*. It was noted by the chronicler Froissart that, during the English Peasants' Revolt of 1381, the followers of rebel leader Wat Tyler marched, "each with his bow ready to shoot."

For this reason, the French aristocracy preferred to keep longbow use to a minimum. Thus, they tried to force military reality to follow social hierarchy, and were to pay for it. So despised was the lowly archer that when the French rolled dice to divide out prisoners, a blank meant a bowman, of no value and likely to have his throat cut rather than be saved by his captor. For their missile launchers, the French favored crossbowmen, usually professionals from Italian city-states like Genoa. The crossbow was a powerful weapon, but expensive, and therefore its circulation in society was controllable. When cranked tight by a winding device, the bowstring could release a steel bolt capable of penetrating plate armor at 350 yards. Its military disadvantage was that it had a slow rate of fire, about one projectile per minute. Also, the French chivalry despised their crossbowmen as of inferior status and underutilized them. An example is at Agincourt, fought in 1415, to which we shall now turn to illustrate some military weaknesses that proved fatal to the hegemony of the knight on the battlefield.

The political and diplomatic history leading up to an English campaign in France need not detain us. Simply, King Henry V wished to take back lands claimed by England in France and won away by the French during the unstable reign of Henry IV, when the English aristocracy had taken to quarreling among themselves. A danger of feudalism was that a heavily-armed upper class finally was as much a threat to peace as a guarantee of it. A good overseas adventure could be expected to unite the English knights and make money. Therefore, on August 11, 1415, Henry set sail from Portsmouth. An armada of fifteen hundred ships carried eight thousand archers and two thousand men-at-arms of all ranks. Henry laid siege to the port of Harfleur, a potential beachhead for further operations.

Things went badly. The city held out until September 22, by which time one third of Henry's army was dead or disabled from wounds and disease. With a depleted force and the summer campaigning season winding down, a major military operation was out of the question. But Henry decided that, for honor's sake, he must march across his ancestral lands to Calais, where he would embark for England. He set out on October 6, but the French blocked his further progress at Agincourt, north of the Somme River crossing, on October 24. They fought the next day.

Both armies were in poor shape, suffering dysentery and pelted with rain the night before battle. The English situation was most precarious. The force had marched a brutal 270 miles in seventeen days, the last eight of which the archers had carried heavy stakes in expectation of imminent attack. The English were outnumbered, with somewhat over five thousand archers and one thousand men-at-arms remaining, versus a French army of perhaps twenty-five thousand, mainly armored men-at-arms. Yet the English won a sharply one-sided victory, killing or capturing up to ten thousand French in return for a loss of about five hundred.

Henry chose a good site for a defensive stand. In front of him were newly plowed fields, now soaked and muddy, to slow down a French attack. To his immediate right and left were woods to shield his archers, some of whom were always placed out on the wings to protect the main body from a mounted flank attack, aimed at rolling up the line and getting in the rear of the army. He then drew his men-at-arms into line, with further wedges of bowmen dispersed at intervals to take toll of an oncoming opponent, somewhat in the manner of later artillery deployment.

The French had learned from earlier encounters with longbowmen not to advance entirely on horseback. But they kept one thousand men mounted to try to drive off the deadly wings of archers on the flanks at the start of the engagement. The rest were drawn up on foot, in two lines eight-ranks deep. Between the lines were crossbowmen. Placing them behind the first line was a contemptuous error; not allowed the privilege of leading the advance and unable to see their enemy to fire, the bowmen were wasted.

The English joined battle by discharging a volley of arrows, which provoked the mounted cavalry on the wings to charge. They were driven off in confusion and, on their way back, caused further disorganization in the French forces by crashing through the first line of foot, now slogging through the mud in their heavy armor to attack the English position. As the French approached, longbowmen on the wings and in wedges along the line showered them with arrows, causing them to flinch together in what is called bunching, a natural emotional herding instinct in reaction to danger, but one that made it difficult for many of the men in the center of the pack to wield their weapons, or even lift their arms. To make matters worse, the French, anticipating the difficulty of marching over muddy, uneven ground, had shortened their lances to make them less clumsy to carry, so that, when they came to "push of pike," the English had a significant advantage in length of weapon.

The front ranks of the closely packed French began to go down in the mud as they lost the exchange of lance thrusts, to be trampled on by those in back trying to get at the enemy. The English archers now threw down their bows and attacked the hapless mass with daggers and the mallets used to drive their stakes into the ground. Soon, the French first line was a crush of men, many exhausted from the difficult march in heavy armor and too terrified to defend themselves, struggling like a stadium crowd caught in a stampede. The French second line, ignoring the military maxim that failure should never be reinforced, now advanced to the attack, pushing on the backs of their friends in the first line and completing their undoing. The battle was reduced to a simple slaughter.

After Agincourt, there could be no doubt that the knight no longer dominated the battlefield. The future increasingly lay with the simple foot soldier, carrying bow or pike, which would soon become fused into the bayonetted musket, still in modern form a basic tool of the infantry. So Agincourt is important. But it was not more so than, say, Crécy, fought in 1346, or Poitiers, 1356, where the English inflicted equally clear-cut defeats on the French. What Agincourt had, and why it stays in memory, in addition to its military importance, is a spectacular interpreter, William Shakespeare, whose play *Henry V* contains some of the finest images in the English language of humanity exalted and devastated by war.

There have been two fine modern movie versions of the play. In each case, the return to *Henry V* was stimulated by events that appeared to be as momentous as those described by Shakespeare. His play became a vehicle for expressing the feelings of interpreters living much later. The first movie, starring Laurence Olivier and released in 1945, is an exuberant expression of Anglo-American pride in the recent Allied victory in World War II, a war often seen as the "Good War." Filmed in color, still a luxury, and with marvelous special effects for the period of arrows flying in air, this is a celebratory piece, with burnished armor and plenty of pageantry. The French, whom the British held in contempt for their 1940 surrender to the Germans, are portrayed as effete, rather silly, quite inferior to the stolid, salt-of-the-earth Anglos.

The 1989 remake by Kenneth Branagh is quite different in tone. It postdates the ugly regional wars that ended Western colonialism and mired the U.S. in Korea and Vietnam. Here the armor is truly "besmirched with rainy marching in the painful field," the ground is muddy and bloody where men tear and stab at each other. In this film, both English and French are victims of a shared inhumanity. Branagh returns to the screen a particularly wrenching scene, removed by Olivier, in which military usage dictates that Henry must execute for pillaging some of his own men, personal drinking companions of his youth. Beaten up and blood-ied by the provost's guard, they strangle by hanging. Probably both films contain elements of truth about the nature of war but, whichever version one prefers, they help to keep fresh the memory of a battle that illustrates some important military reasons for the death of knighthood.

———◆———

Shakespeare, along with Sir Thomas More and others, made memorable another king's reign and another battle that further illustrate weaknesses, both military and political, in the feudal structure. The reign is Richard III's and the field is Bosworth, 1485. This battle demonstrates the grow-ing importance of the mercenary in war. But it also suggests the fragility of a crucial link in the feudal political structure, the personal oath bind-ing vassal to lord, usually given when a contract was made exchanging a deed of land in return for military service. Feudalism functioned for cen-turies to provide military defense and a workable governmental struc-ture at the national and local levels. But, finally, its own instability threatened the public peace.

Under the feudal system, the head of state leased land to great nobles in return for their political allegiance and the military service of them-selves and their retainers. The nobles subcontracted land and subsistence to others who, as their vassals, fought in their military establishment and helped govern their locales. Thus, the nobles were both captains of war and the most powerful political figures in the land under the king, a dangerous equation: if one or more nobles turned against the king, they precipitated not only a political but a military crisis, for there was every chance that their vassals would follow them into battle and not the king, a far-away figure they might never have seen and to whom they had sworn no immediate oath. The danger posed by the potential disloyalty of great men explains the swiftness of trials and executions for those at the top of the feudal hierarchy, a litany of judicial slaughter that shocks the modern reader of Shakespeare.

Fearing their great underlings, kings came when they could to rely on less well-born men as their counsellors, self-made types whose personal loyalty could be guaranteed, so long as they received good pay and advancements. Such new men were William Marshal, Henry II's great military administrator, and Thomas Cromwell, Henry VIII's powerful chancellor. For the same reason, as we have seen, it made increasing sense to hire mercenary soldiers directly from funds in the royal treasury, rather than trusting to the feudal bond to hold good. Thus, feudal flaws promoted capitalist hiring practices in both government and the army. Of course, the nobles resented this. Magna Carta, the great charter of 1215, is not so much a statement of liberties for all subjects as it is an attempt by King John's leading barons to make him recognize them as his peers and stop operating the royal government outside their purview.

The dangers of fighting among the nobles at the top of the feudal order were intense in the fifteenth century. Ties of blood and marriage became so complex that more than one great family could legitimately lay claim to the throne, increasing the odds that powerful men would violate their oaths and risk battle to gain a kingdom. The likelihood of civil war was increased because the feudal order was inherently warlike: it elevated soldiers in the social order. This militant brotherhood demanded outlets for its professional energies, hence jousts, which were war games, quite often lethal, played to keep the knights battle-ready and to allow for professional advancement—the losers might pay not only with life or limb but with loss of status, including armor, mount and equipage, even lands and treasure.

To channel violence away from society, crown and church encouraged crusades against the "infidels" who held the sacred lands of the Bible. Foreign political adventures also helped to unite a realm; we saw this in play with Henry V's campaign in France. The strategy might have worked, but Henry died unexpectedly and his successor, Henry VI, was weak. His reign became a political debacle. The factionalism among England's ruling politico-military families came to center on the aspirations of two great houses, York and Lancaster. Henry VI was of the latter. Fortunes swayed back and forth in a sporadic civil war that occupied the mighty for much of the fifteenth century. The fighting was called the Wars of the Roses, as the heraldic device of York was a white rose and Lancaster a red one. Finally, Edward, the Yorkist leader, triumphed in battle at Tewkesbury in 1471, killing the principal Lancastrian claimants, and inaugurating a period of seeming stability as King Edward IV. The remaining Lancastrian generals took refuge abroad.

Edward ruled well from London and his younger brother, Richard, Duke of Gloucester, governed the north with equal soundness. Then in April 1483 Edward died suddenly of heart failure and the political situation destabilized. The king's eldest son, Edward, aged twelve, was too young to rule so his uncle, Gloucester, was named Protector. Before Richard could reach London from the north, the king's widow, Elizabeth Woodville, moved against him. By this time, the position of aristocratic women had improved and some were important political players. Elizabeth feared Richard, for she had a major role in the 1478 execution for treason of his brother Clarence. She hoped for a Council of Regents in which Richard would be only one among many, with his power diluted.

Faced by this threat, Richard and his major supporters, most notably the powerful southern peer, the Duke of Buckingham, moved to seize power. On his way south, Gloucester arrested and later executed Earl Rivers, the queen's brother, and Thomas Grey, her son by a previous marriage. He then placed his nephews, Edward V and Richard, in protective custody in the Tower of London. Apparently, Richard and his supporters still did not feel fully secure, for they now moved to have the two boys declared illegitimate (a plausible allegation as Edward IV had been promiscuous) and removed from succession to the throne. These actions left the way open for Richard to be crowned on June 6, 1483.

His coronation was a fateful step. Shortly, rumors spread that the king had murdered his nephews. To reassure his subjects, Richard set out on a tour of the provinces but, on September 11, he heard of a rising in the southern counties, led by his erstwhile ally, Buckingham, now in league with Elizabeth Woodville and leading Lancastrians. The reasons for Buckingham's disenchantment and defection, breaking his feudal oath, are unclear. The rebellion was crushed and Buckingham executed. The southern shires were ruthlessly punished and northern men, from Richard's power base, were put over the lands of the dead traitor rebels to assure loyal government. Richard set about cementing his reign with legal and fiscal reforms. But an air of darkness clung to him. When his son died in 1484 many took it as a sign of divine retribution. Richard's portrait shows him to be nervous and careworn, waiting for the crisis.

The king knew that the Lancastrians in France planned an invasion led by Henry Tudor, stepson of Lord Thomas Stanley, a powerful northern noble, whose wife, Margaret Beaufort, was an ally of Elizabeth Woodville. Sir William Stanley, Thomas's brother and strong in Wales, was also suspect. It was to Stanley lands that Henry sailed on August 1, 1485, with two thousand French mercenaries and some seasoned Lancastrian generals, most notably the Earl of Oxford. In Wales, Henry picked up more men, mainly mercenaries, and advanced east to meet Richard.

The king called upon the feudal host, a dubious reliance because the links in the chain of hierarchical loyalty were faulty in key places. The Stanleys were false: when Richard ordered Lord Stanley to contest Henry's advance from Wales, he begged off, pleading the "sweating sickness." All the king could do was take hostage his son, Lord Strange, against future good behavior. Richard did have some solid noblemen to rely on, such as the Duke of Norfolk. But others, high and low in the feudal structure, were doubtful, especially the southern levies seething from Richard's harsh handling of Buckingham's rebellion.

The armies met outside the city of Leicester at Bosworth village. Richard had the benefit of numbers, with eight thousand men to Henry's five thousand. But Henry's forces were mainly mercenaries, experienced professionals. Henry drew up in a valley and Richard deployed opposite, on the gentle rise of Ambion Hill. The king's army was in three divisions, drawn up in echelon from front to rear of the hill crest. Norfolk commanded the van or forward division, composed of infantry. Behind him, in the center division, was Richard with cavalry, knights, and mounted men-at-arms. In the rear was the Duke of Northumberland with more foot. This noble's loyalty was also suspect. Between the two armies, off to one side, were the retainers of the Stanleys, seemingly committed to neither cause.

Norfolk advanced down the hill to start the battle and Oxford moved forward to engage him. After some skirmishing, many of Norfolk's southern vassals ran away, breaking their feudal oath of allegiance and leaving the duke, along with his principal officers, to be overtaken and butchered as they tried to wade back up the hill in their heavy armor—the first broken link of treason and betrayal. Seeing Norfolk's men break, the Stanleys moved to join Henry—the second breach of faith. Richard was urged to flee but he was determined to see the issue out and end the intolerable stress of the past months. The king led the cavalry charging down Ambion Hill in what historian Michael Bennett in his 1985 *The Battle of Bosworth* called "the swan-song of medieval English chivalry." Now a third betrayal occurred—Northumberland failed to bring his division to the king's aid. Seeing this, some of Richard's companions lost heart and faded from the field. Others fought on, like Sir Percival Thirwell, who bore the royal banner aloft until his legs were hewed from under him. Richard died fighting in the field, repeatedly crying treason until Welsh mercenaries dragged him down and killed him.

It was a hard end to the reign and a graphic example of how infidelity could destroy the effectiveness of the feudal political-military system and bring a government crashing down. There was sordidness enough to share around. Whether or not Richard killed his nephews, he had made them illegitimate and had dealt harshly with opponents. His enemies were no better, breaking their plighted word. In an astonishing act of political duplicity, Henry had his reign (as Henry VII) backdated to the day before the battle, so that the lives and property of any who fought against him under their feudal oath to King Richard were forfeit. Richard's body was carted into Leicester and dumped in a horse trough. Completing the sorry tale, in 1489 Northumberland was assassinated in Richard's north country. A note left by the body said the murder was retribution for Northumberland's "disappointing" of King Richard at Bosworth.

In this summer of 1485 when, in the last great engagement fought in medieval England, a crowned king died in battle betrayed by his nobles and foreign mercenaries overwhelmed the chivalry of England, an ironic event occurred. On July 31, William Caxton, printer of Westminster, published the most lasting evocation of knighthood in our literature, Sir Thomas Malory's *Le Morte Darthur,* or the death of King Arthur, to which all modern versions of the Arthurian legends trace their ancestry. That this book should have been published at this time is not actually surprising for *Le Morte* is not a triumphal piece celebrating a current reality but a requiem for an ideal that is fading, that of knighthood.

Malory himself illustrated why knighthood failed as a social and military order. Born around 1410 of an old Yorkshire family, Thomas inherited lands and was for a time a member of parliament. Trained to arms, he served honorably in the 1436 siege of Calais, bringing with him one man-at-arms and two archers. Yet, in the troubled times of the civil wars, he appears to have been outlawed. Crimes charged against him included attempted assassination, robbery with violence, cattle theft, extorting money with menaces, and rape. He was jailed eight times and may have died in Newgate Prison during 1471. His book was at least partially written in prison, for twice he begs the reader to pray for his release: "Praye for me whyle I am on lyve that God send me good delyveraunce. And whan I am deed, I praye you all praye for my soule." And again: "[For] this was drawyn by a knyght presoner, Sir Thomas Malleoré, that God send hym good recover. Amen." Malory had written his book as an act of contrition and in hopes that what mattered about the idea of knighthood could be willed to future generations, living long after its demise. His wish has been fulfilled. But what is it about the figure of the knight that has given the concept its resilience, even in the computer age?

To begin, both during the period of knighthood and for centuries after, to be mounted conferred social status. The horse was a symbol of physical and social power. While most aspired to ride, few could afford to keep a stable, and so the horse was an immediate indication of elite status. To some degree, this is still true in civilian society, where riding to hounds or playing polo are marks of inherited wealth and breeding. Within the army, the mounted arm continued to play an important role on the battlefield but, as the weapons of the foot improved, cavalry became less effective for offensive shock purposes and were relegated more to reconnaissance activities. By the American Civil War of 1861–1865 and the Franco-Prussian War of 1870–1871, a saber-swinging mounted charge was very dangerous against modern rifles. Yet cavalry remained the highly prized showcase regiments of European armies, into which the sons of the most aristocratic houses sought entrance. All British officers were expected to ride and play saddle games—polo, fox hunting, and pig-sticking with spears in India—the expense of which kept the officer corps exclusive into World War I. Even in the more egalitarian U.S., service in the cavalry remained helpful to an officer's prospects. Witness the public attention given George Armstrong Custer and his legendary Seventh. Robert E. Lee, John Pershing, and George C. Patton are other examples of officers associated with the cavalry.

By World War I, a cavalry charge was suicidal, yet horse regiments in every army continued to carry lance and saber and to wait behind the front lines for the galloping breakthrough that never came. The French even continued to wear metal breastplates and ornately-crested brass helmets in a war dominated by technological weapons of mass destruction. As late as 1939, at the start of World War II, the Polish threw lancers against German armor. The truth was, as Winston Churchill, a onetime cavalry officer put it in his 1930 memoir, *My Early Life,* the establishment had clung to the horse because war had been a gentleman's game for so long, at least since Hastings, and it would lose its pageantry when it became fully industrialized, the province "of chemists in spectacles, and chauffeurs pulling the levers of aeroplanes or machine guns." The class consciousness in Churchill's comment is clear.

The mounted figure also is alluring because the horse, until automobiles, conferred an uncommon mobility upon its rider. The knight errant of literature was freed from the confinement of place; he could ride out on quests and crusades, to the envy of the less fortunate. The American cowboy was his successor, the Lancelot of the West, as Owen Wister, the great writer of Westerns, dubbed him. The connection was made too by John Steinbeck, a modern writer on the West, who turned to the Arthurian legends late in his career. The knight and the cowboy, not tied by the mundane toil of the manor house or the frontier homestead, appear to enjoy a special kind of individual freedom as they go forth on adventures, relying on their signature weapons, the couched lance or Winchester repeating rifle, the sword or six-gun, to deal with all occurrences. They ride literally and symbolically above it all.

Aspects of knighthood still seem to have great contemporary meaning. The ideals of chivalry, the medieval gentleman soldier's code, were succinctly set out by Geoffrey Chaucer in his unfinished poem, *The Canterbury Tales,* written mostly after 1387. The knight, he said, near the start of "The Prologue," was one "Who from the day on which he first began / To ride abroad had followed chivalry, / Truth, honour, generousness and courtesy." These values remained the qualities of the gentleman and the lady for centuries and are still within the code of the professional officer. Although knighthood in some senses encouraged conflict, the chivalric code functioned, and still can, to curb some of war's more vicious and barbaric aspects.

The accent on personal values also suggests the importance of individual character. With the urbanization and industrialization of the nineteenth century came a concern that individualism was being lost. People dressed more alike through off-the-peg clothing, lived in houses with mass-produced furnishings, perhaps worked in monotonous surroundings with hundreds of others in office buildings or factories, ate alike, and thought alike through the printing revolution that made newspapers, popular books, and magazines readily available. Social commentators increasingly worried about the conformity and uniformity of modern life. The image of the knight errant riding out on an adventure seemed to offer an antidote to modern monotony and sameness.

Robin Hood, the forest bowman who defied convention, exerted a similar appeal. Thus, in Howard Pyle's 1883 book, *The Merry Adventures of Robin Hood,* Robin exhorts a tinker or traveling salesman to give up work and "lead a right merry life in the greenwood; for cares have we not and misfortunes cometh not upon us." Similarly, a tanner does "away with tanbark and filthy vats and foul cowhides," joining the band "for a merry life." The nineteenth century saw a revival of interest in all aspects of medieval life that reflects a nostalgia for a seemingly more colorful, less uniform stage of history.

In warfare, anonymity came increasingly to characterize the battlefield. Modern weaponry relies for its effectiveness on a hail of unaimed fire, pumped out rapidly in the direction of the enemy. Rarely does either side see the opponent clearly, or even at all, and individual targets are not chosen. It is the weight of fire that counts. Under these circumstances, individual acts of heroism are difficult, even irrelevant. Flag waving counts for nothing in the face of a storm of steel and the noble die along with the ignoble, picked out by random ballistics.

As modern technology allows us to kill in this machine-like way with rapid-fire weapons, so has technology allowed us to replace the fallen soldiers in a similarly efficient bulk manner. Modern transportation and food preservation let armies swell in size to number hundreds of thousands, even millions. These trends were clear by the American Civil War, a slaughterhouse of mass armies. The famous nurse Clara Barton, watching long columns of Union soldiers march through Washington in 1864, noted "that man has no longer an individual existence, but is counted in thousands, and measured in miles." Similarly, in Stephen Crane's 1895 novel, *The Red Badge of Courage,* his protagonist, Henry Fleming, describes the advance of his regiment to the front as like being trapped in a moving box, a good metaphor for the anonymity of modern war, perhaps of modern life, especially during rush hour.

Under these circumstances, the concepts of knighthood served to reassure even common men and women that there was still room for individual character and prowess on the battlefield and in life. The images and attitudes of chivalry permeated Victorian society. Buildings, from mansions to prisons, echoed medieval castle architecture. The romantic historical novels of Sir Walter Scott were devoured on both sides of the Atlantic. And probably the most famous work of England's poet laureate at the time, Alfred Lord Tennyson, was his 1859 Arthurian epic, *Idylls of the King.* Medieval jousts were held by gentlemen in frock coats and ladies in crinolines, from Baltimore, Maryland, to Nottingham, England. Even Arthur Conan Doyle, who invented the prototype of the modern scientific detective, Sherlock Holmes, was more proud of his tales of chivalry, such as *The White Company* (1891), which detailed the adventures of a knight's company in the fourteenth century. "Let us pray to God that we may ever hold their virtues," wrote the author.

Victorians perpetually used the language of chivalry to praise admired military leaders, and soldiers liked to describe their colleagues as knights. There were enough small wars against weak, ill-equipped native opponents to give the British in particular the illusion that individual soldiers could be Christian paladins like the crusaders of old, and that one heroic individual could still make the difference. Such a one was the eccentric Charles Gordon, who died at Khartoum, stubbornly disobeying orders in an attempt to stop a Sudanese independence movement from Egypt. He became an international icon in the West and is still portrayed this way in the 1966 movie *Khartoum,* starring Charlton Heston as a chivalric warrior and unique man of destiny, clearly at odds with the utilitarian politicians in black frock coats.

Both sides in the American Civil War strove to place a chivalric veneer on the fighting. George Freeman Noyes, a Union captain, in his 1863 *The Bivouac and the Battlefield,* remembered that on a night march to the bloody battlefield of Antietam, September 1862, the troops seemed bewitched by moonlight: "No longer Yankee soldiers of the nineteenth century, we were for the nonce knights of the ancient chivalry, pledged to a holier cause and sworn to a noble issue than Coeur de Lion [Richard I of England, a compulsive crusader] himself ever dreamed of."

In the other camp, Gen. Robert E. Lee was perpetually described as a knight without peer, with a chivalry beyond reproach. This hearkening back to chivalry worked particularly well as a morale booster for the South, the weaker side in the war, which had to hope that superior character might offset inferior material resources. In 1861, at the start of the war, many Southerners claimed that they were the descendants of the Normans and that Northerners were the wretched offspring of Saxon churls who became the underclass after Hastings. Thus, the families of both General Lee and Gen. George Edward Pickett claimed a lineage dating to knights who were thought to have fought under William at Hastings.

The delusion that the Confederacy would triumph through superior chivalry led Mark Twain to curse Walter Scott, with his blood-stirring tales of knighthood, as the inspiration for Southern daydreams of glory. Even Jefferson Davis, the worn-out and humiliated ex-president of the Confederacy and going to federal prison in 1865, was described by Southerners as King Arthur being spirited to Avalon. In Richmond, Virginia, there was built a Confederate Memorial Chapel called the "Battle Abbey of the South," an allusion to the abbey William erected, in gratitude to God, on the site of his victory at Hastings. The rebel chapel had a set of murals, devoted to the South's Lost Cause, which were supposed to rival the Bayeux Tapestry. In Montgomery, Alabama, the inscription on the monument to the dead Southern soldiers reads:

> The knightliest of the knightly race
> Who since the days of old
> Have kept the lamp of chivalry
> Alight in hearts of gold.

Twain, as we have noted, thought all this preposterous and tried to warn his culture about what happened when medieval attitudes met modern weapons. In his 1889 novel, *A Connecticut Yankee in King Arthur's Court,* a New England mechanic, miraculously transported back to medieval England, massacres the whole chivalry by applying modern science to the battlefield. In a sense, Twain was predicting the slaughter of World War I, to which the combatants went dreaming of crusading glory. The British, for example, often pictured their soldiers as charging into battle mounted, with swords and lances, or as Saint George, the patron saint of England, slaying the "hun" dragon, who was accused of committing despicable, unchivalric atrocities in Belgium, including baby-killing and the rape of nuns. Chivalric imagery helped to make the conflict initially popular among the warring peoples.

However, for those actually involved in the organized, mass slaughter of the Western Front, knightly imagery could not always survive the muck and blood. But the illusions were retained on the home front, where soldiers were seen as heroic warriors dying in grand acts of individual combat and were remembered in war memorials that often pictured them as knights in armor. And at the front, knighthood took to the air, where the German fighter ace, Manfred von Richthofen, the Red Baron, and his opponents reinvented the joust fought among an elite club of gentlemanly equals.

Tales of the "Olden Days"—before industrialism and social uniformity—found fresh expression after the Great War in the work of authors like J.R.R. Tolkien, a somewhat retiring British professor who hated the grimy ugliness of the modern industrial landscape with its factories filled by toiling, anonymous workers. He was appalled by the war, which had used technology and modern organizational methods to rob individual human life of dignity and meaning in a massive slaughter. He created an alternate setting, Middle Earth, where unique beings could still perceive, and perhaps attain, a special destiny by going forth to test character against great obstacles for worthy goals, all with the hope of returning home wiser and stronger. Tolkien's stories have been endlessly appealing, especially to youth, and have been partly the inspiration for the computer games that pit knights and ladies against trolls and demons. In 2001, *Lord of the Rings* was filmed for the second time and proved to be highly popular with international audiences of all ages. Although Tolkien ventured away from the standard Arthurian fare, his basic concepts are not far from *The Song of Roland* or the eighth-century Anglo-Saxon epic poem of warriors and monsters, *Beowulf*.

Tolkien has been accused of creating an unhealthily regressive escape literature. One professor of education, Alan Chedzoy, writing in the *Guardian,* January 12, 1972, concerned by the many students in America and Britain who read Tolkien, asserts that they must be weaned from "the supreme ostrich writer of our time," who reinforces innate timidity, sticking one's head in the sand to avoid the real world. This criticism may miss the point. Faced with the humdrum of modern existence, what British writer Alec Waugh called "the long littleness of life" in the twentieth century, and constantly pressured to conform to popular norms, many of us may need imaginative guides to fuller lives. Young people, as they develop, need to understand that it is legitimate, even essential, to stretch and extend individually beyond the peer group, the adolescent pack. Even adults, as we go about our daily labor, worrying about mortgages, health insurance, grub worms in the lawn, our children's grades, and the boss's attitude, can find life stressful and tedious, lacking adventure or bold challenge. In these circumstances, it is not necessarily unhealthy to have models of behavior that can help us give our doings a larger shape and purpose, help us to live, even in the suburbs, in such a way that life has a heroic cast.

This is the hero quest, as defined by the anthropologist Joseph Campbell, who, in his books and 1988 interviews with television journalist Bill Moyers, introduced the concept to millions. For our purposes, the hero is the knight, or perhaps a bowman in forest green, setting out to explore what is over the horizon beyond the village. He, or she in this metaphorical context, is someone who determines that simply doing what everyone else does is not enough; there must be an individually fulfilling purpose to existence. The purpose may take the form of a unique kind of job or hobby, perhaps moving to a different region or country, dressing in a way that is out of fashion, or rejecting mainstream values.

To live a fulfilled life, we must overcome our character failings, the censure of others, and personal misfortunes; in moving forward, we must go into the dark woods that border the road of personal development, where we fight monsters and dragons. These may take the form of liberating ourselves from possessive or abusive family members, getting over an addiction, or coming to terms with our real abilities and needs. To leave the village and lead independent lives is frightening and not for most people; they will stay where it is safe in the warmth of the crowd. The hero quest takes significant personal courage, and the risks of exhaustion and failure are great; hence the sustaining image of the knight riding forth. As the newsletter of the contemporary group the National Registry of Medieval Roleplayers in the U.S. suggests, the knight was someone "to be reckoned with, admired," often "weary but defiant" as he "turned to view his opponents across the field of honor."

Two stories linked to 1485 illustrate different aspects of the hero quest and demonstrate that knighthood still has lessons to teach us. The first is Shakespeare's *Richard III,* which suggests that we can be too ambitious and fail if, on our quest, we do intentional harm to others and put success above chivalry, which is committed to uphold humanity. Richard is one of the greatest villains in literature. Physically deformed, he decides he is not fitted for civil pursuits but will plot his way to the throne, using murder to cut a path. Like most writers before the current era, Shakespeare suggests, regrettably, that physical handicaps are a reflection of inner evil; however, Richard remains a remarkable creation, witty, clever, forceful, strong in character. Shakespeare has him kill a good sum of people to achieve power, including the Lancastrian prince Edward, his own wife, Anne, his brother Clarence, and the princes in the Tower. Only the last is possibly true but the others make a good story, and we view with horror a man whose hero quest has led him into the worst excesses and sealed his own fate. It is a cautionary tale and, played well, it leaves a lasting impression.

But Shakespeare doesn't leave it here. He has another lesson to teach. As he comes to Bosworth, Richard is pretty certain that he will die in battle. But he does not flinch from the encounter. Indeed, in the climax of battle, he is willing to trade the whole kingdom that he has achieved through murder to someone who will give him a horse so that he may cross swords with Henry one more time. He will not fly the field but dies as a king and, in so doing, is partially redeemed. The moral, perhaps obvious, is an important one: we can't always choose our fates, but how we face them is in our hands; we can meet them nobly and with dignity.

Because this ending is so important, the final scene of the 1995 Ian McKellen film, which mistakenly places special effects above dramatic value, does not work. As pyrotechnic explosions light up the screen, Richard, laughing maniacally, is sucked into a surreal vortex. The final depiction of the king steals from the fallen hero the dignity with which he meets the fate he has brought upon himself and thus robs us, the audience, of gaining from his lesson and sharing in the human tragedy. Richard is also played as a twentieth-century fascist dictator in a mythical 1930s Great Britain, which denies us the understanding that part of the hero's tragedy is that he has forsaken the values of the knight during his life and is redeemed by embracing them in his final stand. Perhaps this is why a false ending had to be tacked on to the movie; the original no longer had meaning in the film's displaced context. Whatever the case, the movie makes the condescending assumption, common when staging Shakespeare, that the modern audience cannot cope with the Bard on his terms, but must have his work jazzed up and relocated to be accessible.

The second story linked to 1485 that illustrates a different version of the hero quest is T.H. White's 1958 rewriting of Malory, *The Once and Future King*. Perhaps of all versions of the Arthurian legends, White's has the most moral fervor in its creation. Written in the wake of two world wars, the book strongly urges us to find peace through a common humanity. *The Once and Future King* was made into the 1960 musical play *Camelot*, which was filmed in 1967 with Richard Harris and Venessa Redgrave. The story of Arthur's life is written as a hero quest in search of the nobility of peace.

As a boy, the orphaned Arthur is hidden for safety. He emerges as a young man to claim the throne that is rightfully his, and, with the help of the magician Merlin, sets about ending the internecine warfare of the barons, that weakness in the feudal order. From his apprenticeship in bringing peace, Arthur invents the concept of the Knights of the Round Table, a companionship of equals who will use might, not for self, but in defense of right. Arthur's dream crashes when his son, Mordred, conspires to catch the king's wife, Guinevere, and his best friend, Lancelot, making love. Above revenge, Arthur is nevertheless trapped by circumstance into making the war that he hates. He feels that all has been for nothing. Yet in a boy, Tom of Warwick, who is the young Malory, he finds a disciple who will carry on the story of the Round Table and Arthur's struggle to end the reign of brute force.

The story thus takes us through the life cycle, from youthful idealism to the disillusion of middle age when it appears that much we had hoped for will not be accomplished. Mortality beckons. However, if the life has been lived well, if the quest has been truly followed, there comes at the end the final consoling knowledge that something of what we have aspired to will carry on, albeit in the behavior of our children, the lives of our students, the work we have done, or our contributions to the community. Arthur's, unlike Richard's, is a successful quest, even though he too will end his life in battle. The difference is in the moral worth of the quest which each pursues.

The idea that we might revisit Arthur's kingdom to reinvigorate our essential idealism centered for some 1960s youth on the imagery of John Fitzgerald Kennedy's presidency, an aura of idealism that became more pronounced after Kennedy's death, when the divisions brought about by Vietnam and the disillusion with Richard Nixon's incumbency produced a longing for what had seemed a fleeting glimpse of Camelot.

In America, the Cold War had been cast in chivalric terms, as a clash between ultimate good and evil. Such a portrayal was not hard, as the excesses committed by the Soviets made it easy to see them as black knights or even monsters. William Casey, a specialist in covert operations, extolled the Central Intelligence Agency as a new order of Teutonic Knights, a medieval religious-military guild that fought against the Slavs. Casey cut his teeth on covert operations in the Office of Special Services during World War II, America's "Good War" crusade against totalitarianism, leading him to believe that the U.S. was on a knight's quest to save the world for freedom.

Some of the youngsters who went to fight in Vietnam were deeply moved by the movies of their era, not only John Wayne's inspiring *Sands of Iwo Jima* (1949), but also such tales of warrior nobility as MGM's *Knights of the Round Table* (1953) and *Ivanhoe* (1952), based on Scott's story of Norman and Saxon chivalry in contest. Such an idealistic youth was Philip Caputo, a young college graduate from the suburbs of Chicago, who joined the Marine Corps and fought in Vietnam, 1965–1966. He described his experiences in a 1977 memoir, *A Rumor of War*. Caputo thought that the corps would reincarnate the companionship of knights and that the talk in the mess hall would be "something like the gatherings of Beowulf's warriors in the mead hall," where stories of great deeds were retold.

Tragically, Caputo's tour in Vietnam proved to be a misbegotten quest. The young soldier went from idealism to disillusionment, finally being tried for murder after his men killed friendly Vietnamese in a bungled covert operation. At one point, Caputo was what he called "the officer in charge of the dead," who had to count and then lay out for inspection by American generals and visiting politicians the bodies of Vietnamese who could be counted as Viet Cong by any feasible stretch of the imagination. Often, these corpses were no more than unfortunates who had been in the fire zone at the wrong moment. Caputo's grail quest ended in disappointment and self-doubt but, fortunately, he refused to let this be the end of his saga. He went on to write about the war and to explain to others what it is like to endure the ordeal of combat in a fight where the moral lines are not clear.

One vital bond that sustained soldiers in Vietnam, as in many other conflicts, was the buddy system, the camaraderie of the front lines. This unwillingness to let down one's fellows in a crisis, more than faith in an abstract cause, or thoughts of defending home and fireside, has kept many combat soldiers from going mad or deserting in the face of the enemy. The buddy system is the cement that guarantees small-unit cohesion which, in turn, keeps armies from disintegrating. Caputo described this feeling of togetherness, of special closeness, by quoting the lines, "We few, we happy few, we band of brothers."

These words are taken from Shakespeare's *Henry V,* when Henry encourages his men on the eve of Agincourt. The scene is important because it is the first instance in early modern literature where the importance of comradeship to solidarity in combat is recognized. Henry says that all the soldiers of the English army, no matter how humble, will be wrapped in the pride of having stood together on this day; in this context—even the common bowmen are his brothers. The idea has had great potency as a cement holding together the stability of military units.

Ironically, Shakespeare wrote his memorable lines some two centuries after Agincourt and employed a burgeoning sense of English nationalism to suggest a feeling of commonality that Henry would not have felt at the time. Much as he relied on his bowmen, they were still commoners; he belonged to the same order of knighthood as the French nobility across the lines, a fraternity that crossed state boundaries. Illustrating the point, the pathetic petition of a crippled English bowman begs the royal court years after Agincourt for some modest relief from his miserable poverty that Henry had failed to alleviate. The brotherhood of battle had severe social limits.

Nevertheless, no matter how romantic his image of medieval battle may be, Shakespeare captured something important about why war can appeal to one side of human nature. Living in the great age of Elizabethan nationalism, which saw an explosion of aggressive energy resulting in successful conquests in Ireland and America, he wanted to express the exuberant pride in a common identity felt by English adventurers of his time. In so doing, he ably described something vital to humanity's satisfaction in war: the felt sense of having shared an experience more thrilling, more bonding, than anything available in civilian life. To belong to an embattled band of heroes seems a privilege. Henry's words on the eve of battle echo through history, to William Barrett Travis's stirring 1836 appeals for help from the beleaguered Alamo, to Winston Churchill's famous tribute to the British Royal Air Force pilots who won the 1940 Battle of Britain and prevented a German invasion of the island. Never, he said in a direct evocation of Shakespeare's happy few, had so much been owed by so many to so few.

Powerfully appealing to many, the concept of the intimate male sharing of exposure to war unfortunately tends to exclude women from the club of heroes. Indeed, in the nineteenth-century knightly revival this rejection of the other sex was a major attraction for men. As the sexes drew into different spheres, partly as a response to the Industrial Revolution's sharp delineation of men as producers and women as homemakers, men sought same-sex companionship, as did women. For men, knighthood was a perfect, positive symbol of this separation; it emphasized qualities then associated with manliness—muscular strength and assertiveness, patriarchal protectiveness, physical courage, a steely control of feelings. Armor kept men safely protected from exposure to women, an idea found in a genre of Victorian painting that depicts men fully shielded in armor engaged in various relations with nude women, who are either coquettishly trying to distract the knight from noble deeds of masculine endeavor or are stripped and bound, in need of rescuing from the clutches of dragons and blackguards. It was a perfect scenario for the male who could both view the increasingly mysterious female body and be protected from a similar exposure. The idea was still viable if a little bizarre when John Boorman, in *Excalibur,* had Uther Pendragon, Arthur's father, rape a naked noblewoman while wearing full armor.

Yet the hero quest and knighthood do not have to be exclusively male. Military-style companionship, the buddy system, can encompass women, and homosexuals, as it has increasingly embraced African Americans. A female nurse, describing what had been important to her about Vietnam, told a *New York Times* reporter, "I think about Vietnam often and I find myself wishing that I was back there. Life over there was so real and in some ways so much easier. There was no such thing as black or white, male or female. We dealt with each other as human beings, as friends. We worked hard, we partied hard, we were a unit. A lot of us, when we left, wished we didn't have to come home" (March 23, 1981). The buddy system she describes is a direct descendant of Shakespeare's band of brothers. The concept's simplification of life's normally complex propositions down to the basics, kill or be killed, may appeal to women as much as to men; life seems easier when survival alone is the end pursued. In the 1998 animated feature *Quest for Camelot* the daughter of a slain knight of the Round Table sets off on her own hero quest to find the magic sword, Excalibur, suggesting that the universally appealing model of knighthood can be adapted to changing gender roles.

Knighthood's resilience, its refusal to die out from our collective imagination, suggests that at its best chivalry tapped into the most enduring and inspiring human values—civility and courtesy, personal character and an honorable demeanor, generosity to the weak, protest of the exploiter and the bully, willingness to stand up in a good cause no matter the odds—qualities that Malory wished to preserve for posterity.

So did another soldier-writer, who took part in the often sordid, less-than-noble wars at the end of the medieval period and was a victim and perpetrator of their cruelties, Miguel de Cervantes. The figure he created, Don Quixote de La Mancha, does not have the heroic stature of, say, T.H. White's King Arthur, yet he shares the same tragic dignity and refusal to give up chivalric qualities because they are out of fashion. It is hardly coincidental that Quixote's story became a musical play, *Man of La Mancha,* shortly after *Camelot* and was made into a movie in 1972, with Peter O'Toole as the protagonist. Recently, in 2000, *Don Quixote* was filmed for television audiences by TNT.

In trying to explain why Don Quixote has survived through the centuries, Spanish critic Miguel de Unamuno suggests that the knight and his squire, Sancho Panza, followed a seemingly impractical path, the way of disinterested idealism and self-sacrificing honor in a milieu that most highly rewards expediency and self-gratification. The worldly, who live in the satisfaction of the immediate moment, have laughed at Quixote's folly. Yet, in the long fight that pitted the lonely knight and squire enlisted in the noble cause of defending universal values against those who would exploit the world for instant advantage, which side is remembered? Who is it that is ultimately a victim of illusion, the servant of today, prepared to do anything that turns an immediate profit, without ethics or compassion, or the person who strives to find and follow eternal verities? Those who mock Quixote, says Unamuno, turn to dust, but Quixote and his squire live on forever through their enduring principles.

In the end, then, the knight lives on because the concept of chivalry captures the idea that certain verities, which we perceive as universally valid, are worth standing up for. This willingness to be counted in the struggle for higher values began with a military order, but it no longer need be defined that way. The resilience of chivalric themes in our popular culture suggests that knightliness can be a quality of mind, a sought-after elevation of the spirit.

TWO

✛

Brutal Soldiery

We usually don't realize when we hear contemporary Americans voicing distrust of their government, along with related fears of conquest by a tyrannical New World Order, that these concerns are linked historically to social traumas produced by political-military developments in the English-speaking world of the seventeenth and eighteenth centuries. In this chapter, we shall trace the roots of current thinking to early modern Anglo-American hatred of mercenary soldiers and the developing regular or standing army of the central state.

The English writer and social critic H.G. Wells commented in his 1909 novel *Tono-Bungay* that, "Civilization is only possible through confidence, so that we can bank our money and go unarmed about the streets." Judged by this criterion, Americans must lack confidence in their civilization, or at least their forces for order, as they are the most heavily armed society in the developed world. Most comparable nations today have strict gun controls. Yet there are approximately 230 million guns in private hands in the United States, owned by more than 70 million people. Many weapons are not made for hunting: by 1989 Americans possessed nearly 4 million military-style rifles and carbines. Some gun owners keep an arsenal not only to deter criminals but to inhibit the central government and its agents. As a T-shirt on sale at gun shows in 1995 proclaimed: "Patriots Awake! Before It's Too Late. / I love my country but I fear my government."

Loose carping about the policies and methods employed by government is undoubtedly a universal human pastime. In the United States, disgruntlement often takes the relatively benign form of political tirades against the evils of Washington and speeches on the traditional wisdom of small government. Some states put constitutional restraints on the time that their legislators can spend in session and limit the terms governors may serve to minimize the damage that can be done during their incumbency. Grousing about the Internal Revenue Service and public waste of money are also safety valves for frustration about the quality and probity of public services.

But hostility to government in America goes beyond disdain. Central authority is regularly accused of systematic opposition to individual rights and of having a set plan to introduce authoritarian controls. Walter Williams, a university professor and syndicated newspaper columnist, charged in a widely printed article on September 4, 1994, that the IRS and the Environmental Protection Agency use terrorist methods. Describing the tactics of the Bureau of Alcohol, Tobacco, and Firearms, along with the Fish and Wildlife Service and the Corps of Engineers, as gestapo-like, he quotes Thomas Jefferson on the need of the people to keep and bear arms, "as a last resort, to protect themselves against tyranny in government." Williams appears to advocate here armed resistance to federal authority.

This sense of crisis, of being in liberty's last ditch, recurs frequently in America's comparatively brief national history, leading inevitably to violent encounters between citizens and the forces of authority. Some clashes have been serious enough to warrant the label of revolt, starting with Shays' Rebellion of 1786–1787 and the Whiskey Rebellion of 1794. Angry, violent denunciation of central government has not been the exclusive stance of any one political party or persuasion. In the 1850s, radical abolitionists denied the legitimacy of a government that upheld slavery and, building on the ideas of earlier English radicals, they appealed to a higher law of conscience, above federal law, that could justify using force to oppose tyrannical policies. Southerners, too, opposed a government they deemed to be dictatorial. In 1836, Nathaniel Beverley Tucker, a Virginia social commentator, published *The Partisan Leader,* a futuristic novel warning that Martin Van Buren of New York, as president, would use federal bayonets to end the republic. America is saved from despotism only by the leadership of a Virginia soldier who, following the folklore path of George Washington, leads a partisan or guerrilla force of militiamen against the regular army, the tool of tyranny. Roughly following Tucker's prophecy, from 1861 to 1865, the Confederacy fought what it considered a war of liberation from the dictatorship of Abraham

Lincoln and the Black Republicans, who resisted slavery's introduction into additional states.

A century later, in the turmoil over the Vietnam War, young leftist radicals again depicted the federal government as tyrannical. In 1965, Carl Oglesby, president of Students for a Democratic Society, justified resistance to the military draft by citing Thomas Jefferson and Tom Paine on the inalienable right of the citizen to oppose an illegitimate use of power. The following year, resisters from the Free University of New York, called before the House Un-American Activities Committee, likened themselves to the Green Mountain Boys, Revolutionary War militiamen who had fought Britain's standing army. One student appeared in a blue colonial militia uniform.

The right wing is currently the most concerned political group about the encroachments of government. In the 1990s, private militias sprang up, with roots in earlier paramilitary movements, such as the Minutemen, a private army of the 1960s wedded to the ultra-conservative views of the John Birch Society, as well as the Posse Comitatus and the expanded Ku Klux Klan of the 1980s. These groups stated a willingness to use force to oppose government intervention at various levels. Many militia members were heavily armed; for example, the Texas Reserve Militia was equipped with assault rifles.

Militia leaders made clear what these arms were for. Doug Fales, a Californian militia head, in opposing any limitation on the availability of weapons, asked, "How can you defend against the government if you have inferior arms to the military?" The militias of Montana and Michigan warned that they would violently oppose any government attempt to disarm civilians. Militia groups also threatened to forcefully prevent abortion and enforcement of environmental legislation. Although much of the talk was rhetorical posturing, at least one militia group mobilized to shoot down black helicopters of the National Guard, associated in their catechism with the coming New World Order. Serious confrontations ranged from individual gun battles with federal agents, such as Randy Weaver's fight at Ruby Ridge, Idaho, in 1992, to the larger encounter with the Branch Davidians at Waco, Texas, in 1993, and Timothy McVeigh's 1995 assault on a federal building in Oklahoma City. The Branch Davidians received via UPS over forty thousand dollars worth of arms, including machine guns, rifles, and hand grenades. Cult members believed the federal government to be a satanic force trying to enslave the globe.

The idea is not a new one. In the 1960s, fears of a hostile takeover of America, with government collusion, focused on a worldwide communist conspiracy. When, in the wake of President John F. Kennedy's 1963 assassination, a congressional bill was introduced that would tighten federal control of mail-order arms, an Arizona man drove to Washington in January 1964 to testify before the Senate Commerce Committee that the legislation was "a further attempt by a subversive power to make us part of a one world socialistic government." In the same year, Republican minority whip, Senator Thomas R. Kuchel, revealed in the *New York Times,* July 21, 1963, that he received about six thousand letters a month warning that top government officials were communists about to hand over America to a United Nations dictatorship. Some correspondents said that Chinese or other communist forces were poised on the Mexican border to effect the coup.

With the collapse of the Soviet Union, the specific source of the alien threat became harder to define. But the government was still seen as subverted, a tool of totalitarian forces working to create a New World Order. This term, used by both sides in World War II, was refurbished by President George Bush to describe the ultimate goals of the coalition forces in the 1990 Gulf War, and was then seized upon by militias and other disaffected groups to describe a loose but potent international alliance of government officials, Jews, Arabs, American minorities, bankers, socialists, and criminals to eradicate freedom. The tools of tyranny were mercenary forces, such as the Gurkhas, tough Nepalese soldiers originally raised to help police the British empire and thus a seemingly fitting symbol of the hireling without patriotic local allegiance. Native police working for the British authorities in Hong Kong fit a similar model of the mercenary, as, in a loose way, did any military working for the UN.

It is tempting to dismiss such scenarios as the products of a lunatic fringe. Yet the Southern Poverty Law Center, which monitors militant groups, estimated that in 1995 there were 857 active militia groups. Kenneth S. Stern, an expert from the American Jewish Committee, believed that there were at least forty thousand Americans enrolled in private paramilitary organizations in the mid 1990s, and that perhaps millions more embraced their political ideas and even approved of their military preparations. Numbers declined by the year 2000, but many members went into more extreme hate groups, often spreading their message via the web.

Important, too, is the role and significance of the National Rifle Association, which has broad ideological influence in America and a growing membership of about 3.5 million. Its original purpose was in part to protect the rights of sports enthusiasts and to prepare Americans to repel foreign invasion. However, its recent rhetoric is alarmist about internal government threats to liberty. Federal authorities are depicted as alien forces bent on banning guns to abridge citizens' rights. In June 1999, for example, the NRA website posted a statement that both President Bill Clinton and Adolf Hitler's Nazis favored gun control. In a fundraising letter dated April 13, 1995, Wayne LaPierre, then head of the NRA, said that the semi-automatic weapons ban "gives jack-booted government thugs *more power to take away our Constitutional rights, break in our doors, seize our guns, destroy our property, even injure or kill us.*"

Many of the alienated today, as in the past, have real grievances, stemming from social displacement, loss of a strong voice in public policy-making, and economic decline. But what matters here is not the substance of complaint, but the model many Americans use to voice their anxieties, a framework that encourages rather than assuages distrust and tends toward strident confrontation and visions of violence. Such a model predicates an innate tendency in government toward authoritarianism, presaging an assault on citizens' rights using a conglomerate mercenary force with no patriotic allegiance. Although Americans are often accused of having no sense of history, of living only for the present or even the future, this world view is in fact deeply rooted in the history of the English-speaking peoples at the very time when American culture was forming. If Americans are to diminish the high level of violence within their society, one important step will be to recognize that the way many citizens express their disagreement with government indicates they are held in the grip of a historical pattern that molds their reaction to change.

Many Americans are aware of the historical dimension of the terms they use to express the tension in their view of government. The touchstone for articulating government's threat to their well-being is the Second Amendment to the Constitution, which they believe guarantees the right of all Americans to bear arms in maintaining a free society. If guns are restricted, then freedom will fail. Americans are alone among developed nations in believing that private gun ownership is a guarantor of, rather than a threat to, democracy.

David Gregg, writing in *American Rifleman,* the journal of the NRA, June 1991, stated that without the Second Amendment, democracy would be "little more than a ghost haunting reality and praying that it will not be exorcised by the natural forces of bureaucracy, greed, power and corruption." And a gun owner writing in *Newsweek,* June 6, 1994, opposing the new assault-weapons ban, said bluntly, "the Second Amendment was clearly intended to hold tyranny in check by keeping a civilian militia (read farmers, storekeepers, bakers) as well armed as the military." The ban, he wrote, was merely "a cover for firearms confiscation" and "trampled on the constitutional rights of millions."

It is to the intellectual credit of these citizens that they see a historical perspective to contemporary issues. Yet the role of history in forming current thought patterns is much deeper, older, and more complex than they think. America was founded and came to nationhood in a two-hundred-year period, the seventeenth and eighteenth centuries. The epoch was crucial also for resolving the nature of the central state and its relationship to the citizen. Had America been formed in any other major age, its ways of addressing constitutional issues would have been different; in which case its citizens might not be so wedded to bearing or using arms. To understand requires that we pick up our historical narrative thread where we left it in chapter 1, with the feudal world succumbing to capitalism and the mercenary soldier rising as an armed servant of the state. For, at the heart of the idea of the tyrannical central state is the image of the mercenary soldier, the brutal hireling used to destroy the liberties of the citizen.

J.H. Patterson, a British regular army officer, visited the U.S. to drum up support for the Allied cause on the eve of American entry into World War I. He was shocked to find that numerous Americans looked on their regular army not as defenders of democracy but as "lazy, useless brutes." He continued: "It is incomprehensible to me why the average American should have such a strong prejudice against the Army. He seems to imagine that it is some vague kind of monster which, if he does not do everything in his power to strangle and chain up, will one day turn and rend him, and take all his liberties away." A Briton in 1916, who believed that the king's army was saving freedom from the despotic Central Powers, might find the American attitude peculiar. But his English ancestors of the seventeenth century would not.

Much of English and American colonial history in this period was dominated by events in the reigns of the four Stuart kings, a house that ruled from 1603 to 1688, with a break from 1642 to 1660, when there was a civil war followed by a commonwealth under the rule of Parliament and a protector. Elizabeth I, granddaughter of Henry VII, who had won at Bosworth, died childless in 1603. Without an apparent heir to the throne, the English invited James VI of Scotland to take the crown as James I, beginning the Stuart dynasty.

Securing James was a good move in that the quick decision averted any chance of renewed feuding over the throne. The Stuarts had ability, but no experience of the English political system, with Parliament's growing role as the voice of the solid propertied people, the respectable middle class. Also, the Stuarts favored Catholicism at a time when England was decidedly veering to Protestantism. Consequently, much of the seventeenth century witnessed a struggle between the Stuarts and the political representatives of the people as to who should control state policy and its instrument of implementation, the armed forces. The Stuarts were finally exiled, but even then their threat to the peace of the realm forced their successors to maintain a strong standing army, further exacerbating the distrust felt by the citizen toward the central state.

Before going into detail, we need to broadly note the developing relationship between the soldier and society in the early modern period. Well before the end of the Middle Ages, a cash system for exchange of goods and services had become popular, supplementing and then supplanting the feudal reliance on land as the basis of economic arrangements. Many knights had welcomed the opportunity to pay a fee rather than perform military service; merchants paid money to gain privileges and immunities from aristocratic domination; and kings welcomed a cash flow, with which they could hire professional bureaucrats and soldiers.

The growth of central power was positive in many ways. Kings could impose a common rule of law through their agents and soldiers, replacing the often arbitrary and capricious rule of local nobles. This King's Peace allowed trade, agriculture, and learning to flourish, with a concomitant increase in prosperity. Yet centralization also could mean oppression to some people, particularly after the Protestant Reformation of the sixteenth century splintered the Catholic Church, changing religion from a universal social bond to a major cause of conflict. The same authority that upheld the rule of law could impose a state-authorized religion and punish those who dissented.

In military terms, the coming to prominence of paid professionals was a mixed blessing. Until late in the seventeenth century, no major European nation could afford a standing or permanent army with careers spent under one flag. Professional soldiers were usually mercenaries, hired for the duration of hostilities and then released. The arrangement had some strengths. Mercenaries could be assumed to know their trade, unlike many of the rank and file in a militia system, and they embraced the art of war, whereas many knights had turned to peaceful pursuits long before the end of the Middle Ages. Furthermore, hiring the necessary soldiers was more convenient than wheedling a levy out of the major peers of the realm.

But there were also some inherent problems. First, the soldier could rarely afford fixed patriotic or religious ties. The mercenary captains were international contractors, hiring out their companies to the best bidders. If they didn't get paid, or got a better offer, they might change sides. Sydnam Poyntz, an English mercenary quoted in *The Thirty Years War* (1938), who confessed that he changed allegiances without compulsion, said, "I wandered I knew not whither and followed I knew not whom." It was said of sixteenth-century armies that they were reduced 50 percent within six months by sickness and desertion to the enemy.

Soldiers were often short of money, food, and clothing, partly because some captains kept many of the payments intended for their men, but also because the clumsy bureaucratic apparatus couldn't collect and disburse sufficient tax money, and ministers kept the army cash-short to keep it subservient to the civil power. In these circumstances, preying upon civilians for plunder was endemic, armies stripped any region through which they marched, leaving famine, disease, and ruin in their wake. During the Thirty Years War, which plagued Europe from 1618 to 1648, the city of Weisskirchen in Moravia refused shelter and supplies to Gen. Ernst von Mansfeld's mercenary army. An English trooper recalled, "We entered killing man, woman and child: the execution continued the space of two hours, the pillaging two days." Often, the mercenaries made no distinction between enemy and friendly populations. Frederick V, a seventeenth-century king of Bohemia, complained, "There ought to be some difference made between friend and enemy but these people ruin both alike." In 1576, for example, the Spanish garrison in the southern Netherlands, which had not been paid for two years, ran amuck, sacking Antwerp and murdering eight thousand people.

Demobilized troops remained a social problem. Crippled veterans might be given official licenses to beg, but many veterans roamed the countryside in bands, begging help from, and frightening, the locals. "Hark, hark, the dogs go bark, the beggars are coming to town," ran an English doggerel. "Some in rags and some in tags, and one in a scarlet gown." (Scarlet was a popular uniform color.) Men trained in arms resorted in desperation to extortion. In July 1654 two ex-officers of the royal army, named Hussey and Peck, were hanged as highwaymen in Oxford, England. A witness, Anthony Wood, noted that "they had no money to maintain them, which made them rob on the highway."

War, which had been medieval Christendom's highest temporal activity, now appeared to many as a pestilence, and the mercenary soldier as a predator. According to Gregory King, a seventeenth-century economist, the soldier was not a producer and should be catalogued with paupers, day laborers, and others who added nothing to the pool of wealth and from whose ranks the military were often recruited. The many problems associated with mercenaries led the Italian diplomat Niccolò Machiavelli to state in his 1513 political treatise, *The Prince*, that the reliance of the state should be on an army of patriots and not on contractors or condottiere. Although his work was not translated until much later, many English would have agreed with him.

England was largely free of internal warfare from Bosworth in 1485 to the start of the Civil War in 1642. Hence, the English, protected by the seas from invasion, could argue that their main military reliance should be on the navy and the militia, descendant of the Anglo-Saxon *fyrd* with its obligation of all free men to bear arms in local defense. Hiring mercenaries for campaigns on the Continent or in Ireland was tolerable because they would be ravaging other people's lands. The tradition created two problems: because there was little threat of invasion, the militia, or trained bands, as they came to be called, fell into laxity; also, any soldier who desired a serious career had to seek employment overseas as a mercenary. Capt. John Smith, a military and political leader of the Jamestown colony, got his training abroad, fighting against the Spanish in the Low Countries and then with the Holy Roman Emperor against the Turks in the Mediterranean.

The common English repugnance toward professional soldiers derived not only from their predatory habits. The amateur, trained bands were commanded by known and trusted local leaders, the gentry and the propertied middle class, loyal to their districts. Mercenaries, under officers centrally appointed and with no territorial allegiance, could be used as a police force to coerce the people and rob them of the Parliamentary liberties that the English increasingly felt proved their superiority to the authoritarian regimes of the Continent. Consequently, the nature and control of the army became major issues between the Stuart kings and Parliament. On one hand, James I believed that he was divinely appointed and that his God-guided will should govern his people, an attitude he bequeathed to his son, Charles I, on his accession in 1625. On the other hand, the middle class and gentry in the Commons, the lower house of Parliament, felt that they, the propertied classes, should have a major say in affairs of state, including design of national policy and handling of the military.

The contest centered on a few core issues. One was religion. Elizabeth I, seeking to compromise the strife between Catholic and Protestant, had given a Catholic structure with Protestant beliefs to the Church of England, the Anglican state religion established by her father, Henry VIII. Although generally acceptable, some Catholics and extreme Protestants resisted. The latter are referred to broadly as Puritans, because they thought the English Church was not purified enough of Catholic forms. Numerous dissenters feared that Charles would use force to impose uniformity. Consequently, the religious issue was bound up with control of the army.

All this was part of a broad struggle by Parliament to gain a major role in developing national policy and making war. To restrain the king, Parliament sought fiscal control of the army. A crisis came in 1628 when Charles prepared for war with France. He raised soldiers in unprecedented numbers and, as no barracks existed, quartered them on unwilling civilians at private expense. Parliament, apparently more afraid of the king and his men than of the French, replied with the Petition of Right, opposing private quarter or the imposition of martial law. An exasperated monarch dissolved Parliament and for the next eleven years ruled without it, relying financially on the collection of special fees, customs, and excise duties.

In 1640 Charles was forced to recall Parliament because his attempt to impose the Anglican Book of Common Prayer on the Scots Presbyterians had provoked rebellion and the need for an army. Although Charles's personal rule had been relatively benign, Parliament saw their eleven-year suspension as an invasion of liberty and, in the Grand Remonstrance, accused Charles of abusing his office. They answered the king's request for military funding with the Militia Bill, which would give them authority to appoint military commanders and bring control of the trained bands, arsenals, and forts under Parliament. Faced with what he saw as sedition, on January 4, 1642, the king set off for the Commons with a troop of cavalry to arrest the opposition leaders, who wisely fled. Uproar followed in London and Charles felt obliged to vacate the city, riding north to raise forces to coerce his recalcitrant subjects. Parliament also began to recruit, and by the summer the parties were at war.

Charles's attempt to spring a military coup on the elected representatives of his subjects was one of the most traumatic events in the modern history of the English-speaking peoples. Its role in inflaming historic distrust of executive authority was incalculable. The shock of the event was felt in New England, where Puritans had gone, fearing exactly such an abuse of power. This incident directly drives American private militia fears of the federal government; the recurring nightmare of central authority illegitimately using force to abrogate traditional liberties has its incubus in this moment of time. For many years, whenever a sovereign enhanced the home-based standing army, memories of the event would produce such recurring shock waves that we might call it a collective case of post-traumatic stress disorder. The ramifications continue to affect the common psyche.

At the start of civil war in 1642, each side appeared to have some advantages. On one hand, much of the nobility and high-born gentry supported the king. From their ranks, he might draw junior officers, as these gentlemen were used to exercising some authority on their estates. They also would make cavalrymen, because of their training in sword fencing, horsemanship, and the weapons of game hunting. Charles could also hope to attract some of the best European generals who had a natural sympathy for strong personal government. On the other hand, Parliament held London, the great commercial center of England, and had the support of middle-class capital, financial assets that would tell in the end.

Both sides hoped to avoid the large-scale employment of mercenary companies, relying on the patriotism of the people embodied in the trained bands. But, with few exceptions, the bands proved to be poorly trained and lacking in enthusiasm for civil war; thus, the armies had to recruit mercenaries and rely for senior officers on professionals trained in the Thirty Years War. The officers' ranks included the Earl of Essex, Sir Thomas Fairfax, George Monck, and Alexander Leslie. With the coming of mercenaries, England felt the full ravages of war, soldiers taking free quarter, committing rape, murder, and plunder. Hatred of the professional soldier was inevitable and lasting in the English-speaking world.

In addition to hiring mercenaries, both sides tried to recruit likely men for the ranks but the overall quality of recruits was poor, comprising often the unemployed, the alcoholic or criminal, the physically broken or mentally simple. Oliver Cromwell, an up-and-coming Parliamentary cavalry officer, commented bitterly to Col. John Hampden after Parliamentary defeats early in the war: "Your troopers . . . are most of them old decayed servingmen and tapsters [barkeeps] and such kind of fellows." Cromwell and some other Puritan officers proposed a different model: use Parliament's fiscal strength and the rallying cry of religious and political liberty to recruit "the godly," respectable Puritan property owners, and their employees, who might be inspired by a new pride in unit quality, an economic stake in the outcome, and a righteous cause. With regular pay, uniforms, and conditions of service, under firm but fair discipline, they would be removed from the necessity or excuse for plundering. They would be "God's Englishmen," a new kind of model for an army built on military professionalism, piety, and patriotism.

Cromwell believed in promotion through merit. Although he welcomed gentry of good character and ability, he would also take plain-born men "that have honor courage and resolution in them," of "a spirit that is likely to go on as far as gentlemen will go." Good officers would produce good privates: "If you choose godly, honest men to be captains of horse, honest men will follow them." It was a novel idea. To get good men into his regiment of horse, Cromwell recruited in his own district of East Anglia, where he was a member of Parliament and knew his constituents personally. He also appointed officers from New England whose faith and courage had been tested in the American wilderness.

By 1643 Cromwell held the rank of colonel and soon commanded a double-strength cavalry regiment of twelve hundred men. The regiment had high morale, fostered by unit pride and strong discipline, partially self-imposed through a common code of conduct. It was noteworthy that those who swore paid a fine and those who got drunk ended in the stocks or worse. So well behaved were the troopers that an opponent admitted they were welcomed even in royalist districts, "insomuch that the countries where they come leap for joy of them, and come in and join them." The value of commitment and high professional standards was shown at such Parliamentary victories as Marston Moor, fought July 2, 1644, where superior discipline and training played a crucial role, and again at Naseby, fought June 14, 1645. The latter battle shattered the king's inferior army and with it his tottering cause.

By 1645 Parliament had determined to create a genuinely English army upon the lines pioneered by men like Cromwell. In February it authorized a New Model Army under command of Sir Thomas Fairfax. The men would be under one authority, clothed alike in scarlet, receiving uniform pay and rations, carrying standardized arms and equipment. Infantry regiments would have a ratio of two pikes to each musket, the missile-throwing weapon that had replaced the longbow late in the sixteenth century. Cromwell was the senior cavalry officer with over thirty-five hundred men under his command. To leaven the regiments, in which were many new recruits, Cromwell spread his veterans throughout the ranks, a stratagem that paid off at Naseby.

Fairfax marched north from London in April, hoping to threaten the royal base at Oxford. Charles, meanwhile, had taken and sacked Leicester, a victory worse than defeat, as many of his old-model troops became debilitated by debauchery or went off to dispose of their plunder. When Fairfax found the royalists at Naseby, south of Leicester, the king was outnumbered nine thousand to thirteen thousand and his army in poor fettle. In the battle, both sides chose a conventional alignment, with infantry in the middle of the line and cavalry on the wings. The battle opened with a charge by the royal cavalry, commanded by Prince Rupert of the Rhine, a leading Continental mercenary general. On the Parliamentary left wing, commanded by Col. Henry Ireton, some of the horse

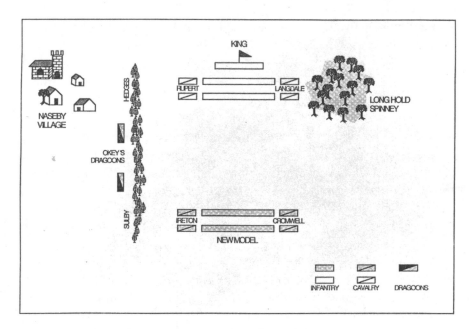

The Battle of Naseby, June 14, 1645. Map by Beth Merten.

drew swords and went forward to meet the charge, while others hung back to fire their heavy pistols at the enemy. Their confusion showed the New Model's lack of experience working together, and the enemy easily drove the dislocated forces from the field. But the mercenaries' lack of discipline and purpose now proved fatal: Rupert's men dashed off to plunder the Parliamentary baggage train instead of exploiting their success with a flank attack on the enemy infantry. On the other side of the field, Cromwell led a disciplined, spirited counter-charge that broke the royal squadrons facing him. Cromwell's men took no plunder. Held firmly in rank, they turned to attack the backs of the royal infantry, which had advanced to "push of pike" with the Parliamentary line. Assisted by Colonel Okey's mounted dragoons waiting in ambush behind a hedge, Cromwell's horse forced the surrender of the royal foot, which, assaulted front and rear, threw down their arms. Charles, his cause lost, would shortly surrender.

Naseby is forgotten because it was not made legendary by a great creative writer or artist. Yet it essentially ended the war. George M. Trevelyan, an early-twentieth-century historian, said that if the battle had gone the other way, parliamentary development would have been curtailed; England would have become part of Continental despotism, with disastrous consequences for the future freedom of Britain and America. Also, the New Model, which got its baptism here, became England's first national army, suggesting the potential for a sound modern military establishment.

Cromwell emerged more sure and powerful, becoming Parliament's greatest general and also a key political figure, the eventual Protector, or president of England. A sound administrator, he was for long a thoughtful moderate in politics, favoring the middle ranks of moderately propertied people. An Independent in religion who had once contemplated emigration to Massachusetts' Puritan commonwealth, he thought Protestant congregations should be free to worship as they chose. Yet, despite the achievement of Cromwell and the godly, they have enjoyed a very mixed press over the generations. We need to examine their reputation, to see what light it throws on their failures and our fears of centralized force.

———◆———

On the one hand, God's Englishmen in Old and New England have been viewed as agents of human progress; some Founding Fathers saw them as models. Embracing Cromwell as a champion of liberty, Connecticut named two fighting ships after him. And John Adams said that Cromwell's Protectorate was "infinitely more glorious and happy than that of his Stuart predecessor." In 1786, while in England, Adams made a pilgrimage to the "holy ground" of Naseby. Although most Americans are no longer familiar with Cromwell or the constitutional struggles of the period, the connection to civil liberty is still made in school textbooks and informs our popular culture. Americans widely believe that the Pilgrim Fathers sailed in 1620 to establish freedom of conscience and democratic government in Plymouth Bay. This benign view of Puritanism pervades Thanksgiving with its rituals of abundance and goodwill.

Other Puritan images are less flattering. Cromwell had voted for the king's death in 1649, becoming a regicide. He and other Puritan leaders were remembered in England and America as brooding, self-righteous killjoys who closed the theaters and banned the secular celebration of Christmas, which was illegal to hold in Massachusetts from 1659 to 1681. The Victorian novelist, Frances Trollope, conjured an image of the

Puritan as "long, black, grim-looking," the very "idea of one of Cromwell's fanatics." Similarly, H.L. Mencken, American journalist and wit, defined Puritanism as the haunting fear that somewhere, someone might still be happy. As late as 1987, John K. Andrews Jr., a critic outraged at Oliver Stone for his portrayal in *Platoon* (1986) of American soldiers in Vietnam as an out-of-hand killing force, akin to the old mercenary armies, likened him in the *Kentucky Enquirer,* February 26, to "the most famous Oliver in history, Cromwell of England, the original zealot out of control."

Pictures of Puritans in power, on both sides of the Atlantic, suggest a strong element of ruthless compulsion. Frances Wright, a nineteenth-century social reformer and feminist, saw the Puritan leadership as exemplary of one male concept of social action, which "sees no motive power but brute force direct." Puritan military operations can appear starkly merciless to modern historians and anthropologists, sensitive to issues of ethnic cleansing. Thus, Puritan colonists used tactics of extermination against Native American tribes in the 1637 Pequot Campaign and 1675 King Philip's War. In Ireland, Cromwell ruthlessly destroyed opposition, which was remembered by the pop group The Pogues, who, in their 1989 album *Peace and Love,* put "A curse upon you Oliver Cromwell / You who raped our motherland." Singer Elvis Costello, in his 1978 recording *Armed Forces,* attacked the modern British military as "Oliver's Army," still hired to shoot Irish and African nationalists. Victorian novelist Nathaniel Hawthorne, haunted by the part an ancestor played in the 1692 Salem Witch Trials, similarly argued that past inhumanities create a cultural pattern that continues to cause harm. In Hawthorne's *The House of the Seven Gables* (1851), the hateful attributes of a magistrate, Colonel Pyncheon, are passed on to a descendant, so that the Puritans' baleful influence continues at work. Appropriately, Pyncheon's portrait shows him with a Bible in one hand and a sword in the other, a conjunction of official force and sanctimony.

The Puritans thus appear puzzlingly contradictory, an enigma made up of the benevolent and the malignant. Actually, the Janus-faced portrait is appropriate. The Puritans did plant liberty, but that liberty was limited, first by their seventeenth-century world view, and then by the dictates of circumstance. They found principle was easier to follow when out of power and, while the dissenting citizen might speak of liberty's extension, a magistrate was likely to emphasize its limits, maintained by military force. Thus, ironically, the Puritans added twofold to our dis-

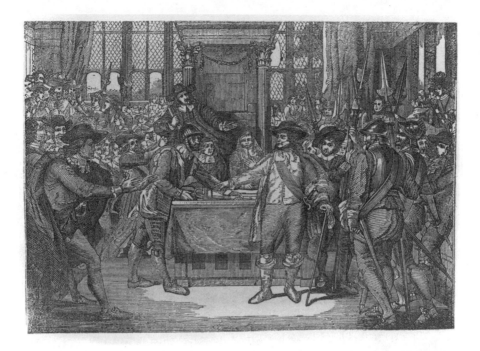

Soldiers assault citizens' liberties. Cromwell and his troops dissolve Parliament and take away the House Speaker's mace, symbol of the legislators' prerogatives. Edward Farr, *The Collegiate, School, and Family History of England*, (U.S., 1849).

trust of central government, first by lasting denunciations of abuse of authority when out of power, and then by the memorable use of brute force when in power.

After Charles's execution, Protector Cromwell hoped to work with Parliament and the army to create a peace built on moderation. But extremists in both bodies forced his hand. Parliament was dominated by Presbyterians, religious conservatives who wanted to replace one religious orthodoxy with another. Their goal offended many soldiers who had fought for extended freedom of conscience. The more radical troopers, called Levellers, also wanted profound social change, including universal suffrage, rights for women, and more equal distribution of property. Such equality terrified Parliament, men of income, who wanted no "heretical democracy," and who now tried to dissolve the army without back pay to break its spirit. Forced to act, Cromwell twice used troops, in 1653 and 1659, to purge the Commons of its most anti-army members. Thus a civil war begun to prevent the use of force in politics ended by endorsing it, and Cromwell added significantly to the popular fear of centralized military power. The poet John Milton, an erstwhile friend of the army, wrote that this was "most illegal and scandalous," tending "to the sad dishonour of that army, lately so renowned for the civilest and best-ordered in the world."

Cromwell also cowed the army, punishing the leading Levellers. Lucy Hutchinson, a Puritan, wrote, "He weeded in a few months' time, above a hundred and fifty godly officers out of the Army." Many zealous rankers went with them, and "in their room abundance of the King's dissolute soldiers were entertained." The army was being transformed from an inspired force for change into a professional standing establishment without ideological commitment. By the mid 1650s, it numbered fifty thousand men and absorbed a military budget three times that of King Charles. The army came to be feared by ordinary people and to reinforce the distrust of central authority instigated by Charles.

Unable to prevent royalist plots by other means, Cromwell in 1655 divided England into eleven military districts under major generals empowered to undertake searches and interrogations, limit public gatherings, and put "idle and loose" people to forced labor. The intent was largely to prevent subversion, but intrusions into private homes, bans on sporting events, punishments for drunkenness, blasphemy, and Sabbath-breaking, enforced by soldiers, appeared to many as an encroaching authoritarianism, particularly as Cromwell also wrested the trained bands from local control, appointing their commanders centrally. The bitter folk memory of this period eclipsed more progressive measures such as support for schools and libraries.

Cromwell's most questionable actions took place in Catholic Ireland. When the stronghold of Drogheda fell in September 1649, the Parliamentarians put nearly three thousand, including many civilians, to the sword. A similar butchery ensued at Wexford in October. Cromwell took six million acres from Irish Catholics, displacing and condemning to exile or starvation thirty thousand people. Clues to the motive for such brutal behavior lie in a ban on English soldiers marrying Irish women, and in the actions of the New Model Army after Naseby. Meeting a party of Welsh women in the rear of the fleeing royal army, the godly troopers mistook them for Irish, as they spoke Celtic. They killed some and abused others, slashing noses and faces, common punishments for whores. Well-disciplined and seemingly decent men could inflict such cruelty because, in their political and religious catechism, the Irish were savages and Catholics, servants of Satan. To spare them was blasphemy and an encouragement of the Devil's work. Tolerance was not an option.

The Puritans believed that God directed their actions; therefore, ruthlessness must be condoned by Him or defeat would follow, a doctrine known as justification by success. Contemporaries noted that Puritan soldiers were unusually fervent in prayers for success before battle and in thanksgiving afterwards, giving God the credit for victory. An officer wrote after Edgehill, 1642, "How admirably the hand of providence ordered our artillery and bullets for the destruction of the enemy." "Blessed be the God of battles," cried another. Cromwell himself, contemplating the win at Marston Moor, wrote, "God made them as stubble to our swords." From the victim's side, Michael O'Suilleabhain, a twentieth-century Irish republican, noted that "it was Oliver's invariable custom, before any fair-sized massacre, or mass murder, to intone a lengthy prayer," ending the butchery with "a second prayer, its length in proportion to the volume of blood which had been spilled."

The surety of God's favor was felt in New England also, where magistrates dictated morality, backed by the sword, and full civic participation was limited to members of the Puritan congregation. The system has been called "tribalism," but the social science term doesn't effectively explain what the "elect" themselves thought they were doing. Their model was Calvinist Geneva, a homogenous little city independent of external authority and self-disciplined to achieve God's purpose. In this context, the Puritans came to America to create liberty in the seventeenth-century sense of that term, meaning the enjoyment of special privileges open only to full members of the group and not to outsiders. John Winthrop, governor of Massachusetts, defined liberty as a collective right to perform "that only which is just and good," and not an individual entitlement to do whatever one wished. The latter was "liberty of corrupt nature, which is affected both by men and beasts, to do what they list," and was "inconsistent with authority, impatient of all restraint." Those who rejected restraint on their individual notions were punished. Roger Williams and Anne Hutchinson, for example, were banished. Witch-hunting functioned partly to curb opposition to the formal will of the community and to punish eccentricity.

Following the precedent set in Ireland, war with "savage" native tribes was total, not limited. Puritan strategy was to attack the enemy heartland, towns and crops, forcing the warriors to fight head-on for defense of their families. Warriors were exterminated; women and children might be spared but typically were enslaved. At the sacking of Mystic Village in 1637, six hundred Pequots perished, a huge proportion of the tribe. The ruthlessness was again justified by success, as showing God's will. Capt. John Underhill, marveling at the totality of Pequot destruction, recalled, "So remarkable it appeared to us, as we could not but admire the providence of God in it." The massacre was not an atrocity because, in the Old Testament, Jehovah placed a Ban, or sentence of extermination, on some enemies; hence, "We had sufficient light from the word of God for our proceedings." Similarly, the Rev. Cotton Mather noted "the marvellous providence of God," seen in "prospering the New English arms, unto the utter subduing of the quarrelsome nation and the affrighting of all the other natives."

The Puritans who had left England to escape coercion by royal authorities now used military force on recalcitrant settlers. Governor Winthrop sent soldiers to shackle an unorthodox preacher, Samuel Gorton, who had called him "The Great and Honoured Idol General," a telling depiction of the governor's police power. Thomas Merton, a free-thinking lawyer, was condemned by Plymouth Bay for establishing a community of outsiders including runaway servants and natives. He was charged with allowing interracial mating, selling liquor and arms to the Indians, and breaking the Sabbath. Miles Standish, a mercenary captain, was sent with the trained band to level the community and bring Merton in irons for shipment out of the colony.

As in England, the use of military police power overshadowed other, more positive qualities. The Puritans made lasting contributions through commitments to education and participatory local government. They practiced civility, opposing blood sports and drunkenness. They did not intend to be tyrannical but struggled with the conundrum of how to act well in a world that contains evil. Because they resorted to force to impose their will, they came to practice the same intimidation that had tainted Stuart rule. In so doing, they added to Anglo-American distrust of central authority and fear of its military police power.

The divisiveness arising from the English Civil War period lived long in folk memory, contributing to American regional consciousness. As David

Hackett Fischer reminded us in his 1989 work, *Albion's Seed*, the old stereotypes, of New Englanders as Yankees bred of Puritans and Southerners as Cavaliers who had followed King Charles, had some truth in them. Much of Northeastern culture was dominated by Puritan migrants. At the same time, Virginia, Maryland, and to some extent Carolina became home to Anglicans and Catholics, supporters of the Stuarts, some fleeing there during the Commonwealth. Mutual distrust fed sectionalism. In the 1850s, Southerners, defending their culture against abolitionist assaults, argued they had created a benevolent aristocracy, based on the personal authority of the plantation owners, descendants of English nobility. Northerners, progeny of Puritan merchants, were too low-bred to appreciate Southern culture. Opponents of slavery, in turn, called for inspiration on Puritan strength in a righteous cause. The Massachusetts poet James Russell Lowell, disgusted by Northern political compromise over slavery, claimed he had been visited by the ghost of Capt. Miles Standish, who told him New Englanders of old "had some toughness in our grain" and knees "that were not good at bending." When John Brown declared war on slavery in 1859, New Englanders remembered that his ancestors had come on the *Mayflower* and they likened his fortitude to that of Cromwell.

When civil war came in 1861, many Southerners saw their opponents as repeating Puritan hypocrisy. Out of power in the 1850s, many abolitionists had wanted separation from the South, just as Puritans had howled earlier to be free of Charles I's interference. Now that the North controlled the central government, these same people were determined to rule the South, just as the elect had dictated to New England. Emma Holmes, a proud Charleston aristocrat, asking herself in 1863 if the South could lose, mused, "We, the free-born descendants of the Cavaliers, to submit to the descendants of the witch burning Puritans. Never!" Confederate general John B. Magruder, bitterly denouncing to a British visitor, Lt. Col. James A.L. Fremantle, the arrogant Northern assumption of moral superiority and the bullying of the South into submission, "spoke of the Puritans with intense disgust, and of the first importation of them as 'that pestiferous crew of the *Mayflower*.'"

Such sentiments were not simply hyperbole and Southern soldiers who affected a Cavalier dress weren't just making a fashion statement. Northern moral fervor against slavery did owe something to the Puritan legacy. Col. Thomas Wentworth Higginson, a soldier and minister of

Puritan lineage, in his memoir *Army Life in a Black Regiment*, compared the godly zeal of his black troops to that of the New Model Army: only in "Cromwell's time, had there been soldiers in whom the religious element held such a place." Southerners saw a parallel between the winners of the English Civil War who had talked of liberty but during the Commonwealth had inflicted their will by force of arms and the Federal government's use of the army to restructure Southern society during Reconstruction. In both cases, government policy was to be implemented through force.

The point is not lost on Civil War reenactors today, over 50 percent of whom live in the South, and some of whom share with private militias a distrust of federal power and a wish to be counted in the ranks of its opponents. When the National Park Service was asked to intervene in a reenactment to prevent gender discrimination, one resentful participant commented that this was typical of federal interference in a private matter, "What we fought the war for in the first place." Journalist Tony Horwitz, in his 1998 book, *Confederates in the Attic*, refers to this genre of reenactors as neo-Confederates. They cherish, he says, the South's Celtic heritage of independent-minded Scots and Irish, versus staid Northerners of English mercantile stock, who used "industrial might and numerical superiority to grind down the South with Cromwellian efficiency." Certainly, both Scots and Irish suffered much in the struggle between Stuart and Parliament.

To return to the Stuarts, Charles II, eldest son of the executed king, was restored to the throne in 1660. A pragmatic politician, Charles accommodated to being a constitutional monarch. He died in 1685 and was succeeded by his brother, James II, who antagonized Parliament by an open avowal of Catholicism and by trying to return to personal rule, going around the legislative arm to issue executive decrees. Suspicious of his intent, Protestants were further discomfited when James stationed a standing army of thirty thousand men, officered largely by Catholics, near London, officially in response to an abortive rebellion by the Protestant Duke of Monmouth, but seemingly also to intimidate Parliament.

Fearing a Catholic resurgence, leading men in 1688 engineered a coup against James, offering the crown to his Protestant daughter, Mary,

Threats of rebellion necessitated a standing army during peacetime. The redcoat destruction of the 1745 Stuart uprising is remembered annually in the Warren County, Ohio, reenactment of Culloden. Photograph of Barton J. Redmon as the Duke of Cumberland, by Michael Snyder, courtesy of *The Cincinnati Enquirer*.

and her husband, William, Prince of the Dutch State of Orange. James fled into a French exile. Philosophical underpinning to this Glorious Revolution was provided by John Locke's argument that the people have a right to resist tyrants and that a government is legitimate only so long as it protects the citizen's life, liberty, and property. From now on, allegiance was conditional upon the monarch abiding by constitutional governance. The Bill of Rights, promulgated in 1689, finally established Parliamentary supremacy, with control of the purse and the prohibition of royal dispensations. Some Protestants were allowed to keep arms to help suppress any Catholic risings for James.

The Stuarts in exile, James and his son James III, worked to reclaim the throne through military means. A 1690 Catholic Irish rising was brutally suppressed by William at the Battle of the Boyne. Scots rose five times, in 1689, 1708, 1715, 1719, and 1745. Thus, by an irony, the Stuarts forced successive monarchs, William and Mary, her sister Anne, and the Hanoverian Georges who followed, to secure the realm with a standing army larger than the one that had terrified people under James. By the mid-eighteenth century, the regular army had a wartime establishment of seventy thousand men.

The Stuart threat was ended finally on Culloden Moor in the Scottish Highlands, April 16, 1746. Here, a government army under William, Duke of Cumberland, second son of the reigning monarch, George II, crushed a rebel army of Scots clan warriors and Irish mercenaries in the French service, under Prince Charles Edward Stuart, son of James III. In gratitude for this vindication of the Glorious Revolution, the English named the flower Sweet William after Cumberland, Franz Joseph Haydn composed "The Conquering Hero" in his honor, and Virginia settlers named Cumberland Gap, Kentucky, for him. The redcoats were popular heroes, but not for long.

To punish the rebellious clans, the military was ordered by the government to confiscate land, burn property, drive out the people, and imprison or even execute ringleaders. So enthusiastically did Cumberland appear to pursue his police work that he earned the title Butcher. Even government supporters became uneasy. Actually, the extent of persecution was exaggerated and, soon, clan leaders were being welcomed into British ruling circles to cement Scottish allegiance. London money was pumped into the Highlands to wed the economy to England's. At the same time, Highland life was romanticized. The clan system had been a harsh feudal structure, under which even the poorest tenant of land was liable for compulsory military service under his clan leaders. Clan raiders had disrupted life in the more prosperous and settled Lowlands, thieving cattle and extorting through blackmail. Yet by the end of the century the clansman was transformed into a lone hero who stood for individual freedoms against the tyranny of government and its redcoated hirelings. The model was Rob Roy MacGregor, a real figure transformed into legend by Walter Scott, whose *Rob Roy* appeared in 1817. Later films such as the 1954 Disney movie, *Rob Roy, The Highland Rogue,* and a 1995 version starring Liam Neeson as Rob Roy continue in popular culture the image of the stoic individual determined to oppose abuse of power. Both movies were popular, suggesting the contemporary resonance of the theme.

It was not hard to cast the redcoat in the role of hired brute. Despite being better regulated than the old mercenary bands and serving in a national force, the regulars were still considered as largely unproductive, at best a necessary evil. Although many men in the ranks actually exhibited a high degree of professionalism, they were depicted as the scum of the earth, recruited from the lowest levels of society, marginal laborers, the unemployed, alcoholic, criminal, and reckless. To many civilians it was unfathomable that any but the most contemptible would willingly surrender their free will to become puppets of the state, disciplined by the lash, a degradation reserved for criminals, slaves, and wearers of the king's uniform. The officer class, mainly younger sons of the landed gentry and children of middle-class professionals, again were often good at their jobs, but the corps contained enough rakes and bullies to earn them the reputation of being immoral and vicious. Jonathan Swift spoke for many when, in his 1726 novel, *Gulliver's Travels,* he denounced the concept "of a mercenary standing army in the midst of peace, and amongst a free people." Regulars were debased beyond the level of criminals, "rascals picked up at a venture in the streets, for small wages, who might get an hundred times more by cutting their throats." Better by far, said Swift, to have a free local militia of sturdy independent farmers and tradesmen under known and trusted local leaders.

These views were fervently embraced in the American colonies, where the settlers saw little of London authority or its soldiery for many years. Redcoat detachments usually appeared only in times of civil disorder, acting in a police role, as when the administration of Virginia governor William Berkeley was threatened by Nathaniel Bacon's 1676 rebellion against central authority. Developing relatively free of imperial interference, the colonies largely made provision for their own military protection, using the traditional militia system. Every freeman was obligated to play a part in local defense, and volunteers were recruited from the mass for extended campaigns or service beyond the colony's boundaries.

The volunteers were the "select" or "active" militia, typically young men needing the generous enlistment bounty to get a stake in society, or servants wishing to escape the oppressive toil of their indenture. Conditions were better than for the redcoats, including higher pay and land grants, lighter discipline, and shorter terms of service. Colonial militiamen also often expected to retain their muskets, a departure from European practice made customary by the ever-present Native American threat. The retention of arms would be a crucial matter of contention in the slide to revolution. Samuel Adams, believing that Americans were about to be coerced by redcoats, warned in January, 1775, "We may all be soon under the necessity of keeping shooting irons."

In addition to local Native American threats, the major American military concern, after the eclipse of Spanish power in the late seventeenth century, was New France, an ambitious colonial empire designed to stretch from Canada through the Midwest to Louisiana. In the first three French Wars, 1689–1697, 1701–1713, and 1744–1748, the colonies relied largely on their volunteer or select militia, with help from regulars in specialized fields like artillery and engineering. The Royal Navy also cooperated with colony forces, as in the successful 1748 New England capture of Louisbourg, a citadel on Cape Breton Island.

The military formula changed after 1755. In the previous year, Virginia troops under George Washington were dispatched to observe French movements in the Ohio Valley, which threatened English expansion westward. The Virginians were captured, a slight to British arms that led in the next year to the sending out of two redcoat battalions and colonial volunteers under a regular general, Edward Braddock. He was also defeated. War with France now becoming worldwide, a far-sighted British statesman, William Pitt the Elder, decided to emphasize the American theater of war, believing that the course of empire and future wealth lay in these huge continental domains. He threw Britain's commercial power into the balance, paying for a massive regular army offensive in America. By 1763 the war was won and Canada joined the British empire.

But from triumph sprang the seeds of revolution. To win, Pitt had resorted to massive deficit spending. Adding to the burden of debt, Britain now had vast new possessions to protect with garrisons. As taxation in Britain was twice that in America, the government determined to raise taxes in the colonies and retrieve some costs of redcoat garrisons through the 1765 American Mutiny (Quartering) Act, which required localities to pay for the soldiers' food and accommodation. Using the precedent of the Stuart Parliament's denial of the right to tax without representation, colonists steadily resisted government policy.

Reacting to their opposition, the government in London looked for cost-saving options. Remembering how the Stuarts had fomented rebellion through Scots' resentment of English cultural dominance, the government gave civil rights to Canada's seventy thousand French Catholics, effectively winning their begrudging loyalty and cutting the need for garrisons. The extension of rights made sense in London but to Protestant New Englanders, the alliance with hated "Popery" seemingly negated the recent victory and stirred memories of Stuart deviance. Anti-Catholic riots in Boston and elsewhere provoked sympathetic responses in England, particularly East Anglia, a staging ground for earlier Puritan migrations. Redcoats were called out to protect threatened property and, in doing so, manhandled some protesters, further inflaming the sense of distrust and fear of impending tyranny. When redcoats were sent to Boston in 1768, writes Barbara Tuchman in *The March of Folly* (1984), Andrew Eliot, a citizen, cried, "To have a standing army! Good God! What can be worse to a people who have tasted the sweets of liberty."

A second defense economy measure spread the discontent beyond New England. Reasoning that the other major security threat, besides Canada, lay in the encroachment of white settlement on Native American lands, the government drew an imaginary line down the crest of the Appalachian Mountains and banned settlement west of that marker. Again, drawing a boundary appeared in London to be an enlightened policy but citizens of Virginia and Pennsylvania felt it arbitrarily robbed them of huge new opportunities.

Further, as the colonists objected to paying for the upkeep of frontier garrisons, the government pulled them back to seaboard cities where they could be supplied more cheaply from Britain. But, even in the more conservative southern colonies, the citizens refused accommodation to the regulars. Henri Bouquet, a redcoat officer, commented that whites saw the troops as slaves, "making little difference between the soldier and the negro." And the pioneers on the frontier believed that they had been deliberately deserted by an uncaring and perfidious government overseas.

As relations deteriorated, colonists without a voice in Parliament resorted to the traditional method employed by the disenfranchised to express resentment: they formed mobs. Called the Sons of Liberty, these were neither the howling, mindless crowds portrayed by conservatives or the boyish rascals of Disney's popular 1957 movie *Johnny Tremain*. They were well-organized paramilitary groups, containing seasoned militiamen, and carried out carefully planned acts of political provocation. A retailer of British goods might be roughed up or his furniture smashed. A zealous customs officer could be ridden on a wedge-shaped rail, after being coated with boiling tar and feathers, treatment causing permanent injury or death. As there was no professional police force, the military had to adopt its hated police role. The militia was unreliable, as it merged with the mob, so regulars had to be deployed in the major cities, hotbeds of dissidence.

The worst excesses took place in Boston, antagonized by Catholic tolerance and a British tax on sugar that affected the sale of rum. A concentration of regulars played into the hands of radicals convinced that America must be free of British dictates. Samuel Adams, a brilliant pioneer of urban terrorism, provoked incidents that milked the negative image of the standing army to cast the authorities in the worst possible light. Adams's motto was "Put your enemy in the wrong, and keep him so, is a wise maxim in politics, as well as in war."

The most famous incident orchestrated by Adams and the Sons was the so-called Boston Massacre of March 5, 1770. A regular protecting the customs house, deliberately provoked by a radical in the guise of a delivery boy, fetched the youth a musket blow to the head, at which a crowd of Sons gathered and menaced the soldier. More innocent by-passers joined in the haranguing. Capt. Thomas Preston tried to rescue the sentry with a redcoat squad, but the mob hemmed the soldiers in, throwing rocks, brandishing firearms, and chanting, "Damn you, you sons of bitches, fire!" Finally, a soldier was knocked down and fired his musket, the others following suit. Preston quickly intervened but the damage was done. Eight people lay dead or wounded. The redcoats were tried for murder. Their legal counsel was John Adams, who felt that the tactics of his cousin Samuel would taint the American cause. He got the regulars acquitted.

People act not on what is objectively true, but on what they perceive to be true. Although only a minor police action, the incident became in the hands of a master artist, able to dramatize the potential symbolism in the event, a brutal act of calculated repression inflicted on a free people. Paul Revere, a gifted metal worker, engraved a dramatic picture of the brutal soldiery calmly firing volleys into a peaceful crowd. The vivid print electrified the provinces, and its powerful imagery is still familiar to most Americans today.

On December 16, 1773, Sons of Liberty, disguised as Native Americans, dumped ninety thousand pounds of tea, worth millions of dollars and nominally taxed, into Boston Harbor. The regulars, fearful of handing the radicals another propaganda triumph, failed to intervene. But,

The militia on Lexington Green disperse, but keep their weapons. Many Americans have been reluctant to part with them ever since. Amos Doolittle print of *The Battle of Lexington, April 19, 1775*, courtesy of the Connecticut Historical Society, Hartford, Connecticut.

when the British government learned of the vandalism, it overreacted, closing Boston Harbor and suspending the Massachusetts legislature until the tea was paid for, high-handed acts that gave the Sons another political victory. The Massachusetts legislature met independently and put the militia on a war footing. Sir Thomas Gage, the ranking regular in America, was sent to Boston as governor, a further error as the appointment of a soldier to civil authority could only provoke visions of martial law and the loss of remaining rights.

Gage was actually a decent man who wanted no war, as he was married to a colonist and held American lands. Trying to find a peaceful solution, he reverted to Scottish precedent in which, to prevent further risings, the military had confiscated the claymore, a lethal broadsword, and the bagpipes, a weapon of morale. Through late 1774 and into 1775, Gage sent out military patrols to clean out the militias' arms dumps. He could have done no worse. Not only did New Englanders feel the traditional English loathing of a standing army, they had come to associate keeping arms with security and liberty. They were sure that disarmament was a prelude to being murdered in their beds by the king's men.

On a routine police sweep to seize a cache of weapons at Concord, regulars were confronted by militia on Lexington Green. Textbooks say that Maj. John Pitcairn, commanding the redcoat advance guard, ordered the rebels under Capt. John Parker to disperse. As gun advocates well know, he said more: he told the militia to surrender their weapons, shouting "Lay down your arms, damn you!" Parker, at the last minute, appears to have told the militia to disperse, but neither he nor his men intended to leave their guns. In fact, some were used in the ragged exchange of fire that now began a civil war. Resentment of government intrusion had reached its logical conclusion. Gage's policy, well intentioned as it was, struck a raw nerve in the American psyche, propelling forward into the future an emotional equation between keeping guns and retaining liberty that remains axiomatic for many today.

———◆———

In the ensuing struggle for independence, the Patriot war effort was handicapped by traditional distrust of a standing army. In the summer of 1775, Congress authorized a Continental army with George Washington in command. The federated regular army bore the long-term burden of opposing the redcoats in conventional battle. Yet the Continentals never had adequate numbers or support. Contempt for a standing army discouraged enlistment, and both Congress and the states begrudged a liberal expenditure on the troops. The states already supported the militias, their first line of home defense, and Congress feared nourishing a bloated monster that would enslave the people. As the Declaration of Independence stated: "A standing army, however necessary it may be, is always dangerous to the liberties of the people." The resulting parsimony largely created the suffering at Valley Forge in the winter of 1777–1778.

Benedict Arnold, a talented and courageous Continental officer, felt that "the insults and neglects which the army have met with from the country beggars all description." The army, he said, "is permitted to starve in a land of plenty." He attributed the lack of support to fear of a military coup. Congress "acted as if any military officer who dared to complain about their actions was a veritable Oliver Cromwell, bent on destroying free republican government." The traumatic memory of the Protectorate remained a potent political force.

It was partly a sense of hurt that led Arnold to return to his British allegiance. But on that side of the Atlantic, too, there was horror at using a standing army to coerce English subjects. The hiring of thirty thousand German mercenaries to supplement the regulars provoked further opposition. Lord Camden denounced in Parliament this "mere mercenary bargain for the hire of troops on one side and the sale of human blood on the other." In America, Patriot propaganda easily convinced people that the dreaded Hessians would actually eat their children.

When the war was won, Congress, fearing hired professionals, quickly decreased the standing army to a skeleton force. Many soldiers were released without their back pay and the Continentals might have aped the New Model and marched on the legislature, but Washington and other senior officers intervened to avert a crisis. The Articles of Confederation, under which the nation operated from 1781 to 1789, reflected traditional fear of central tyranny. The Congress could raise volunteers in an emergency to supplement the tiny regular forces, but arms and financial backing had to be requested from the states. As always, the major reliance was on the universal obligation of militia service.

The practical inadequacy of America's military arrangement was shown in Shays' Rebellion of 1786, the first armed challenge to the new nation. Disgruntled farmers in western Massachusetts, facing high taxes imposed to retire the state's war debt, rebelled under Capt. Daniel Shays, a Revolutionary War veteran. The rebels thought they were exercising their inalienable right to resist oppression. The state and national authorities disagreed. A number of state constitutions embraced the right of revolution, but only for a majority of citizens. Force was applied, although the actual military showing was downright embarrassing. The U.S. could field no credible contingent and the state militia were inept. Only in January 1787 was rebellion quelled.

The inadequate military response to Shays' rising helped to bring about a new constitution, ratified in 1789, under which there was a serious regular army supported by direct taxes. But fear of tyranny led to distribution of power. Control of the military was divided: Congress held the purse strings, made rules to regulate the army and militia, and declared war; while the president was commander in chief, with the power to make command appointments and call the militia into federal service. As a third check, two provisions in the Bill of Rights, adopted in 1791, addressed the balance of arms. The Third Amendment restricted quartering of soldiers on civilians and the Second ensured the right of the people, collected in the militia, not to be disarmed. This provision reads in full: "A well regulated militia, being necessary to the security of a free State, the right of the people to keep and bear arms, shall not be infringed."

Again, suggesting that Americans do care about the past, there has been great practical interest in the issues addressed in these amendments. In 1850, when Bostonians freed a fugitive slave from jail and President Millard Fillmore threatened to use federal troops to preserve order, Theodore Parker suggested he not try on General Gage's cloak: "The Bostonians remember how that business of quartering soldiers on us in time of peace worked in the last century." Given that troops are now housed in government barracks, the Third Amendment is not controversial, but the Second is. The NRA has argued consistently that this provision guarantees the individual private ownership of weapons as a direct legacy of the Revolution. "The Revolution wasn't fought over taxes; it was fought over the British trying to take away people's arms," wrote NRA activist Seth Mydans in the *New York Times*, December 24, 1990. Members also defend on historical grounds the right of civilians to own military-style weapons. A writer in *Newsweek*, September 20, 1999, stated, "Inspired by the Founding Fathers, I believe that private ownership of military-quality firearms helps deter government abuses."

White-male militias took the argument a step further, using the Second Amendment to justify forming private armies, so long as they were regulated from within. Historical precedent was prominently displayed. The Wisconsin Free Militia called themselves minutemen, while Michael Fortier of the Arizona Patriots, an opponent of all gun controls, flew a Revolutionary War "Don't Tread On Me" flag in his yard. Ed Brown, a militia leader, said in Kenneth Stern's *A Force upon the Plain*, "This whole King George thing is very important." Like their forebears on Lexington Green, the modern militia, said Brown, "have answered a call to arms to defend their homes, and their Constitution from some foreign power that threatened to take away, above all, their beloved guns." According to *Newsweek*, April 9, 2001, Timothy McVeigh also felt the resonance of Lexington, stating, "I like the phrase 'shot heard 'round the world,' and I don't think there's any doubt the Oklahoma City blast was heard around the world."

Some legal and constitutional scholars accept the interpretation of private right in the Second Amendment. Daniel Lazare endorsed the idea categorically in *Harper's Magazine,* October 1999, saying it makes "effective gun control in this country all but impossible." Joyce Lee Malcolm, author of *To Keep and Bear Arms* (1994), claims that she can no longer find colleagues to oppose her advocacy of the right to bear arms. The public, hearing about the issue mostly from the NRA, has accepted the claim to private right. A 1991 *Los Angeles Times* poll found that, while 60 percent of Americans would like gun controls, an overwhelming majority accept that the Constitution guarantees ownership. On the other hand, military experts, who study the historical context of practical defense issues in which the Second Amendment was written, overwhelmingly believe that it confers a corporate right only to serve in the state militias.

There is no simple answer to the question, partly because the Founding Fathers assumed a generally understood context and therefore failed fully to spell out their intent. Oscar Handlin, a fine constitutional scholar, notes in *The American Scholar* (Spring 1993) that the Founders were not made of marble and were prone to error and blurred thinking, so that what is meant by "the people," for example, is not clear. In this situation it makes sense to look at the practical military context. Throughout its formal existence, the militia was under public and never private control. Gun advocates correctly point to Gage's role in 1775, but they misunderstand that his opponents on Lexington Green were not simply like-minded individuals privately motivated; they were duly enrolled soldiers in the Massachusetts military establishment, under martial law and the orders of the Assembly. Throughout the Revolution, the militias remained under state authority, an arrangement confirmed in the Articles of Confederation, which asked all states to keep a well-regulated, that is, a duly constituted and properly organized, militia. The Second Amendment may be problematic, but its purpose was clarified by the Militia Act of 1792, which required all able-bodied white male citizens to enroll in the state militia, a public entity.

Washington had earlier stated the rationale for mandatory service in a May 2, 1783, letter to Alexander Hamilton. He argued that, much as he regretted it, standing armies in peace were traditionally seen as a threat to liberty, so "the militia of this country must be considered the palladin of our security," or main defense. Although he would have preferred the services of a regular army, he didn't see militia service as an imposition. Each citizen, he argued, owed the government "not only a proportion of his property but even of his personal services to the defense of it" and consequently must enroll in the state militia. Note that the general saw militia as a compulsory public obligation to guarantee the security of the central state and not as a private option to resist it. Read in this context, the Second Amendment appears to make the same point: it contains a public and corporate right, not a private and individual one.

Every internal attempt to assault the U.S. government has been met with arms, denying in practice the right of private groups or individuals to bear arms against the state. An example is the 1794 Whiskey Rebellion. In 1791, the government laid a heavy excise duty on whiskey, which was bitterly resented in agricultural areas where whiskey was a product so important it was used in place of cash as medium of exchange. Underdeveloped backwoods areas, such as western North Carolina, became areas of resistance to the tax. The resentment persists today: the Southern Poverty Law Center, in its *Intelligence Report* (no. 95, summer 1999), noted that a concentration of extreme hostility to government "in this mountainous part of the state—and in adjoining areas of South Carolina and Tennessee—dates all the way back to the Whiskey Rebellion."

In rural Pennsylvania, revenue men were assaulted and Sons of Liberty groups sprang up in a clear belief that the protesters had by precedent a right to resist tyranny by force of arms. In August 1794 the rebels temporarily held Pittsburgh. President Washington, fulfilling his view of the citizens' military obligation to secure the state, rather than to oppose it, federalized select elements of the Pennsylvania, New Jersey, Virginia, and Maryland militias, some 13,000 troops who quelled resistance and brought 150 ringleaders in chains to Philadelphia, the national capital. Washington declared a national day of thanksgiving for "the reasonable control which has been given to a spirit of disorder in the suppression of the late insurrection." Clearly, the president saw no precedent for a private right to resist the central power.

When John Brown and his followers attacked the federal arsenal at Harpers Ferry, Virginia, in 1859 (representing yet another attempt of individual citizens to resist a government they deemed tyrannical), both the regular army and the Virginia state militia were used to stop Brown, who was then hanged for treason. In the greatest ever challenge to central authority, in 1861 the Confederate States called out their well-regulated militias to oppose what they saw as Lincoln's despotic rule. Their action would appear to be a constitutionally defensible use of the official militias to secure the freedom of the state. But both the regular army and the federalized Northern state militias were used to override this interpretation.

After the Civil War, the militias atrophied. Only some volunteer regiments under state authority remained, used mainly to quell violent strikers. In 1903 Congress passed a law turning these "regularly enlisted organized and uniformed active militia in the several states" into the National Guard, thus closing the book on the history of the militia with its citizen-soldier right to bear arms. It is difficult for a military historian to see how America's history can justify private militias or an individual right to own military-style weapons. The Supreme Court has uniformly agreed with scholars of the military. In the seminal 1939 U.S. vs. Miller, the Court held that the 2nd Amendment intended to provide for the calling out of the state militia to execute the laws of the Union. The Court also has identified the National Guard as the militia of today. Other decisions have further affirmed the right to bear arms collectively, not individually, and only for public bodies, not private militias.

⎯⎯◆◆⎯⎯

The debate over bearing arms has life-or-death consequences. One in three Americans knows someone who has been shot. The vehemence with which U.S. citizens state their right to resist, bully, even kill, government officials has no parallel in other developed nations. "Just as our forefathers purchased their freedom in blood, so must we," argued KKK leader Louis Beam. "There can no more be a peaceful birth of our nation in the 1980s than there was for our ancestors in 1776" (*Dallas Morning News*, May 22, 1988). Similarly, after the passage of the Brady Bill, Kenneth Stern's *A Force upon the Plain* quoted militia leader Norman Olson as saying, "This may be the beginning of a Concord-like confrontation." Some people buy guns to intimidate government: "Only an armed citizenry can exercise power over government," noted an ex-Navy Seal to author James William Gibson at a pro-gun conference in September 1986. Most remarkable of all, Mark Reynolds, a leader of the Washington State Unorganized Militia, said in June 1994, "The reason the Second Amendment was put into the United States Constitution," was "so that when officials of the federal and state and local governments get out of hand, you can shoot them" (*A Force upon the Plain*).

We don't have to posit that Americans are more violent or more paranoid than others to explain such sentiments. Many peoples distrust their politicians, but Americans are more extreme in word and deed because of their place on the time line of history. The first two centuries of American development coincided with the traumatic struggles of the English-speaking peoples to win parliamentary liberties and to bring the central power under constitutional restraint. During those struggles, successive authorities used troops to curtail the people's dissent. The government's use of force against its citizens feels like yesterday to many Americans for whom two centuries are half of (their) history. Thus, a writer in the *Cincinnati Enquirer,* November 23, 1990, citing historical precedent to legitimize his chronic distrust of federal power, said that at some point every government has "turned its power—its police power—against its own citizens, confiscated their property, imprisoned them, tortured them and made a mockery of personal dignity." Thus, George Bush is envisioned perhaps not as Caligula or Hitler but certainly as Charles I, Cromwell, or Thomas Gage. Is it possible, too, that when militants describe their apocalyptic visions of New World Order black helicopters coming to get us, one inspiration buried in the imagination is the figure of a black-clad, military-backed Puritan witch-hunter?

Historians know that while we should learn from the past, no healthy society can afford to be dominated by it, victims of time caught in the sticky web of yesterday's issues. Take the example of Joyce Malcolm who, in building a rationale for the private right to bear arms, stresses the precedent of the provision in the English 1689 Bill of Rights that some Protestants could keep arms. We have seen that the arrangement was specific to helping prevent a successful Catholic Stuart resurgence, a threat ended on Culloden Moor in 1746. Once we have this fact in full historical perspective, do we want to say that it should shape our response to current gun issues? Only because of the historical timing of America's development can this limited English defense provision of the late seventeenth century, aimed at the now defunct Stuart dynasty, be treated as a powerful debating point regarding a contemporary social issue.

Some federal and state officials confess that they live in fear of their lives, particularly since the Oklahoma City bombing. Beyond this, gun violence creates universal danger and anxiety, leading some observers, like Israeli military historian Martin Van Creveld, to describe the American situation as approximating a low-intensity civil war. During the ten-year period of the Vietnam War, 6 times as many Americans died violently at home as in the war zone, up from 2.5 times as many during Korea. In the 1999 military operations against Yugoslavia, gun casualties in America's elementary and high schools alone eclipsed those for U.S. forces in the war zone. Not all of this can be blamed simply on gun ownership or attitudes regarding the 2nd Amendment. But it can be said that the history-bedeviled debate over bearing arms has reached such an intellectual impasse that it helps to paralyze the search for solutions. In this context, seventeenth-century poet John Dryden, depicting the turbulent political-military events of his age, might have described our era also when he wrote, "Such subtle covenants shall be made / Till peace itself is war in masquerade."

THREE

✛

New Men with Rifles

In the following pages, we shall trace the growth of an indigenous American portrait of a new type of fighting man, a profile that was clearly sketched even before the Revolutionary War. The new American warrior was not a mercenary or regular solider but an amateur, a farmer or hunter. He drew his strength not from professional training, but from closeness to God and Nature in the New World environment. A reluctant warrior, the New Man was slow to anger but implacable when roused. In harmony with the environment, he was not ashamed to seek cover behind sheltering trees and rocks, for he had the cunning of a native allied to the innocence of a virgin people. The theme has continuing resonance for the mainstream imagination, providing, for example, the overriding theme for the 2000 movie *The Patriot,* starring Mel Gibson. For much of American history, the image of the amateur fighting man significantly shaped American views on the nature of a proper democratic military establishment, which people felt should be reliant on citizen soldiers and not career professionals. This had practical impact on American wars. For example, at the start of the Civil War, there was not a significant regular army with which to put down the incipient rebellion.

—◦—

If, for the sake of argument, we allow that Americans have a constitutional right to oppose with arms the forces of central government, a puzzling question still remains. How can untrained citizens, armed mainly with hand and shoulder weapons, hope to defeat the enormous and technologically-advanced armed forces of the United States? Successful citizen resistance to the most powerful military in the world is a fantasy, but it is a dream based on a potent American myth of amateur superiority to the professional soldier.

A good example of the theme is provided by the 1984 movie *Red Dawn*, a video hit that remains popular with members of private militias. The plot centers on an invasion of the U.S. by conglomerate communist forces, including Russians, Cubans, and Nicaraguans. Enemy troops spearhead the invasion in unscheduled Cuban commercial airliners that penetrate America's air defenses before the ruse is detected. Defeat of America's armed forces in the theater of war follows. Implausible as the plot may sound, it builds on a longstanding assumption of professional incompetence in the regular forces. Hope is provided by a group of teenagers from the heartland who, taking up their parents' hunting guns and calling themselves the Wolverines after their high-school ball team, wage a war of liberation. Note that the saviors are youthful and are connected through their rural location and group name to the world of nature. They are potent virgin amateurs with hunting weapons.

The theme's core elements, dating back to at least the mid eighteenth century, are central to *The Last of the Mohicans* (1992), a popular movie that is set in 1757. In a key scene, we see Maj. Duncan Heyward, a British aristocrat, leading a redcoat patrol through the forest. He is ambushed by Native Americans. Unable to appreciate that tactics appropriate to an open-field European terrain will not work here, Heyward forms his men in three ranks and they deliver a single volley into the woods. The enemy duck the bullets and rush upon the soldiers with tomahawks and axes. The regulars, their muskets empty, don't seem to have bayonets (a standard-issue weapon difficult for a native warrior to protect himself against); consequently, the soldiers are slaughtered. Only two figures can triumph in this environment: One is Chingachgook, the Native American who has become the white man's dependent. The other is Hawkeye or Leatherstocking, the white hunter close to Nature and adept in native warfare, but also made superior to the savage by his white cultural background. He is the man perfectly placed between the too-savage forest and the decadent city; he represents America in its youth. His superiority to the regular and the native is made manifest in his matchless skill with a long rifle, a peculiar product of American ingenuity, made for the peaceful pursuit of hunting but a deadly man-killer when the hunter is justly aroused. The allure of the long rifle remains potent in the U.S. Many hobbyists fire black-powder weapons, and the National Muzzle Loading Rifle Association boasts over twenty-three thousand active members. The association sponsors gun-training and game-hunting programs and is politically active in promoting the individual's right to bear arms privately.

The image of the New Man came to full development in a roughly eighty-year period between 1755 and 1836, a crucial epoch straddling the American Revolution. During this era, the American people struggled to forge an identity that would model their special qualities and differentiate them from Europe and the mother country they were rejecting. Four military affairs were primary in setting the image of the new American man: Braddock's Defeat (1755); Lexington-Concord and Bunker Hill (1775); New Orleans (1815); and the Alamo (1836). Each posits the triumph of gifted and God-inspired amateurs over venal and arrogant Old World professionals.

In 1754, Maj. George Washington of the Virginia military was sent with a company of volunteers drawn from the militia to deter French activity in the Ohio Valley, which would cramp British expansion westward. He was to destroy Fort Duquesne, at the Forks of the Ohio. Instead, Washington and his command were captured and sent packing. So, in the next year, a regular was sent to do the job, Maj. Gen. Edward Braddock, with two battalions of redcoats and some provincial levies from Virginia and Carolina. He was killed and his expedition routed some twenty miles south of Duquesne.

A mythic version of this battle quickly developed and persists in American popular culture. It can be found in basic American history texts stretching over almost two centuries. According to the legend, Braddock was too arrogant to heed American warnings that he must adapt dress and tactics to the environment, take precautions to avoid ambush, and rely on his Native American and colonial scouts for guidance. Benjamin Franklin said Braddock was ruined by overconfidence, his mean view of provincials and Native Americans, and reliance on European practice.

Supposedly, Braddock haughtily marched through the woods as if on parade in London. A school history of 1877, published by Appleton, said the regulars "all were dressed in full uniform; their polished arms glanced in the sun-light, every move was made with perfect precision; and the full strains of martial music, starting the wild deer from his lair." Although splendid to watch, such a procession would be the worst kind of behavior in the forest where lurked a stealthy enemy. By 1969 Donald Workman, in *The War for the British Empire*, still had the British "resplendent in scarlet and gold," striving for "pageantry" in the forest.

Not surprisingly, so runs the tale, Braddock's highly visible column was ambushed by the French and Native Americans. Then, says the 1967 *American Heritage History of the Thirteen Colonies*, defeat was guaranteed by the "incompetence and ignorance" of the British officers. They refused to disperse their men into the woods but kept the scarlet ranks closely packed on the trail, where they "made fine targets for their enemies who, as usual, hid behind every tree and rock," as an 1898 American Book Company text put it. Picking up the story, Wadsworth's 1994 *America! A Concise History* says that the redcoats "maintained impressive discipline," but their coordinated volleys, fired into the forest, were futile.

Only the Virginians, we are told time and again, had the sense to get behind trees and shoot from cover, in what was called the "American" or native way, the only chance of winning. Thus, Appleton's 1877 text said, "The Virginia Rangers alone retained their presence of mind. Familiar with Indian warfare, each selected a tree and fought the savages in his own style." And the Barnes 1885 history agreed: "The Virginia troops alone sprang into the forest and fought the savages in Indian style."

The essential elements of the story, then, are these: The regulars dressed inappropriately, arrogantly underrated their colonial allies and native enemies, fought in a disciplined but obstinately incorrect manner, and ignored sound tactical advice; their behavior was supposedly typical of European regulars in the New World environment. The Virginians, short-term volunteers rather than long-service regulars, kept their heads, tried to instruct Braddock in forest fighting, and took the only action that could have resulted in victory, namely, aimed marksmanship from behind cover.

In fact, much of this picture is distorted. To begin with, Braddock did try but was unable to recruit sufficient colonials and Native Americans to act as scouts. Those he got were unreliable, going off when they chose and violating camp security. He was accustomed to look for locals to act as scouts—recruiting clansmen as guides in the treacherous Highland terrain was a common practice in Scotland, where he had served. Before leaving their Cumberland, Maryland, base at the start of the expedition the soldiers had removed their parade gilt trimmings and inessential equipment, including their short swords, or hangers, deemed of no use in the woods. They also had browned their white cross belts and dulled their muskets. British scarlet, after months in the field, as on this occasion, faded to a rusty brown, a good color for woodland warfare.

On the march, precaution was observed. The column had men out on the flanks and a guard in advance to avoid ambush. Everyone, including the Virginians, expected an ambush at the difficult crossing of the Monongahela River. When the surprise attack didn't happen, precautions were relaxed a little; the flankers were late getting out. But the advance guard was in its place when it collided with the French and Native Americans on the path. Each side was equally surprised; there was no ambush either way. To understand what happened next, and why Americans then and now have misunderstood what Braddock was trying to achieve, we must take a slight detour into English military practice of the eighteenth century.

Folklore enshrines major misunderstandings. First, no conventional army discharged all its muskets at one time. The weapons were fired either by platoon, a cluster of men in the larger unit, or by rank, one of two to three lines firing in rotation, so that some weapons remained loaded at all times. Most infantry used a smoothbore rather than a rifle, which, despite greater range and accuracy, was slower to load, taking over a minute, and more expensive to make, requiring skilled craftsmanship. A smoothbore, though inaccurate, was cheap, an important consideration when the army was kept poor by suspicious legislators, and it could be reloaded quickly, twice in a minute. When conditions allowed, it was best to use the smoothbore weapon in a concentrated mass, putting out a heavy field of unaimed fire in a restricted but deadly killing zone.

However, the British did not rely on concentrated volley fire alone. In Scotland, for example, the men were trained to operate in small units in the glens, searching out and ambushing rebels. A royal officer reported, in 1746, that the rebels "are greatly surpris'd to find our soldiers climb over their rocks and mountains full as nimble as they can themselves, . . ." European armies, at least from the 1740s, also employed specialized rifle units recruited from gamekeepers and professional huntsmen, but their value was seen as limited.

Reliance on an exchange of fire, as the Virginians wanted on the Monongahela, usually cost lives and often proved indecisive. British officers did not trust the reliability of the flintlock, the firing mechanism attached to both the smoothbore and rifle. By this device, the charge was fired when a flint, held in a lock attached to the trigger, fell down on a metal pan, igniting some grains of powder there, which in turn ran through a touchhole, or channel, into the barrel, setting off the main charge and ejecting the ball. On damp days the gun might fail to fire, leading to the Prussian-army saying, "All skill is for nought when an angel pisses down your touchhole." In the best of conditions a flintlock misfired on average every four of twenty-five shots.

In these circumstances British officers usually preferred to trust discipline and the bayonet to control uncertain battlefield dynamics and prevent a dangerous stalemate. Success depended on gaining psychological mastery of the opponent. Redcoats waited silently for the enemy to come within true killing range of the smoothbore, fifty yards or less, accepting the casualties attendant upon long-range enemy fire. The deep-throated British battle cry, a series of huzzas, then betokened one to two shattering volleys followed by a bayonet charge, the men screaming to destroy remaining enemy resolution. The momentum-shifting counteroffensive was usually enough to determine the outcome of battle. A perfect example of this technique is the 1759 Battle of Quebec. Gen. James Wolfe cautioned his men not to fire until the French were within forty yards; two volleys then preceded the bayonet attack accompanied by lusty shouting. The main action was over in fifteen minutes, with a complete French rout.

We are now in a position to appreciate what Braddock and his officers tried to achieve on the Monongahela. When the advance guard under Thomas Gage ran into the French and Native Americans, they waited for the enemy to close and then delivered a sharp fire into their faces, unnerving them. The British then delivered the battle huzza and advanced with the bayonet upon the wavering foe. But their opponents were rallied by a charismatic officer, Lt. Daniel Dumas, who directed them down natural defiles running on each side of the British. From here they poured a disconcerting fire into the redcoats. At this point the moral advantage changed sides. The British, many of whom had no battle experience, stopped cheering and refused to go forward. Gage recalled that "a visible terror and confusion appeared amongst the men." Bereft of offensive momentum, he fell back upon the main column, disrupting Braddock's efforts to get the main body from column of march into a more flexible offensive formation.

For the rest of the action Braddock and his officers tried vainly to get the men to break out of their encirclement with a bayonet charge and place the enemy on the defensive, instead of huddling together, firing ineffective volleys into the woods. A British officer recalled that the troops "threw away their Fire in a most indiscreet Manner," and that, "They kept in a mere huddle in spite of the most ardent Endeavours of many brave officers." Many of the men, inexperienced and from poor quality drafts, simply went to pieces. They were not the iron-disciplined redcoats of legend. Confusion was actually increased by the Virginians urging the regulars to disobey their officers and seek shelter in the woods. It is probable that some of the regulars, baffled, and terrorized by the colonials' campfire tales of Native American cruelty to prisoners, shot their own officers who tried to force them forward. Thus, far from illustrating redcoat discipline under fire, the Monongahela provided an example of its failure.

Why, then, did the folklore version of the action come about? In purely military terms, the Americans, not used to working with regulars, failed to grasp what the redcoat officers were trying to do. When John Bach McMaster, a nineteenth-century American historian, said that the "British fought bravely; but Braddock would not let them hide behind trees in Indian fashion," he missed two points. The regulars were clumped together through terror, not bravery, and it was not obtuse arrogance that made Braddock refuse to let them shelter, but the typical British officer's conviction that the defensive was sterile, potentially fatal. The Virginians may have been right in going to ground, but so may have been Braddock in refusing to do so. In July 1756 at Oswego Col. John Bradstreet ended several hours of indecisive fighting behind trees by leading a bayonet attack that routed the French and Native Americans. Unfortunately for Braddock, he didn't live long enough to explain to the Virginians what he was trying to do.

At a more symbolic level, the American version of the action gave confidence to a developing people. The account became a highly positive, potent myth of great value to young America. British officers had little respect for provincial troops, reflecting a broader European view of colonials as bumpkins. Europeans had more polish, more tradition, more exquisite manners. But these accomplishments proved a liability in the New World environment, where the Americans' more simple style was an asset, especially for the future, which surely lay to the west in America's vast and fertile stretches.

Americans had something Europeans envied, contact with a virginal wilderness, a glimpse from a world grown jaded into a new Garden of Eden. How affirming for Americans if events proved that the untutored colonial, immersed in this setting, was shown to be superior to the best products of European education and training. Moreover, in a period when many people saw war as a pestilence, the idea that Americans were not regulars, hired assassins, but volunteers who served only when justly provoked by wicked enemies had a pleasing tone of moral superiority to the decadent Old World.

This model is what the Monongahela appeared to endorse. On the one hand, the redcoats had to be cast as the finest representatives of Old World culture. In fact, because Parliament feared a standing army, regular units were kept skeletal until an emergency. So, when Braddock's battalions left Ireland for America, they had to be augmented by drafts from the rest of the Irish establishment, usually the worst men that commanding officers wanted to be rid of. Then, when the force arrived in America, the ranks, depleted by sickness from the ocean voyage, had to be fleshed out with raw provincial recruits. They were not the proud redcoat host of myth, but their haughty demeanor could make them appear so.

On the other hand, the provincial troops were not just "the hardy class of men," pictured by McMaster, "who were by turn farmers, hunters, and fighters, as occasion required," a breed "rough, brave, daring; caring nothing for the refinements of city life." They were, in fact, paraprofessionals recruited from the militia in Virginia and Carolina's settled areas, usually landless young men willing to be soldiers for a time to make a living, and not that different from the redcoat rankers. Though not as sternly disciplined as the regulars, they were men professionally trained in the rudiments of fighting, often veterans of a campaigning season or two, and not the peaceful settlers of myth.

The positive intellectual power of the juxtaposition between redcoat and hunter is demonstrated in the works of James Fenimore Cooper. Writing in the early national period, Cooper was trying to help establish not only an American identity, but an American literature that would exemplify national characteristics. His first literary attempt failed, as he aped the English setting of a developed country estate used by novelists like Jane Austen. But then he hit upon the figure of the frontiersman operating in the wilderness, shaped along the lines of Daniel Boone, a hunter and scout who was at the Monongahela. In fiction, the frontiersman became Natty Bumpo, the Hawkeye, and perhaps the first distinctive national type in American literature. He was a symbol for the new nation.

One further creative invention completed the transformation of Braddock's Defeat into usable myth. George Washington, disgruntled by lack of pay and prospects, had resigned his Virginia commission after the 1754 debacle. But he was with Braddock as a volunteer aide in 1755. Although he did not play a key part in the battle, his significance on the Monongahela was redefined later when his importance to the founding of a new nation became clear. Pictured as a simple farmer close to nature, he became a man of destiny, called upon to observe British failure and gain from the 1755 lesson when, as a Continental general, he became an architect of America's great future.

Supposedly, Washington had fruitlessly warned Braddock of his errors and coolly directed the Virginians under fire. Without his efforts all the redcoats would have died. He led a charmed life; four balls cut his coat and two horses were shot from under him, but he was unscathed. According to an 1877 history, one disappointed Native American chief said that Providence looked out for him: "Some mighty Manitou protects him." An English survivor was reported, in D.H. Montgomery's *The Beginner's American History* (1902), to have said, "I expected at every moment to see him fall," but, said the text, "he was to live for greater work." Providence was with the New Man in the land of the future.

The regulars and the provincials continued to misunderstand and underrate each other. The redcoats tried to adapt to wilderness warfare. They were used to change, a point missed by Americans who looked at the conventional encounters on the European continent rather than the military experience in Scotland, where the regulars adapted dress to the bleak, wet mountains, wearing woolen caps, gloves, and leggings.

Their weapons changed too. After the English Civil War the pike had disappeared, being replaced by a pike-head, or bayonet, plugged into the end of the musket, much as a bottle cork plugs into a bottle. Thus, the qualities of the gun and the pike had become united in the bayoneted musket. But at Killiecrankie in 1689 Gen. Hugh Mackay saw his men cut down by charging, sword-wielding Scots Highlanders as the redcoats tried to plug bayonets into their muskets after firing at the rebels. Consequently, he invented a bayonet that could be fixed to the musket and still allow it to fire, the ring bayonet, which fitted around the gun's muzzle. Now, no time had to be lost fixing the bayonet after discharging the weapon. The new model was used in all major armies until the late nineteenth century. The redcoats also introduced a new bayonet thrust to wound the Highlander in his underarm as he raised his claymore for the downward sweep.

They also demonstrated adaptability to circumstance in America. After Braddock's failure to recruit sufficient provincial and Native American scouts, it was decided to regularly enlist local ranger battalions, another concept developed in Scotland, to scout, harass the enemy, and provide intelligence for the army. Rangers were usually dressed in green, armed with shotguns or smoothbores and tomahawks, and encouraged to operate with individual initiative. Rogers' Rangers were the most famous unit. Unfortunately, they were expensive, commanding higher pay than an equivalent regular battalion. Also, the American rangers proved ill-disciplined and unreliable, choosing to do as they pleased. So, starting in 1757, one regular company per battalion was turned into light infantry. These were physically agile, better-educated men, trained to fight individually, and sensibly clothed in short jackets with jockey caps. Regular infantry, too, wore a modified uniform, ceasing to wear hair long and powdered, modifying their tri-corn hats, and shortening their long-tailed coats. In 1758, a British officer wrote home, "The art of war is much changed and improved here. Our hair is about an inch long; . . . hats are worn slouched . . . coats are docked."

In 1756 a new regiment was raised to fight the Native Americans, the Royal Americans, comprised entirely of colonials, with experienced Swiss mercenary officers, under the command of the brilliant Henri Bouquet. But the bayonet, still emphasized for all units, proved a winning weapon, both against the ill-trained French-Canadian militia and the native warrior who, once brought to bay, could not defend himself against the seven-foot-long spiked musket. The Royal Americans' flexible fighting force played a crucial role in the French and Indian War and shattered Pontiac's rising of 1764, when Bouquet routed the warriors with a surprise bayonet attack at Bushy Run.

Despite these adaptations, provincials nerving themselves for a confrontation with Britain in the 1770s needed to reassert the reassuring myth that regulars were rigid automatons who couldn't fight in America. Thus, a ballad popular in the revolutionary year of 1776, "The King's Own Regulars," still mocked the redcoats for Braddock's Defeat: "It was not fair to shoot at us from behind trees, / If they had stood open, as they ought, before / Our great guns, we should have beat them with ease."

On the other hand, the regulars too easily discounted the fighting qualities of provincial troops, which cost them in the Revolution. They lumped all colonial units together, failing to differentiate between the universal short-service militia, poorly trained for home defense, and the volunteer units that served for longer periods and were often sound in battle. The regulars read provincial resistance to harsh regular discipline as lack of spine, when it was more the traditional freeborn Englishman's resistance to arbitrary authority. When a provincial unit left for home at the expiration of its term of service, British officers interpreted the departure as lack of patriotism, when it was in fact a colonial faith in the sacrosanct nature of the legal contract, which had been the foundation stone of all the colonies.

The provincials didn't look like much. Often slovenly and ill-clad, their camps were dirty and pest-ridden. Despite their reputation as eagle-eyed hunters, provincial recruits often had no prior familiarity with firearms and, even after training, failed to stand up to a well-delivered bayonet charge. But their shortcomings blinded the regulars to the fact that a solid provincial volunteer battalion was capable of inflicting significant damage when led by trusted, capable officers into battle on its own ground.

The regulars' contempt was expressed in a song popular in the ranks on the eve of Revolution, "Yankee Doodle Dandy." Here, the colonial volunteer, a bumpkin riding on a pony instead of a war horse, sticks a feather in his hat and thinks doing so makes him a dashing fellow, a "macaroni" (at the time fashion was set in Italy, the home of pasta, and "macaroni" was slang for a high dresser or dandy). So, the term is used ironically to mock the provincial's clumsy attempt at cutting a military figure. A comic figure, he is warned not to overrate himself but to get to the kitchen where he really belongs, "and with the girls be handy." But, as the regulars learned at a price, it was a mistake to underrate what the experienced American volunteer soldier could accomplish, enlisted in a strong cause and on home ground.

The American myth of provincial military superiority, seeded in the

French and Indian War, was greatly enhanced by events in the revolutionary year of 1775. On April 19 regulars marched from Boston to seize militia weapons stored at Concord, fighting a skirmish at Lexington along the way. They were then harried back to their base. The redcoats were again portrayed as the Old World's finest professional army. Conversely, their militia opponents were depicted as plain country folk, the minutemen of legend, hating war, driven to it only by rank injustice, and with no prior military experience. A leading character in the 1987 movie *April Morning*, based on Howard Fast's 1961 novel, says that the Americans are blacksmiths and farmers who "have never shot and killed another man," whereas the enemy are "the very best army in the world."

Nevertheless, these colonials routed their enemy, "moving in relentless pursuit with deadly accuracy of fire," as popular historian Barbara Tuchman put it in *The March of Folly* (1984). Earlier, in his 1902 *Essentials of American History*, Thomas B. Lawler said the militia "poured a deadly fire on the retreating British." Accuracy with a rifle suggested not only native prowess of a peaceable people, but the help of Providence bestowed on a good cause. The miracle was repeated at Bunker Hill, June 17. Here, said Lawler, "the Americans with deadly aim swept the British line away" twice. A third redcoat attack was successful only because "as the Americans had no powder left they were compelled to withdraw."

The reality was more complex. Once again, many regulars were not hardened veterans but recruits, some enlisted in the colonies. At Concord's North Bridge, on April 19, where a sharp exchange of fire heralded the running fight back to Boston, the light infantry shot high, which, as one British officer observed, was a sure sign of raw troops. At the same time, we mustn't go too far the other way and suggest that the redcoats were utterly inept. Some historians contend that by 1775 all the techniques of the French and Indian War period were forgotten. Yet on Lexington Green the light infantry, leading the British advance out of Boston, properly executed standard battle drill, volleying by platoon in response to ragged militia fire and then charging with the bayonet to complete the dispersal. American bystanders thought the screaming regulars had gone mad, a verdict endorsed by most historians, but they were in fact doing their job.

On the retreat back to Boston the light infantry did their best to keep the rebels away from the column. But doing so proved impossible when the redcoats had to funnel through narrow points such as ravines and bridges, where the light troops had to merge with the column and the

The folklore version of Lexington and Concord. All of the redcoats are in column on the road, all of the militia are behind rocks and trees. From Barnes and Company's *A Brief History of the United States, 1885.*

enemy could get within close range. On occasion the light infantry managed to get at their tormentors and exact payment with the bayonet. General Gage had known that such a march, through hostile and difficult country, was potentially costly because only cavalry, of which he had none, could make the raid and extricate themselves quickly. Even then, so reliable a source as the 1969 U.S. Army text *American Military History* estimates that it took 75,000 rounds fired by militiamen to make 273 redcoat casualties, not an impressive hit rate. Neither side was the force of legend.

The claim that the effete British thought hiding behind rocks, trees, and fences was unsporting, is not true. British officers tried to avoid prolonged firefights from cover, but they did use ambushes and practiced woodland tactics where appropriate. What enraged the regulars on April 19 was that some of the rebels deliberately picked out officers to kill by aimed fire. Sniping of this kind was considered akin to murder by all conventional authorities. It has remained so. Ernie Pyle, the great World War II reporter, wrote, "there is something sneaking about [sniping] that outrages the American sense of fairness." No army extends mercy to snipers.

On the other side of the action, it is true that some of the militia had barely basic training in drill and were good for only a potshot or two. They were close to the virgins of myth. But others were veterans of the redcoat or provincial volunteer forces in the French and Indian War and could fight well. Beyond doubt, more rebels had previously smelled powder than had the king's forces. Perhaps twenty thousand Massachusetts citizens of a total population of two hundred thousand, representing 30 percent of men 16–29, had fought France. Massachusetts had a strong conventional military establishment, some of it well drilled. On April 19 many fought from behind cover in the "American" way but, where the ground was clear and level, coherent militia units also volley-fired in rank. The weight of numbers on the rebel side was enormous. By early afternoon four thousand were in the field, twenty thousand by nightfall. Under these circumstances, the miracle was not that supposedly untried farmers beat the best army in the world, but that Lt. Col. Francis Smith's seven hundred regulars survived at all when faced by superior numbers of partially experienced colonial forces.

Nevertheless, for Americans, the showing made by their "embattled farmers" had great symbolic significance. English tradition had held that the trained bands of citizens were a better guarantee for a free nation than a mercenary force. Now there seemed ample proof that the free citizen enlisted in liberty's cause was a superior soldier to the long-service regular. General Gage was said to have marveled that "The very children draw in love of liberty with the air they breathe," suggesting that the youthful innocence of America was itself a source of power. America, as the home of that innocence, had a special destiny. A letter of April 25, 1775, from a New England gentleman, was quoted in *Lloyd's Evening Post* (London, June 17) as asking a friend if there was any parallel in history where irregular troops had driven picked veterans seventeen miles. He went on, "I view the hand of God in it, a remarkable interposition of Providence in our favour."

Esther Forbes, writing a century and a half later in 1943, could see where America's special mission had led. In *Johnny Tremain* the hero reflects that he hadn't thought farmers could beat the British military machine with "their perfection of equipment, discipline, grand gaudy uniforms." Yet, "We beat them. We Yankees did. God *was* with us." As America moved to leadership of the free world against Axis militarism in World War II, Forbes (and Johnny) could see that Lexington-Concord had been "For men and women and children all over the world."

The fight at Bunker Hill furthered the sense of virtue triumphant, especially because the clash was more clearly a set-piece engagement, in which the regulars lost 1,054 to 440 patriots. Redcoat casualties resulted from two root causes. First, Gage was intimidated by rebel numbers and didn't take the early action he should have to clear them away from the hills commanding Boston. He waited for reinforcements from Britain, but by the time they arrived the rebels had built a strong, commanding position on Breed's Hill; any attempt to dislodge them would be expensive.

The second cause was the complacency and arrogance of Gage's new subordinates, fresh out from England, Sir William Howe and Sir John Burgoyne, who failed to reconnoiter the ground properly and recognize that the rebels could be flushed out of their position by a landing in their rear. Instead, a frontal assault was launched, reflecting the dangerously supercilious mentality of Burgoyne, who said, "What! Ten thousand peasants [some sources say 'Yankee Doodles'] keep five thousand King's troops shut up!" With about twenty-two hundred men on each side, the rebels, behind breastworks, had the advantage and drove off two attacks. When the third reached the ramparts, the militia gave way rather than be bayoneted. But redcoat prestige could not weather such costly victories.

Today, most Americans still think it was this militia that won the Revolution, a belief that is not quite true and needs qualification. The bulk of the Massachusetts militia, Tom Paine's summer soldiers and armchair patriots, went home after a while. To win, the rebels needed an army as stable and reliable as that of the British. The Congress must create a "respectable army" of regulars, said General Washington. Writing to his civilian superiors in 1780 he said, "*No Militia* will ever acquire the habits necessary to resist a regular force." Therefore, "To place any dependance upon Militia, is assuredly, resting upon a broken staff."

In fact, Washington never got enough regulars and had to rely partly on militia in every engagement. On the positive side, even poorly prepared units might be good for a volley or two before the sight of closing bayonets broke their resolve. The better units stayed and fought hard.

Also, militia could be relied on for short-term garrison work, transportation of goods, and guerrilla harassment of the enemy. But they weren't long-service professionals and couldn't finally win the war. Before the 1777 Battle of Bennington four hundred of sixteen hundred militia went home. At the siege of Newport, a year later, five thousand militia left, forcing Gen. John Sullivan to abandon his campaign. Summing up, Gen. Phileman Dickinson observed, "perseverance in enduring the rigors of military service is not to be expected from those who are not by profession obliged to it."

The despised and ultimately forgotten regulars of the Continental line bore the brunt of fighting and sustained the Patriot cause through the long years of defeats and stalemate. Trained by European mercenaries like Baron Friedrich Wilhelm von Steuben, the regulars were aided immeasurably by European professionals after France in 1778 and Spain in 1779 declared war on Britain. It is indicative of the American army's profile that when Lord Cornwallis surrendered his army at Yorktown in 1781 his opponents mustered six thousand Continentals, six thousand French Line, and only three thousand Virginia militia, merely one fifth of the army.

If the Americans have been mythologized as untrained neophytes, the British continue to be stereotyped as effete aristocrats typical of the decadent Old World. In the 1985 movie *Revolution* Al Pacino stars as a simple man of peace, Tom Dobbs, forced to become a reluctant warrior. He gets to witness a good reenactment of a British bayonet attack. But, spoiling this realism, the British officers are caricatured as cruel and vicious fops in rouge and tight pants who enjoy raping colonial women and buggering their drummer boys. New York Tory ladies, entertaining the king's men, wear fantastic hairdos incorporating forts, artillery batteries, and warships. Based on eighteenth-century cartoons spoofing current fashion and having no place in reality, these creations are in the movie to suggest the effect of European moral viciousness on simple American manners. Dobbs and his son do not become Continentals, who are shown as only less brutal than the British regulars. Instead, they serve in the forest alongside Native Americans. In the last scene, Ned leaves for the virgin land of the new frontier in the West.

The frontier ending is appropriate because, as America expanded after the Revolution, the tri-corn hat and knee-breeches of the eastern farmer, symbolizing the citizen soldier, gave way to the coonskin cap and

The New Man, armed with a rifle, and clad in homespun, faces the virgin frontier of the West. From Thomas B. Lawler, *Essentials of American History*, 1902.

buckskins of the frontier hunter. The New Man was heading for the setting sun. Journeying from Kentucky and Tennessee, he would shortly appear in Louisiana, fighting the British for a second time.

The War of 1812 disappointed Americans' best hopes. Some naval victories in small-unit actions barely compensated for the failure of plans to conquer Canada. In 1814 a British expeditionary force burned the public buildings in Washington in retaliation for the torching of York, Ontario. The local militia defending the capital gave way so precipitately at Bladensburg that the battle became known as the "Bladensburg Races." An outraged American naval officer, Capt. Joshua Barney, said they "ran like sheep chased by dogs." They faced regulars who, said one militia survivor, "moved like clock-work. The instant part of a platoon was cut down it was filled up by the men in the rear."

However, this rigid Old World discipline would shortly appear to be a deficit against the canny New Man fighting on well-chosen ground. After failing to reduce the forts defending Baltimore, the British moved on to New Orleans, intending to block midwestern trade from exiting the country here. The force would then move up the Mississippi River into the American heartland. After destroying American naval defenses, Gen. Sir Edward Pakenham landed seven miles from the city on December 23. Then, in January 1815, came news of a great American victory. The invaders were repulsed with over two thousand casualties, the Americans suffering only fifty-two. Even though peace had already been signed at Ghent, Belgium, on December 24, the victory was welcomed because it renewed American pride. The triumph was attributed to the backwoods militia of Kentucky and Tennessee, in coonskin caps and homespun, fighting under Gen. Andrew Jackson, also a westerner from Tennessee.

Most people today know little about the battle except that it is the theme of "The Battle of New Orleans," Johnny Horton's popular 1950s song that begins, "In 1814 we took a little trip / Along with Colonel Jackson down the mighty Mississip.'" The narrator identifies the Americans specifically as firing "squirrel guns," hunting rifles, rather than the smoothbores associated with regulars. The character of the event is also fixed by a "tall tale" of the kind told around frontier campfires. One such story had Davy Crockett grinning down a bear. In Horton's song, the militia fire their cannon until the barrel melts down and then they fight another round by filling an alligator's head with cannon balls, powdering his behind, and lighting the charge. To complete the association with the backwoodsmen, they finally set their hunting dogs on the fleeing British.

The same core elements can be found in an earlier piece, "The Hunters of Kentucky," first performed in 1822 and effective in Jackson's 1828 presidential election campaign. Here, Pakenham soon repents the folly of invading because, "Jackson he was wide awake, and wasn't scared at trifles / For well he knew what aim we'd take, with our Kentucky rifles." Despite their "martial pomp," the Britons can't match "Old Kentucky."

A British staff officer at the New Orleans battle also attributed victory to the frontier sharpshooter. Moving forward, he saw "a tall man standing on the breastworks, . . . with buckskin leggings, and a broad brimmed hat. . . . gazing intently on our advancing column." The sharpshooter fired, sniping one officer after another. The horror and confusion caused was so great that, the officer concluded, "the Kentucky rifleman contributed more to our dft., than anything else." Generalizing the point, John Bach McMaster said in a 1917 history that the Americans "were, almost every one of them, frontiersmen and fine shots with a rifle."

Correspondingly, the redcoats were depicted as having just conquered in Europe. A 1918 school text said, "the English had twelve thousand trained troops, many of them having fought against Napoleon." So the primal contest was clear. "The British were tried and disciplined troops, while very few of the Americans had ever seen fighting," said an 1871 popular history. But "our men were accustomed to the use of the rifle, and were the best marksmen in the world."

The reality was less archetypal. Jackson had a composite force built on two battalions of regulars, supported by U.S. artillery manning twenty cannon, winning weapons in a good defensive position. Contingents of the New Orleans city militia, including a company of free blacks, plus some Kentucky and Tennessee units, as well as river pirates, completed the force. The British had just over five thousand, not twelve thousand men, many inexperienced garrison troops from the empire's fringes. To slow the British advance, Jackson attacked on December 23, achieving the desired effect of making Pakenham cautious. When he finally renewed his advance on the 28th, Jackson had prepared a strong defensive line, 1,000 yards long. He had deepened an irrigation ditch, throwing the mud up to make a nine-foot-high parapet. Both ends of the position were protected to prevent a flank attack; on one side was an impassable cypress swamp, on the other the Mississippi River. On the opposite west bank of the river, Jackson also built a redoubt with artillery to anchor the position.

Pakenham, making the best of a bad job, prepared a pre-dawn attack on January 8, 1815. Two columns with fascines, or bundles of stick, to fill in the ditch and scaling ladders to mount the mud wall would attack the main line. Light infantry would cross the river, take the redoubt, and turn the guns on the Americans precisely as the main attack went in. The plan was too complex for inexperienced troops and went badly awry. The river, tidal at this point, fell twenty feet in the night and the light infantry's boats couldn't be launched from the levee on time. They were late taking their objective. The main columns were headed by the Forty-fourth and Ninety-third regiments, both raw. The Ninety-third had been on garrison duty in Africa since 1805. The scaling ladders and fascines were forgotten so that the British, caught in the open at point-blank range, were cut to pieces by artillery and volleys from the regulars. Aimed fire was neither necessary nor possible on most of the field, as a heavy river mist was soon thickened by clouds of gun smoke. Many infantry, including militia, equipped with smoothbores, fired buckshot, a scattering fire deadly at close range. Ironically, about the only success achieved by the British was at the west bank redoubt where 1,000 Kentuckians bolted before 450 regulars.

Jackson's choice of a defensive position and the fighting qualities of all his troops, especially the disciplined behavior of his regulars, accounted for the victory. But in myth the army bluecoats were denied their share of credit for the victory because they were seen as mercenaries. If they had simply butchered with machine-like precision the somewhat immature and incompetent British, where was the symbolism? It had to be the peaceable settler alone who smashed Europe's finest, affirming America's special destiny as New World example of ordinary men triumphing through democratic virtue. "That regular troops, the best disciplined and most veteran in Europe, should be beaten by undisciplined militia is, almost incredible," said Congressman G. Troup. Many thought that God must have protected America's experiment in republicanism. It was "one of the miracles of *Heaven*" said one patriot, and Jackson saw the "wonderful interposition of Heaven." America's virgin environment had a hand, too, in nurturing these invincible men. Jackson, said Sen. Hugh Lawson White, was not a formally-trained soldier but "educated in Nature's school." His men, said Maj. L.A. Latour, the general's chief engineer, were "modest and simple sons of nature," not drilled but "instinctively valiant."

The backwoodsman, more than the Massachusetts farmer-craftsman, was an ideal representative figure for a young America forging a new identity. Europe had age, the antiquities of Greece and Rome, medieval Church learning and architecture, great libraries, art galleries, and universities. It had opulence and high fashion. The British regulars represented that rich Old World tradition. Each regiment had unique uniform facings, battle honors, badges, and special customs. The American regular, whose uniform closely followed the British, seemed simply a copy with less of a past. But the frontier citizen soldier wore distinctive domestic products, the coonskin cap and buckskins. His long rifle portended an ability to master nature and assert republican man's individual autonomy, free of kings and regulations. If Europe had the past, in the wilderness Americans were carving the future cured of yesterday's errors. Utopian communities would arise, such as Pleasant Hill, Kentucky, and New Harmony, Indiana. Old World cities, like York, England, were already congested by traffic in their narrow medieval lanes, with no room to expand or change. New cities, like Cincinnati, Ohio, were spacious, laid out on a grid system showing modern man's ability to make rational progress. The frontiersman, the architect of change, was destiny and the future was with him.

Those who shaped symbolically the American victory at New Orleans were not guilty of outright lying. The British officer did see a marksman, but his importance was magnified by the horror of sniper fire directed at one important group, the general's staff. Americans who mythologized the battle worked in a vacuum of information because there was little accurate battle reporting. Most news came in letters from participants. Not until William Howard Russell, of the *London Times,* covered the Crimean War in 1854 would there be professional newspaper war coverage. So wishful thinking could fill in the gaps in knowledge, in order to give a meaningful pattern to current events.

The locus of public power from the Revolution to the Civil War was moving westward with the frontier, from the gateway of Kentucky into Tennessee, Ohio, Indiana, on to Illinois and the great beyond. The first presidents were gentlemen born, from the old states of New England and Virginia. These states had property qualifications for voting and holding office. But, starting with Kentucky in 1792, every western state entered the Union with universal white male suffrage. This was the age of the common white man, growing up with the expanding country. In 1828, their representative, Jackson, defeated by a landslide John Quincy

Adams, the educated, patrician offspring of John Adams. Although the son of a Founding Father, Adams's eastern background and aristocratic demeanor no longer fitted him to be the representative American. The general had no platform, only his aura as a self-made westerner who had pushed the Indians out of the way of expansion and whipped the British. George Bancroft, an enthusiastic Democrat and historian, viewed the hero proudly in 1827 as "the unlettered man of the West, the nursling of the wilds . . . little versed in books, unconnected by science with the tradition of the past, raised by the will of the people." That Jackson was a prosperous slave owner whose mansion, the Hermitage, was decorated with fine imported wallpapers was downplayed. Jackson served two terms, and the Alamo was fought during his second, in March 1836. By now, the New Man, represented by James Bowie of Kentucky and David Crockett of Tennessee, had reached Texas.

Historically, the Alamo might seem to provide poor material for sculpting onto the national saga. The whole garrison died in a gruesome slaughter. The battle shouldn't have happened. The Alamo was a church compound, not designed as a fort, and couldn't hold with a garrison of 182 men; Mexican general Martin Cós and 1,000 men had failed to defend it in 1835. The usual rationale for the Texan stand, that it slowed down Mexican president and commanding general Santa Anna, bleeding his troops and giving Texas time to build an army, doesn't stand scrutiny. The crux of the argument is that Santa Anna couldn't bypass the Alamo, which lay across his line of communications to Mexico; he had to storm it. In fact, the Alamo had little offensive capacity; its one possible strength, a dubious one, lay in twenty-odd cannon mounted for defense. The garrison was essentially immobilized. Two to three squadrons of lancers could have contained the Alamo, making it a prison while its garrison starved.

As it was, the battle didn't cripple Mexican offensive capacity. Contrary to myth, which put Mexican losses anywhere up to 2,500, about 600 became casualties, of whom perhaps 275 died. The Alamo's defenders gave a good account of themselves, but did not inflict a fatal wound. Also, the thirteen days of time they bought by occupying Santa Anna were squandered by Col. James Fannin at Goliad and Gen. Sam Houston at Washington on the Brazos. Houston was on a drunken spree during some of the Alamo's last days, which, he admitted, was "a bad business. I hated it." As the Houston anecdote implies, the Alamo was abandoned to its fate, despite passionate appeals from its commander, Col. William Barret Travis, who tried to force the Texas leadership to concentrate their force at San Antonio. Only thirty-two volunteers from Gonzales joined the garrison. Col. William F. Gray, despairing of mounting a relief force from Washington, wrote, "The vile rabble here cannot be moved." Legend says Travis and company made a deliberate decision to die but, chances are, they hoped to live and couldn't believe until too late that Texas would refuse them aid.

The causes of the Texas revolution are complex, not entirely the simple struggle for freedom against tyranny of American folklore. Santa Anna, as president of Mexico, thwarted progress toward democracy, aborting the 1824 Constitution, modeled on that of the United States. Americans migrating to Texas chafed at the lack of representative government. They also had to take Mexican citizenship and adopt Catholicism. Some new arrivals openly despised Hispanic culture, calling the people "greasers," and made it clear that their only motive for immigration was land. They brought their slaves, in violation of Mexican law that had abolished bondage. One reason for the 1835 Revolution was that leading Texans, such as Stephen Austin, Bowie, and Fannin, were slave owners and traders. Finally, in 1830, Mexico tried to prevent the influx of disruptive and rambunctious foreigners, who continued to stream in, exacerbating the tensions producing war.

Despite its complex history, the Alamo story had elements of usable myth, once pared down to a simple plot structure. The setting was classical, a fort on a plain with a doomed garrison. A memorial tribute from the citizens of Nacogdoches, dated March 26, 1836, said, "Travis and his companions will be named in rivalry with Leonidas and his Spartan band." The struggle seemed clear-cut in many American minds: Anglo New World freedom versus Spanish Old World decadence and tyranny. The protagonists included James Bowie and David Crockett, self-made frontier heroes representative of the New-Man type carving out a republican civilization in the West. They would be seen "as founders of new actions, and as patterns of imitation," said the *Telegraph and Texas Register* on March 24, 1836.

With their long rifles and love of freedom, they stood in the American Revolutionary tradition. "The same blood that animated the hearts of our ancestors in '76 still flows in our veins," cried Reverend W.P. Smith, a Texas patriot who claimed to have fought at New Orleans, an experience conferring special esteem in Texas circles. The legendary sharpshooter of New Orleans lives on in a description by Mexican captain Rafael Soldano of a Texan in a buckskin suit and coonskin cap, who used the Alamo's low parapet to "rest his long gun and fire, and we all learned to keep at a good distance when he was seen to make ready to shoot." In line with this legendary pedigree, the garrison could not be allowed ordinary deaths. Although about sixteen hundred Mexicans fought in the battle, one early historian claimed there were eight thousand and the battle lasted all night. The mighty Crockett surely died last, and, said the *Columbian Sentinel* on May 11, 1836, he fell with "a smile on his lips—his knife in his hand, a dead Mexican lying across his body, and twenty-two more lying pell mell before him."

Although some Texans had prior military experience as regulars in the American, British, or French armies, in myth they were all citizen soldiers. They enlisted only for honor, not land or pay, according to Herman Ehrenberg, a private in a volunteer outfit, the New Orleans Greys. He held regulars in contempt because they cherished neither honest work nor liberty, but were "mainly whiskey-loving foreigners." The Mexicans were portrayed as a highly-trained, long-service professional army on the European model. Cementing the image, Santa Anna was said to be in league with the crowned heads of Europe to overthrow the American republic. They were, said Texas leader Francis W. Johnson, "met in unholy enclave to devise the means of crushing liberal principles."

Santa Anna had no such luck. Many of his soldiers were new conscripts, "snatched away from crafts and from agriculture," according to Mexican officer José Enrique de la Pëna, men "who usually do not make good soldiers." Their only connection with Europe was the worn-out British Brown Bess smoothbores and Baker rifles they carried, sold off cheaply at the end of the Napoleonic War in 1815. Mexican officers, like their British counterparts, put no faith in these weapons and ordered reliance on the bayonet, which probably caused most of the wounds in the Alamo. The same Brown Bess was used by some Texans, as Cós abandoned four hundred in San Antonio in 1835. They may have been better off than defenders with long hunting rifles that could not be fitted with bayonets, because the Mexicans quickly gained the interior of the compound, where the fighting was at close quarters.

The Alamo found early fame, but no great artist memorialized it with brush or pen, so over time it slipped from popular consciousness. Its example of sacrifice in the cause of American liberal expansion was not needed after the U.S. completed its western conquest. By 1900 most of the adobe structure had decayed, leaving only the stone chapel. Books and films achieved only modest success until, in 1955, Walt Disney presented *Davy Crockett: King of the Wild Frontier.* Aired as part of Disney's weekly television program, the show was then released as a film and met huge, unexpected success. The production was low budget and Fess Parker, who played Crockett, was relatively unknown. But Disney executives employed forward-looking marketing techniques, now considered standard.

In 1953 MGM had released *Knights of the Round Table,* a chivalric epic accompanied by a corresponding toy figure line. Disney did a more comprehensive sales job, promoting Frontierland at the soon-to-be-opened Disneyland in Anaheim and advertising a large line of theme products during its TV show. Related toys included long rifles and coonskin caps, powder horns and bullet pouches, even buckskins. The film's theme music, "The Ballad of Davy Crockett," was a hit, selling ten million copies, and is still remembered fondly by adults who were kids then. *The Alamo Journal* (April 1994) records that when film producer David Zucker told President and Mrs. Clinton that he was contemplating a Crockett movie, they broke into a spontaneous rendition of the ballad.

Marketing is not the whole answer to the film's success. The movie also met the immediate emotional needs of an America that, if not facing an identity crisis, was short a measure of confidence. America's military self-image of innocence-aroused had been questioned by domestic critics after atom bombs were dropped on two Japanese cities in 1945, indiscriminately killing thousands of noncombatants. Further shaking America's sense of well-being, in 1949 Russia exploded an atomic weapon, meaning the U.S. faced the prospect of extermination despite a national myth of inevitable progress. In 1950 came the Korean War, a seemingly indecisive struggle during which some American prisoners of war broadcast anti-Western messages. America's destiny and purpose seemed unstable. The Alamo perhaps provided an object lesson in how to stand up under terrifying shadows.

Resurrection of the Alamo coincided with a need for surety, for clarity in values between good and evil, a return to America's roots in once-virgin soil. Crockett, with his "first make sure you're right, then go ahead" philosophy that was heavily worked in the film, seemed an excellent model to dispel doubt and remind Americans of their basic goodness and the soundness of democratic values. In the words of television critic Steven D. Stark in his 1997 book, *Glued to the Set,* Disney excelled in a kind of "nostalgic optimism" that used the past to provide positive support in the present. To further this goal Disney scriptwriters contemplated not letting Crockett die at the Alamo. But, knowing historians would cry foul, they did the next best thing and left him swinging his long rifle as he retreated up the Alamo steps.

It is doubtful that the Disney production had overriding political motives. But John Wayne's 1960 wide-screen epic, *The Alamo,* which built on Disney's success, served as a vehicle for Wayne's conservative viewpoint. Frustrated by the indecisive nature of the Cold War, so different from the total victories in the World Wars, Wayne worried that "We're getting too soft." Ironically, although Wayne had no war service, he doubted the toughness of newly-elected president John F. Kennedy, himself a veteran of the Pacific Theater. The Kennedy glamor seemed to reflect a glossy prosperity that was eroding America's moral fiber. Spoiled 1950s youths, in particular, were soft. Russell Birdwell, one of Wayne's publicists, said that the Alamo was "the greatest single event, perhaps, that has transpired since they nailed Christ to the cross." It would serve, like the Crucifixion, as an object lesson in how to sacrifice for a faith. In 1836 Americans knew what they stood for and how to fight for it. "There were no namby-pamby pussy-foots, malingerers or skedaddlers in that brave band," said the Duke in a publicity release for the film.

Although Wayne would claim defensively that he had included land hunger as a motive for the Texas Revolution, *The Alamo* as message had to show a clear-cut sacrifice for good against evil, liberty against tyranny. To underline the point, a prominent cross was placed on the chapel roof. The problem of slavery was dealt with by having Richard Widmark, as Bowie, free his slave, who chooses to die in the Alamo, a free man. In fact, a slave in the fort, Travis's Joe, was freed by Santa Anna after the battle. Thus, although the film was billed as "a chapter of true-life history," the story had to be more edifying than the actual messy details of history ever can be.

The key change was to have Houston, who in 1836 advised the evacuation of the Alamo, now order Travis to hold it to the death; no longer fighting to live, the command is now deliberately dedicated to dying in the cause of freedom. They are tragic heroes facing their chosen fate. Matching this epic theme, the Alamo was impressively recreated on a Texas ranch along with a sizeable representation of San Antonio. Surveying the mass of extras set for the last battle, Wayne said, "Look at all those troops. That gives you a better idea than any description [in books] what the men in the Alamo had to look at. . . ."

In fact, the film is bigger than history. Where the Mexicans only had ten light field pieces at the Alamo, they now have massed batteries of cannon, including a huge gun destroyed by a cunning Texan frontier commando raid. There is not one battle for the fort but two, both in broad daylight to cameo the defenders' skill with the long rifle. In reality, the Mexicans got to the walls in the darkness, before the garrison knew they were there, and the fighting was over in thirty minutes before daylight. Most killing was done by the Alamo's cannon and the Mexicans' bayonets. To show the titanic nature of the struggle, authors Donald Clarke and Christopher Anderson estimate that Wayne had over five hundred more Mexican soldiers than were at the 1836 battle. In the film, all the Texans fight to the end in the compound, fulfilling their death pledge, although we know historically that three groups, comprising about a third of the command, tried to break out and were killed by lancers, while about five men surrendered and were executed.

Each leader dies magnificently. Travis, whose slave said he was shot in the forehead at the start of the fight, possibly the first Texan to die within the walls, now dispatches several Mexican officers before he is cut down late in the battle. Bowie, who history says was dying of disease, probably typhoid, and was bayoneted in his bed while unconscious, rouses himself in the film to kill several enemy with his gun (a marvelous seven-barreled affair) and knife. The dramatic finale is provided by Wayne as Crockett blows up the Alamo powder magazine in the chapel before being the last man to die, run through by a lancer. We really don't know how Crockett died, but it certainly wasn't this way, because the explosion would have killed all the noncombatants sheltering in the building and would have destroyed the only structure that is preserved today. Wayne's point, obviously not historical realism, was to show the lengths to which Crockett, the American frontiersman as representative democratic common man, would go in sacrificing for the cause of liberty. As Wayne said, he wanted to show the world that Americans could be "savagely cruel against injustice."

Perhaps not the most appropriate symbol for a superpower. The beleaguered Alamo garrison is put to the bayonet. Frederick C. Yohn, *The Battle of the Alamo,* circa 1913, courtesy of the C & A Insurance Company.

The film has dramatic strengths. The clash between haughty Travis and earthy Bowie, over whether to stay in the Alamo or wage guerrilla war outside, is a legitimate vehicle for exploring the difference in approach between a regular dedicated to following orders and a frontier volunteer with a more flexible approach to authority. Wayne's crusty individualist philosophy is more robust than much of the self-consciously prim family values talk of the 1990s. Few public figures today would risk defining a republic worth dying for as a place where one could come or go, drunk or sober.

In other ways, Wayne missed a perfect opportunity to showcase real American strengths to the world. The historical Alamo was a melting pot of different nationalities and ethnic groups. Wayne's garrison is strictly Anglo. Juan Seguin, a Mexican cavalry officer in the Texan service, is refigured as a sympathetic but passive older civilian, not a young freedom fighter. So ethnocentric was the movie that the Mexican government banned its distribution. Wayne also lapsed into silly Hollywood comic routines, a poor parody of frontier humor, and a soft sentimentalism that undercut his own call for toughness. The birthday party for

Captain Almeron and Susannah Dickinson's daughter is a sugary implant straight out of 1950s suburbia. *Newsweek* rated the movie B for Banal, and despite hints from the movie's publicists that to vote against it would be unpatriotic, the film did not net Wayne the Oscars that would validate his vision.

Perhaps part of the problem was that although the overworked Alamo story could strengthen American confidence in the short term, it was not a sustaining metaphor for a superpower. The U.S. after 1945 was rich, strong, and mature, yet the Alamo related to a young nation, relatively weak and beset by potentially powerful enemies. Constant recurrence to the Alamo betrayed a siege mentality. Beleaguered president Lyndon Baines Johnson, mired in Vietnam, tried to use the Alamo as a rationale for his policy. He claimed, incorrectly, that his grandfather had died in the mission fortress and vowed the abandonment would not happen again. "It's just like the Alamo," he said, referring to military support for South Vietnam. "Somebody damn well needed to go to their aid." The problem with the analogy was that the Alamo couldn't be held.

John Wayne agreed with Johnson. In a message to LBJ, he pointed out that a Crockett speech in his movie, saying that Santa Anna would soon be in Tennessee if Texas fell, was a rendition of the domino theory: Texas was Vietnam, Tennessee the rest of the free world. Sen. J. Strom Thurmond made the point literal when he said that his fellow South Carolinian, Travis, had held the Alamo "with 3,000 Russians threatening to attack." In the end, the Alamo wasn't that helpful an image for a superpower, because it had the feel of being trapped in one's own massive fortress, harassed by darker-skinned enemies, and made uneasy by the threat of impending (nuclear) doom.

The difficulty with the Alamo as metaphor is demonstrated in the last major Alamo production, 1987's *The Alamo: Thirteen Days to Glory*, a TV mini-series based loosely on Lon Tinkle's 1958 book with the same title. Reflecting uncertainty over America's contemporary mission and the Alamo's significance in the immediate post-Vietnam era, the film isn't sure what points it wants to make. At times, it aims for historical accuracy. Houston and Fannin fail dismally to aid the threatened garrison, and Travis is correctly portrayed as something of a hothead who has personally brought a terrible fate on the command.

Yet the movie also contains large elements of traditional patriotic myth. Wayne's cross remains on the Alamo chapel roof, a symbol of

God's providence, and in tribute to the Duke, his son, Ethan, has a minor role, wearing his father's coonskin cap. Inaccuracies in Wayne's film are reproduced: there are two battles for the fort, both in daylight, and all the garrison die fighting, the camera lingering on their heroic dying moments. Travis, who actually used a shotgun, again dies sword in hand as an officer and gentleman; Bowie goes down standing; and Crockett, in a reversion to the earliest legend, is last seen gutting Mexicans galore with his knife. Suggesting how film refers to film for inspiration and thereby creates its own cinema folklore, Wayne's one cannon sabotaged by a commando raid now becomes a whole battery. Such weak repetition, failing to make an intelligent point about a beleaguered garrison that in reality lacked the suggested offensive power, undercuts the film's pretensions to accuracy.

The movie fails also by having Travis, played haltingly by Alec Baldwin who never seems convinced by the role, declare outright that the fight is "not about land or money" but only freedom. The statement is repeated in a voice-over after the last battle, as the movie's parting statement. A chance was missed to offer a more complex and accurate view at a time when some Americans would have accepted that mundane issues like land and oil were reasons for war and that Americans might not always be totally innocent or pure. Instead, the film is finally a more confused and less attractive version of the legend than Wayne had produced. It succumbs to the danger in commercial products of condescending to the public's intelligence through the assumption that offering a more complex vision with less overt patriotism will offend the audience and hurt sales.

Overall, the New-Man image of the civilian soldier, voluntarily leaving the plow or forest hunt to fight for liberty, is a poor fit for the world's largest conventional military establishment. Missiles may be called Minutemen or Patriots but they remain inanimate killing mechanisms, less akin to the individualist aura of the militia than to the corporate image of the regulars, conceived as a rigidly disciplined robotic killing machine. Romantic poet William Wordsworth described eighteenth-century redcoats in this vein, destroying Scots "shepherds and herdsmen" in "cold mechanic battle" during the 1745 rebellion. Modern high-tech militaries cannot easily be configured as blacksmiths or hunters, but can be seen as waging an emotionally-removed mechanistic battle, like the redcoats.

The military occasionally tries to use New-Man images regarding its elite ground troops. The Vietnam-era Green Berets attempted a Rogers' Rangers motif. A photograph accompanying a 1962 article in the *Saturday Evening Post* shows the Green Berets paddling directly at the reader "like a canoe full of Rogers' Rangers emerging from the forest streams of the American past," as cultural critic John Hellmann later noted in *American Myth and the Legacy of Vietnam* (1986). The 1962 article comments that the soldiers could use modern high-tech weapons but also the bow and arrow, symbolically linking them to Chingachgook and Natty Bumpo. Perhaps, but the image of the hawkeyed forest fighter actually has been more potent for those who believe that America was betrayed in Vietnam by the Washington establishment: the immensely popular *Rambo* is the modern Natty, a man more at home in the forest/jungle than the natives themselves, and whose real enemy is the U.S. government and its professional-army generals, inept and probably evil.

The New-Man image often has most resonance for those who distrust the federal government and envisage a threat to individual autonomy by the mercenary forces of the New World Order. Private militias frequently refer to themselves as minutemen and patriots. As "The Ballad of Davy Crockett" reminds us, it is the citizen militia that America's popular military myths celebrate:

> Andy Jackson is our gen'ral's name
> His reg'lar soldiers we'll put to shame,
> Them redskin varmints us Volunteers 'll tame
> 'Cause we got the guns with the sure-fire aim.

The National Rifle Association cites the Alamo in its literature as an example of citizens prepared to use their private weapons to defend their freedoms. It doesn't take a great stretch of the imagination to see the Branch-Davidian compound at Waco, Texas, not far from the Alamo, in this context.

For some ordinary white Americans, especially men, the 1980s and '90s involved a search for identity quite as intense as that accompanying the birth of the republic. Faced by major modifications in gender roles and unable to keep pace with the educational and high-tech changes that increasingly defined access to the American Dream, some white Americans felt a deep need for the reaffirmation of their value. They found it in the image of the New Man, the self-reliant individualist who is controller of his environment. The image was correspondingly less attractive to minority elements who wished a greater role in shaping America's mainstream character. The English writer D.H. Lawrence, referring directly to the forest hunter figure, said that the American hero was stoic, alone, and a killer. His description might happily fit a male who admired the Rambo model, but many American women, for example, couldn't comfortably embrace such a self-definition.

The concept of the citizen soldier as hero was exclusively white and male. Fitting the era of the American as a revolutionary public figure creating a new republic based on democratic values, it essentially barred all women and black men from such a role. Their exclusion was reflected in the constitutions of western states like Kentucky, which in 1792 gave the franchise to all white males, but excluded all women, and affirmed the legality of slavery. Blacks did not figure as people in the national saga. White women could share the stage only in subordinate support roles to the male actors, masking their separate story. In Wayne's Alamo movie, Susannah Dickinson, a female survivor of the battle, is portrayed rather as a frontier Betty Crocker, tall, blonde, mature, wholesome, and totally devoted to her husband Almeron's soldierly point of view. The real Susannah, fifteen at the time, frightened, puzzled, and traumatized by the mass violence, became so emotionally unstable that she went through four husbands and became a prostitute. Her daughter, Angelina, the "Tennessee Babe" of Wayne's production, also became a prostitute. The costs of war paid by women are neglected in this mythic story of male valor.

The prominence of a warrior element in the mythic image of young America had political implications. The Constitution wisely made a civilian, the president, commander-in-chief. But, to ensure some experience in the role, Americans tended to elect soldiers who fit the modest republican image, rather than the Cromwellian or Napoleonic military-dictator mode. Thus, Washington was depicted not as a professional soldier but as Cincinnatus at the plow, a farmer yearning to be back at Mount Vernon. Jackson was a professional soldier as well but was indelibly linked to the frontier and his modest beginnings. William Henry Harrison also made use of a backwoods military image, specifically his 1811 frontier victory over the Native Americans at Tippecanoe, Indiana. Zachary Taylor ran as a Mexican War hero, but under the homely sobriquet of "Old Rough and Ready." Even Abraham Lincoln, on the election trail, referenced his tour as an Illinois militia officer in the 1832 Black Hawk War, though he had the integrity to treat the minor experience with deprecating humor. Ulysses S. Grant, although a graduate of West Point, was born in an Ohio-frontier log cabin, drank considerable hard liquor, and looked distinctly the common man in his blowsy choice of military attire. He, too, was successful.

These presidencies established a tradition of appropriately democratic military service being a qualification for high office. The problem for women and blacks is that, until recently, they have been denied opportunities for frontline military service, or their contribution has been ignored. The free blacks who fought at New Orleans were written out of the story. Thus, in many minds, key minorities have not appeared to be qualified as commander-in-chief and, hence, president. As a volunteer marching song of the Civil War put it, the male private might aspire to be colonel but not the woman: "She can't be captain, that must not happen, / She can't be captain, but play the second fife." It was the woman's role to be second string.

Perhaps the figure who most came to represent the New Man, other than Andrew Jackson, was David Crockett. Through his writings and life history we can perhaps further explore the possible strengths and weaknesses in this definition of the American. The wide-open frontier allowed Crockett to utilize his talents to the utmost, both as a hunter and as political representative of the common man. A mediocre farmer, Crockett excelled as a game hunter. His long gun gave him power over nature, the ability to earn a living, and individual autonomy. He said in his 1834 autobiographical *Life,* "I love a good gun, for it makes a man feel independent, and prepared either for war or peace."

As a citizen soldier, Crockett served initially against the Native Americans and British. His service helped his political career, and he became a congressman of some standing. Although Crockett on the stump declared himself a family man, soldiering also entailed twice leaving behind wives fearful of their ability to cope alone on the frontier. The second lived to hear of his death. The first, who had watched one husband struck down by warriors, pleaded unsuccessfully with David not to go fight the British. Said Crockett, "the entreaties of my wife were thrown in the way of my going, but all in vain, for I always had a way of just going ahead at whatever I had a mind to." "Just doing it" was part of Crockett's appeal for a people who tended to value action over reflection.

Reflexive action, bereft of introspection, is also a form of innocence in motion. The New Man, as minuteman or frontier fighter, was an innocent, who knew nothing of killing until roused to righteous fury by aggression. Then, as Richard Slotkin has pointed out, he sought moral regeneration through violence. He was often uneducated and knew little of military lore. His ignorance was a good thing in that, uncorrupted by the sophistries of European writers, he was instinctively virtuous and his cause was naturally just. Actually, the reality of early American warfare was more complex, less innocent. At least one redcoat at Concord was scalped, perhaps while alive. The taking of hair was a frontier custom on all sides, and border warfare, where differing ethnic groups and cultures clashed, was inevitably cruel and far from innocent.

At the Alamo, Santa Anna burned the enemy bodies, partly as a sanitary measure but also out of contempt and hatred. The Mexicans were repaid at San Jacinto, where Texans took teeth, scalps, and other body parts as trophies. Quarter was denied. A drummer boy, shot through both legs, begging for his life, was pistoled in the head. Houston, trying to stop the mayhem, shouted, "Gentlemen, I applaud your bravery, but damn your manners."

Despite employing a light tone throughout, Crockett gives candid glimpses of frontier warfare in his *Life*. He took part in the destruction of a native village on the Coosa River in Alabama. Soldiers in a hollow-square formation surrounded the dwellings and slaughtered the inhabitants. "We shot them like dogs," Crockett recalled. Houses were burned with people in them. A boy with a broken thigh lay "so near the burning house that the grease was stewing out of him." He was left to cook. The next day the militia came back and ate the enemy's store of potatoes, roasted in the grease of burning bodies, which "had run down on them and they looked like they had been stewed with fat meat." Perhaps Crockett remembered this episode starkly because it edged toward cannibalism.

Innocence, the closeness to a state of nature, is associated with youth and the rejection of prior authority. The New Man stood for young America's experiment in throwing off the weight of past practice. Crockett acknowledges in his autobiography that he cut school as a boy, denying the usefulness of received learning. When his father tried to punish him, the youngster ran away, laughing at the old man's efforts to catch him, "puffing and blowing as though his steam was high enough to burst his boiler." The archetypical American is youthful, while the experience of age is irrelevant, even funny.

Crockett actually learned enough in school to continue his own education later, but he deliberately professed to little learning, boasting that he had natural-born, or common, sense instead. Like other representative common men, Crockett posited learning and common sense as being in conflict; the former destroyed the latter. He affected to despise grammar and spelling, bragging that while others were doing composition, he and General Jackson, also depicted popularly as a man of little formal learning, were out in the real world, "fighting in the wars." Crockett rejected an honorary degree offered by Harvard University, maintaining that LLD (Doctor of Laws) meant "lazy, lounging dunce."

The idea that an ordinary person can make a go of almost anything, even without formal training, is positive in many ways. America was freed from the stifling European guild system of craftsmen, and the innovative were set loose to create. American energies were released in a dynamic, confident, can-do sense that led to invention and productive improvisation. Talented people were able to rise, instead of being condemned to obscurity in Europe by humble origins. Perhaps the most magnificent example is Abraham Lincoln, surely one of the greatest political leaders of the modern world.

But the same concept fed anti-intellectualism, even within education. G.P. Quackenbos, although a Doctor of Literature, wrote admiringly in his 1877 *Illustrated School History* that Crockett "had enjoyed but two months' instruction at a country school; but his strong common sense and indomitable courage made him very popular among the people." Jeff Long, an authority on Texas history, says Quackenbos actually meant that, "Crockett made bumpkinhood a badge of honor."

The idea that one should help one's self, triumphing over disadvantages and using natural ability to achieve success, is a positive encouragement to human endeavor and makes the U.S. a dynamic and creative culture. It has encouraged Americans to rise above poverty and class barriers, avoiding the human cruelty and waste of talent inherent in, say, the British class system. But there was, in New-Man ideology, a related tendency to distrust centers of established learning and those who possessed it as snobs and elitists, out of touch with the people, even un-

American. Jacksonian America emphasized the abilities of the untrained common man to such a degree that it is still not unusual to find members of school boards and university governing bodies in America who do not have college degrees, have no experience in education, and do not respect intellectual pursuits separate from job training. The result can be policy and budget decisions that have grievous consequences for those in the business of opening minds. Crockett's attitude lives on in the motto of a contemporary Kentucky Parent Teacher Association, the neighboring state to David's home of Tennessee: "An ounce of common sense is worth a pound of learning." Thus continues the assumption that common sense and learning are conflicting and not complementary qualities.

Distrust of intellect and learning is at the basis of the difficulty dramatists have had in dealing with Travis. He is typically depicted as a Southern gentleman, if not quite an appropriate frontier model, at least a recognizably respectable, even romantic, past American male type. Travis in fact was from a poor background and struggled against debt all his life. He went to Texas because he bankrupted. Not an aristocrat, he was nevertheless a reader, both of the law, which he practiced, and of Romantic writers like Walter Scott, whose works influenced his ideas and writings. The problem for dramatists is that to be learned was not only to assume a position elevated above the mass, but to be unmanly, effeminate. How could Travis be this? To deal with the problem, Wayne sketched Travis as an arrogant gentleman, but not a reader, to allow him a recognizably masculine ethos.

Attacking narrow university pedantry and ingrown scholasticism is legitimate, but an indiscriminate contempt for intellect, which is a negative aspect of our legacy from the New-Man myth, handicaps our search for understanding and the cultural enrichment acquired through intelligent dialogue. In 1978 Dan Kilgore, president of the Texas State Historical Association, published *How Did Davy Die?*, positing the accuracy of accounts by Mexican officers saying that Crockett surrendered and was executed. Kilgore was subjected to an avalanche of vilification. One outraged citizen called him "a mealy-mouthed intellectual." The *World Weekly News* asserted that the surrender story was put about by "smarty-pants historians" as part of "a commie plot to trash our heroes."

Kilgore said he wouldn't have minded the abuse, but it wasn't based on thoughtful information. "Nobody even read the damn book." A case in point was Peggy Dibrell, chair of the Daughters of the Republic of

Texas Alamo Commission, who said in the *San Antonio News Express,* March 6, 1985, that everyone knew Crockett was lanced to death as he went "to blow up the gunpowder placed in the main shrine." Dibrell's version appears only in Wayne's movie and has no basis in history. Film is a wonderful stimulus to the imagination, but it is often an untrustworthy authority if not supplemented by serious reading in the printed sources.

Contempt for specialized schools as towers of elitism led, during the Jacksonian era, to earnest attempts to close down the U.S. Military Academy at West Point as a breeder of aristocrats with undemocratic values. Crockett was a leader, excoriating the Point as a bastion for "sons of the rich and influential" who were "too nice to work." As he saw it, "The volunteer goes into the war for the love of his country," but the regular had no commitment beyond his military fraternity. He suggested that the school be abolished, dividing the savings "among the poor and downtrodden, instead of fostering institutions for the wealthy and powerful."

The criticism was not altogether absurd. Not all cadets were to the manor born, but they learned the code of the officer and gentleman, which was potentially class-conscious and inimical to the values of the common man. The tension had consequences for performance in the Mexican War and, more particularly, the Civil War. Mutual mistrust harmed the ability of volunteer and regular-army officers on both sides to cooperate well. On the one hand, the appointment to high command of civilians who were perceived as being representative common men and therefore natural warriors, despite little or no prior military experience, often proved fatal for their troops. On the other hand, regulars' contempt for the undisciplined common man and his political leaders created unnecessary alienation and dissension, particularly in the Union army. Well-bred officers from the old gentleman class, such as Maj. Gen. George B. McClellan, could see no merit or ability in the seemingly uncouth western common man, Lincoln, their war leader. As a result, they radically underrated his administrative ability and strategic vision, and performed poorly for him. They also downgraded the effort of their democratic volunteer armies against the Confederates, stereotyped as backwoods riflemen led by Southern gentlemen.

The resistance of old-style gentlemen like McClellan to the ascendant common man was reactionary in many ways. But it produced a minor progressive strain. Gentlemen of the Northeastern establishment, seeing their political power wane, went into social and moral reform movements as an alternative form of public action. Some became abolitionists and formed an alliance with African Americans that did much to make possible the Union colored regiments. Paradoxically, for a short while, the highest and the lowest in the social order would be struggling together to redefine American freedom though arms, trying to force the common white man to share the civic stage. Their aspirations would be highlighted in the flashes of gunfire that illuminated the July 1863 night attack on Fort Wagner in Charleston harbor.

FOUR

✣

Unlikely Heroes

In 1854 and 1863, two actions were fought by British and American forces that were clear defeats. Neither probably should have been fought as they were. Each involved poor judgement or weak communication, or both. Yet each came to be seen by important cultural interpreters as examples of sublime heroism in the service of important common values, and therefore worth the price in lives. These engagements were the Charge of the Light Brigade of British cavalry at Balaclava, October 25, 1854, and the Union assault on Fort Wagner in Charleston harbor, July 18, 1863. Together, the two actions suggest a significant shift in Anglo-Americans toward a much more positive attitude about the cultural benefits of war. Some seeming advantages of strife were coming to be seen as offsetting the more negative aspects of peacetime society such as selfishness and lack of community.

Once introduced to the public consciousness by important cultural communicators, each battle was subsequently available in our imaginative lexicon as a useable piece of the public past, to be creatively refigured as necessary to meet the notional needs of succeeding generations. Of the two actions, Balaclava was for a long time by far the better known on both sides of the Atlantic. Recently, it has begun to fade from public recognition for reasons that we will attempt to explain. Wagner, on the other hand, dropped from the consciousness of all but a minority for about a century. Yet, even in the shadows, it continued to be memorialized by talented artists and humanists, so that it retained a continued existence as a cultural artifact, never quite lost to light, and ready to be brought forward and refurbished brightly when an appropriate moment arrived.

From the Renaissance or early modern period, war had been seen as a necessary evil, embarked on at times to achieve diplomatic or economic ends, but hardly an uplifting or morally improving activity. Capable of producing noble deeds, it largely brought suffering through wounds and diseases, disruption of economic life, civilian misery, and destruction of property. The regular soldier, the mainstay of armies, was regarded as little better than an indigent brute. This attitude was tempered by faith in the citizen soldier, the amateur who was a reluctant warrior, raised above the level of mere butchery by his amateur status and civic virtue. Americans could celebrate their success in the Revolution as a victory for human progress, but few saw the details of war itself as more than an expanse of suffering, filled with wounds, disease, and hardships.

Perceptions began to change by the mid-nineteenth century. War, hitherto seen as a blight upon civilization, was being reconfigured as an antidote to the corruptions of peace. The ordinary soldier had been society's outcast, disparaged as a waster, a potential rapist and murderer, the enemy of civic liberties. Now, he was being reshaped into a model of honorable duty, a public servant who put the common good above personal profit or well-being, even above life itself. Even the ex-slave could be transformed into a hero to some by donning the army blue coat.

A second model of selfless action was the middle-class woman, imagined as an "angel in the house," the "light of the home," a pillar of morally correct conduct. But her sphere of action was private, the family, so that the soldier offered a more public model for right action. The idea that war is a good, arousing the public spirit that lies dormant in peacetime, remains with us today in the United States, perhaps as a somewhat guilty response to the overwhelming attraction of consumerism. In Europe the concept was tarnished by the slaughter and inhumanity of two world wars. America was not as fully immersed in World War I and came to see the second global conflict as a "Good War" productive of civic virtue and national strength. Eclipsed by the division over Vietnam and the defeat of American aims there, the positive view of war has reemerged strongly since then. Many saw the onset of the 1991 Gulf War as a healthy exercise to bring society together and promote communal pride. Since September 11, 2001, many media commentators have seen such overt symbols of pro-war patriotism as the flying of the flag from vehicles and buildings in an equally positive light.

In the Crimean War, from 1853 to 1856, an alliance of nations, principally Britain, France, Turkey, and Sardinia, fought Imperial Russia. The causes of the war were complex but, essentially, Imperial Russia was trying to expand in the Balkans and eastern Mediterranean at the expense of Turkey. Its goals threatened Britain's imperial and commercial interests and challenged a traditional "balance of power" policy that no state must become too dominant in a vital geographic area. Napoleon III of France, a military adventurer who needed a foreign success to endear him to his people, backed Britain. These two powers sided with Turkey, and Sardinia also joined the alliance.

Allied strategy was to force the czar to the conference table by seizing the naval base at Sebastopal, a valuable property in the Russian Crimean province, on the northern shore of the Black Sea. An invasion force landed north of the city and defeated Russian defensive units dug in on the hills overlooking the Alma River on September 20, 1854. The Allies then failed to break through Sebastopal's strong fortifications and the campaign settled into a siege. A deep-water port, needed to supply the Allies, was located at Balaclava, south of the city, and from it a long, vulnerable road ran to the front lines.

The generals understood the vital importance of the road; if it were cut by a Russian army moving to relieve the city from the east or interior of the province, the Allies, taken in rear, and without means of supply, would be forced to surrender. The likely direction of attack was across the Causeway Heights, a long, rolling ridge of hills along which ran the main road from the interior to Sebastopal. The Heights divided the plains below into two basins, known as the North and South Valleys. Through the latter ran the Balaclava supply road. If a Russian army seized the Heights, they could launch a two-pronged attack, moving south to cut the road and possibly capture Balaclava, and also northwest to take the Allied siege lines in rear. To prevent this, the Allies built a series of redoubts, earth forts mounting cannon, along the Heights. But, because they needed their best men in the siege lines, they manned the redoubts with Turkish conscripts, ill-treated and demoralized, supported by British gunners. When the Russians attacked from the east, on October 25, 1854, the Turks bolted and the forts were lost.

Following their success, the Russians moved a strong cavalry force south toward Balaclava. They were met by the Sutherland Highlanders, Scots infantry drawn up in a long firing line and using the minië ball, a new and deadly bullet, as fast to load as a smoothbore round but with the accuracy and clout of a rifle shot. Rolling volleys drove the enemy back in disorder. Meanwhile, a second Russian mounted thrust headed down North Valley toward the Allied main lines was stopped by the Heavy Brigade, British cavalry under Sir James Scarlett. Big men on large horses, the Heavies could be used to break up enemy formations at short-range. Six hundred of them charged into thirty-six hundred Russian troopers, poorly deployed in a close-packed mass. The disconcerted enemy retreated to the Heights. Lord Raglan, the British commanding general, had the satisfaction of witnessing all the action from the Sapoune Ridge, a tall hill due west of the Causeway Heights, which gave a panoramic view of the whole battlefield.

Raglan's equanimity was short-lived. He presently observed the Russians preparing to remove the cannon from the Causeway redoubts. He also observed the Light Brigade of cavalry sitting at the near end of North Valley, unused in the battle so far. Light cavalry were light men on fast horses, used like light infantry for scouting and special operations. They were perfectly suited for a lightning attack to save the departing guns. Noting Lord Cardigan, commander of the brigade, talking with Lord Lucan, chief of all the cavalry, Raglan sent Capt. Louis Nolan, an aide, with an order to "advance rapidly to the front, and try to prevent the enemy carrying away the guns. . . ." Shortly, the brigade advanced, but toward the wrong guns. Instead of slanting up out of the valley onto the Causeway, the cavalry went straight down North Valley, at the far end of which the Russians had placed a strong force of artillery, supported by infantry and cavalry. Incredibly, the Light Brigade advanced over a mile and a half into the enemy position, sabred some gunners, battled the cavalry, and then rode back. But only 195 of 673 men survived the attack. The Light Brigade was ruined to no practical purpose.

What had happened to instigate such a blunder? First, Raglan's message was imprecise, specifying neither which guns were the object, nor their location. Like most of the British home army, he had not seen active service since the Napoleonic Wars ended in 1815, and his skills were rusty. He forgot that, while he could see the crest of the Heights from his vantage point, Cardigan and Lucan, at a much lower elevation and blind to happenings on the Heights above them, could only see the guns at the

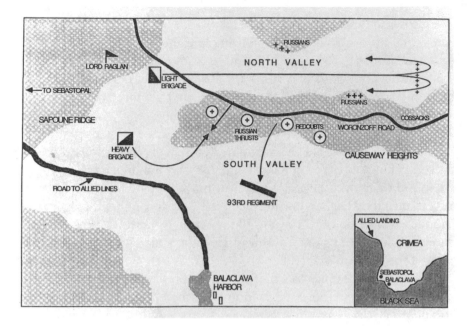

The Charge of the Light Brigade, October 25, 1854. Map by Beth Merten.

---

farther end of North Valley. Second, it was probably a mistake to send Nolan with the order. Chosen because of his horsemanship, which allowed him to safely negotiate the steep descent from Sapoune Hill, he was also short-tempered and impulsive. Both Lucan and Cardigan questioned what appeared to be a suicidal order. Nolan, impatient to have the order carried out, and probably disoriented by the difference in aspect of the terrain from the valley bottom, apparently gestured impetuously in the wrong direction while pointing out the target. He got no chance to correct his mistake as he was the first man killed in the advance.

The initial reaction to the defeat was shock. Colonel Henry Clifford, a staff officer watching from the nearby hills, wept openly as "murderous fire" poured into the brigade. He drew a stark sketch of a horribly mangled lancer disemboweled by a solid iron shot that also killed his horse. But emotion concerning the slaughter was soon to assume a celebratory tone, and the defeat would be remembered, while the successful charge of the Heavy Brigade was forgotten. Key in articulating this development was

Alfred Lord Tennyson, the national poet laureate. The stage for the reception of his work was set by other communicators who made the Crimean War, more than any which had preceded it, a media event. William Howard Russell, a correspondent with the troops, wrote graphic dispatches to the *London Times,* which fired the popular imagination, while Roger Fenton captured the war in photographs, bringing the visual image of the conflict to the public.

In "The Charge of the Light Brigade," a poem that appeared on December 9, 1854, and was famous for many years, Tennyson capitalized on public interest to suggest a dramatically improved view of the man in uniform. Generations of schoolchildren would learn the lines as an example of nobility in action to be emulated in their adult lives. Central to the poet's laudatory view of the soldiers was the fact that, although they knew a mistake had been made, they did not waiver from their duty. Tennyson wrote:

> Was there a man dismay'd?
> Not tho' the soldier knew
>   Some one had blunder'd:
> Their's not to make reply,
> Their's not to reason why,
> Their's but to do and die:
> Into the valley of Death
>   Rode the six hundred.

The image was based on a reality of the troopers' dedication. When Cardigan addressed the survivors, he said in apology, "It was a madbrained trick; but it was no fault of mine." "Never mind, my lord," came a voice from the ranks. "We are ready to go again." A little earlier in history, some critics would have acknowledged such courage in the ranks, but others would have viewed such devotion as merely the brute courage that one would expect from near-animals trained through savage discipline to perform in the macabre circus of war. Now, many responded to Tennyson's exhortation that they "Honour the Light Brigade, / Noble six hundred!"

What had changed in the social context to make the lowly shilling-a-day rankers appear noble? We can approach the question by looking at another piece of imaginative work that also appeared in 1854, Charles Dickens's novel *Hard Times.* At the time, Britain was the most industrialized nation in the world. First water and then steam power had been harnessed to machines in factories that poured out manufactured goods of all kinds. After the American Eli Whitney and other engineers perfected the machine tools to make interchangeable parts, everything from furniture to rifles could be turned out economically to standards consistently higher than those achieved by individual craftsmen. Brian Donkin, a British steel maker, pioneered the modern process for canning goods, giving us the first convenience foods, and equally inventive producers marketed off-the-peg clothing. A revolution in automated printing methods enabled publishers to cheaply publish books and newspapers, along with wallpapers and prints to decorate the home. In short, the Victorian period was a great age of materialism, enjoying a hitherto unheard of supply of consumer goods and improvements in everything from transportation, with the steamship and railroad, to cooking stoves and building supplies.

These improvements appeared so beneficial, bringing widespread comfort and prosperity, that some businessmen and economists, based in the industrial city of Manchester, England, maintained that production and international trade would so happily unite humanity that poverty and wars would soon be ended. In a radical departure from the idea of selflessness as noble, the profit-absorbed businessman was seen as automatically advancing the public good, providing jobs and a better quality of life by selfishly pursuing his material interest. Dickens was not so sure. In *Hard Times,* he attacked the Manchester School for its utilitarian insistence on defining the quality of life entirely in material terms. He accused the business leadership of overvaluing economic self-interest, placing no value on the spiritual development that produced art, poetry, and the higher sentiments of love and charity. The product of their philosophy in *Hard Times* is the spiteful youth Bitzer, a disciple of the factory owners, who states cynically, "What you must appeal to is a person's self-interest. It's your only hold. We are so constituted." The world created by the manufacturers is Coketown, a dismal, dirty factory city where workers toil endlessly, exploited for profit and shut off from the healthful influences of nature and art.

Tennyson also despised the Manchester School. He believed that self-interest was destroying character. Even patriotism was being reduced to a matter of sound trade agreements. What about courage, honor, sacrifice for a cause? In lines "Suggested by Reading an Article in a Newspaper," the poet assaults "the hogs, who can believe in nothing great," who sneer "at all things human and divine," as they go over "their scrips and shares," wallowing "bedridden in the down of Peace." An antidote for the greed and crassness of peace might be war and the soldier who risked his life for about eighteen cents a day. He appeared to be comparatively selfless.

Tennyson made the point in a second poem written in 1854, *Maud*. Here, the protagonist wanders through a human wasteland of cheating and exploitation, which drives him into a mental breakdown. He glimpses hope through meeting Maud, his childhood sweetheart, but her brother marries her off to a nouveau-riche coal baron. Happiness is barred when the hero kills Maud's brother in a fight. Reduced to despair, he contemplates death, but is saved by news of the Crimean War breaking out. He volunteers. Tennyson concludes that this salutary call to patriotic action will force the English to put aside the selfishness of the many and the alienation of the dissenting few for a while in a common cause. The nation "has lost for a little her love of gold, / and love of a peace that was full of wrongs and shames." Not war, as we might expect, but peace is "Horrible, hateful, monstrous, not to be told."

As the protagonist's encounter with Maud implies, Victorians saw another potential antidote to the devouring greed in modern commercial culture, the middle-class woman cast as the angel in the house or light of the home. She was the nurturing homemaker who created a haven in a heartless world for her husband and children, a place where giving, gentleness and compassion held sway. Here the male could retire from the harsh competition of the marketplace to be soothed and replenished with virtue through his wife's devotion and example.

A woman who came close to uniting the roles of angel and soldier was Florence Nightingale, who pioneered in the Crimea military nursing as a field for women and became beloved as "the lady with the lamp," tirelessly checking on her patients through the night. Through her compassionate nurturing she was the light of the home, but in her ability to endure hardship, and her willingness to fight against red tape and official callousness, she had the toughness of a soldier. She was so mentally and physically strong that she often wore out her assistants. Her heroes, according to her biographer, Cecil Woodham-Smith, were the common soldiers whose "world was not ruled by money, and she detested materialism." She admired the character that enabled a man to sacrifice himself for a cause or comrade with no hope of material reward.

The idea of transcendence through fighting got a full airing in World War I, which was initially embraced as a marvelous opportunity to shed the materialism and selfishness of peace for noble sacrifice in the public interest. But, as the killing dragged on, and millions of young men became the victims of seemingly uninspired plans concocted by unimaginative generals, leaving grieving relatives and dependents filled with emptiness, the appeal of Tennyson's celebration of death in futile military action soured somewhat. When, in 1936, between the World Wars, Warner Brothers made a movie about the charge, it was no longer attractive as a blunder, albeit a redemptive one. Nor could Tennyson's rejection of materialism be expected to excite an audience suffering through the deprivations of the Great Depression.

Yet the battle, still familiar to audiences through Tennyson's poem, continued to have cultural vitality, and the movie was a popular success. A new plot was given to the film. In it, the charge is made to kill Surat Khan, the sinister emir of an Indian provincial state who has earlier massacred a British community at Chukoti, a probable borrowing from the actual Cawnpore Massacre of 1857. The gallant major Geoffrey Vickers, played by Errol Flynn, has survived the massacre and leads the attack for revenge.

At one level, Warner Brothers was simply following the common practice in Hollywood of making cultural outsiders, particularly non-westerners including Native Americans, into villains. Paramount had done so the previous year with great success in *Lives of a Bengal Lancer.* Warner was pursuing a proven profitable idea. *The Charge* was a hit with white audiences in America and Britain, although its racist tones are now disturbing. At the same time, the plot change is intellectually intelligible. The Great Depression had swept America and Europe, leaving the strength of capitalism itself in doubt. The British Empire, which America had helped to save in World War I, was under assault by nationalist movements, including that headed by Mahatma Gandhi in India. Fascist and communist authoritarianism posed threats to the progress of liberal democracy. Appropriately, the Russian commander at Balaclava, ally of the emir, looks very much like Joseph Stalin. With verities collapsing everywhere, the movie gave audiences reassurance, as Flynn, the classic clean-cut Anglo-American type, triumphs over evil. The death of his character in the process provided a remaining link to Tennyson: artistic and moral inspiration from heroic sacrifice.

In the 1968 English remake of the film, after another costly world war for Britain and a messy, bloody retreat from empire, inspiration through heroic sacrifice is missing. The movie is much more factually accurate than Warners' but goes to the opposite extreme in viewpoint, relentlessly pursuing the incompetence and callousness of the generals, the unrewarded loyalty and wretched plight of the rankers. It is a parable for Britain's postwar plight, with a paper-thin prosperity that was collapsing, while the political establishment seemed incapable of a viable vision for recovery. Moreover, neither Britain's counter-insurgency campaigns in Kenya and Malaya nor America's involvement in Vietnam had made war look attractive. There is no glory in the 1968 version. Raglan, played to bumbling perfection by John Gielgud, rambles about the prettiness of table linen while the charge is taking place. The Light Brigade now functions dramatically as a devastating social critique of official ineptitude.

"The Trooper," a heavy-metal song by the group Iron Maiden, similarly offers no moral compensation for the blunder: "The Bugle sounds and the charge begins / But on this battlefield no one wins." The trooper is shot down and dies, numb and thirsty, "forgotten and alone." Interestingly, the visual images that inspired Steve Harris of the band to write the song were from the 1936 film and not the 1968 version; the mood or message of a movie, like the event it portrays, can be read differently over time and space, according to the changing emotional needs and perspectives of the viewer. Flynn, dying to prop up the British Empire, no longer impressed youth. Yet the visual recreation of the charge retained its vitality as a stimulator of cultural commentary.

Although many Americans today are not familiar with the Charge of the Light Brigade, for decades the event served as one yardstick by which to measure heroism and as a metaphor to evoke the invigoration of war versus the lethargy of peace. In June 1861 Mary Boykin Chesnut, the sharp-witted wife of Sen. James Chesnut, a fire-eating South Carolina secessionist, wrote in her diary of the war fever in the South: "We had all led such prosperous quiet uneventful lives—we were ready to rush into any thing for change & excitement—even as the six hundred rushed 'into the Jaws of Hell.'" Tranquility and prosperity seemed to go hand-in-hand with boredom.

While the rich might suffer from ennui, factory labor found life physically wearing, machine-like, and soul-destroying. Even white-collar office jobs produced what German economist Karl Marx called alienation of labor. Herman Melville imaginatively describes the problem in his 1853 story "Bartleby the Scrivener." Here, a clerk goes from sorting dead letters to the endless copying of legal documents. He is a human duplicating machine who finally loses his reason and dies in the workhouse. War, with all its horrors, could provide an alternative to such long littleness as life. Melville captures the yearning for adventure at the start of *Moby Dick* (1851), picturing New York's docks crowded on weekends with "thousands of mortal men fixed in ocean reveries," poor souls, "of week days pent up in lath and plaster—tied to counters, nailed to benches, clinched to desks."

American critics echoed Tennyson and Dickens in believing that capitalist endeavor was cruelly exploiting the worker while making the wealthy soft and undermining their public spirit. This concern was acute in the Northeast, the nation's most industrially advanced region. Yankee descendants of the Puritans had been associated traditionally with hard work, shrewd bargaining, and thrift. But now the drive for profit seemed to be subverting all other human motives; making money, rather than being a means to good works, had become an end in itself, dulling the moral sense. In January 1860 a shoddily-built factory in Lawrence, Massachusetts, notoriously dangerous, collapsed, burying five hundred workers. George Templeton Strong, an aristocratic lawyer from an old, established New York family, wrote in his diary on January 11: "It becomes us to prate about the horrors of slavery! What Southern capitalist trifles with the lives of his operatives as do our philanthropes of the North?"

That slaves appeared to be better maintained than free workers was a sad comment. Strong was no lover of the South, believing slavery wrong and the plantation spokesmen bullies, such as Preston Brooks of South Carolina, who beat Sen. Charles Sumner of Massachusetts senseless for his intemperate attacks on the slave owners. Yet the Northeast's need for cotton to manufacture into cheap cloth seemed to make businessmen partners in Southern crime. On April 5, 1861, Strong wondered if any outrage could "stiffen up the spiritless, money-worshipping North? Strange the South can't kick us into manliness and a little moderate wrath. Southerners rule us through our slaves of Fifth Avenue and Wall Street."

The sense of humiliation was particularly keen among Strong's class, professionals and gentlemen farmers of old pedigree. They had held power in the early republic but had been shouldered aside by aggressive new men like Andrew Jackson of Tennessee and his ally Martin Van Buren of New York, from a new breed of seemingly unscrupulous machine politicians. Francis Parkman, a patrician New Englander, thought his class was becoming degenerate through ease and security. Aping the New Man of the frontier, in the 1840s he took the Oregon Trail to renew his animal vigor. He also thought a war would be useful, looking on the pacifism of some neighbors as an indication of their decline in character. After touring a British ship of war, he wrote approvingly in his journal, December 24, 1843, "There is no canting of peace. A wholesome coercion is manifest in all directions," with cannon balls piled ready for action. How different, he thought, from the "feeble consumptive wretch at home, who when smitten on one cheek literally turns the other likewise."

Some Northerners felt an upsurge of hope when John Brown, of New England extraction, attacked the U.S. arsenal at Harpers Ferry, Virginia. Later judgments often label Brown's plan as insane, but at the time it was understood to make military sense. Brown hoped to use the captured guns to arm runaway slaves and poor whites living in the mountains, hostile to the planters, and begin a hit-and run guerrilla war from this rugged base. After Brown's capture, his declaration of principle at the trial and his heroic demeanor on the way to execution inspired pride. His actions became material for the pens of noted literary figures like Ralph Waldo Emerson, Herman Melville, and Henry David Thoreau.

Thoreau was a Massachusetts thinker who feared that his people were imprisoned by materialism, chained by their worldly goods and by the gold made in the Southern cotton trade. Brown's action gave him hope and, in his 1859 "A Plea for Captain John Brown," he suggested that the assault on the arsenal showed superior character to the Charge of the Light Brigade. Thoreau did not ordinarily embrace collective violence as a social good. He had opposed the Mexican War as a scheme to extend slave territory. And he saw the regular soldier in traditional terms as a mercenary shirking real work. He did not agree with Tennyson's viewpoint on the Light Brigade, saying that their dying in response to a mistaken order was simply "proving what a perfect machine the soldier is." Such an unthinking puppet was "a fool made conspicuous by a painted coat." But Brown's action was sublime because it came from conscience and not merely in blind obedience to a command. Brown "was a superior man. He did not value his bodily life in comparison with ideal things."

———◦•◦———

Northeastern gentlemen were deeply relieved when young men of their class responded readily to President Lincoln's call for volunteers, following the April 1861 Confederate attack on Fort Sumter. Henry Ward Beecher, a leading religious and cultural figure, wrote retrospectively on September 6, 1863, "Our young men seemed ignoble; the faith of old heroic times had died." But then, "The trumpet of this war sounded the call and O! how joyful has been the sight of such unexpected nobleness in our young men." Such a privileged youngster was Oliver Wendell Holmes Jr., the future Supreme Court justice. Another was Robert Gould Shaw, son of a prominent Boston family.

Before the war, Shaw had exemplified the unsettled yearning of the comfortable. He became jaded by his studies at Harvard and left before finishing his junior year. After a little wandering about sightseeing, he was placed by his family in the New York mercantile firm of an uncle. He was not happy in an office job, describing himself as a slave and saying at one time that it would be more exciting to be a chimney sweep. He dreamed of going on a trip west, but his emotional salvation was the breakout of the Civil War, which gave his life direction and purpose. Shaw enjoyed army life as an officer in the Massachusetts Second. He fought at Antietam in September 1862 and was then appointed colonel of the Fifty-fourth Massachusetts, one of the first colored regiments. He was killed on July 18, 1863, leading an assault on Fort Wagner.

Although not as blatant an error as the Charge of the Light Brigade, the conception of the attack was faulty and it is doubtful that it could have succeeded. The reason for the assault was that Wagner, situated on Morris Island in the bay of Charleston, blocked the southern approach to the city. If it could be taken, Union guns could hit the town itself. The difficulty lay in the approach to the fort, which was over a narrow neck of land between the sea on one side and dunes on the other; thus, the fort could not be flanked and a frontal assault inevitably would be costly.

An assault on Wagner was thought feasible by the commanding general, Quincy A. Gillmore, an engineer who had been impressed earlier in the campaign by the great damage that Union cannon had done to Fort Pulaski, at the mouth of the Savannah River. However, suggesting that technology changes faster than humanity's ability to fully understand it, Gillmore failed to see the limitations of the new rifled shells. Against the brick walls of Pulaski they were devastating, drilling huge holes in the masonry. But Wagner was of sand and supple palmetto logs that absorbed the shock from the projectiles. The Rebels, whom Gillmore expected to suffer great casualties during the Union bombardment preceding the attack, were in deep bombproofs, quite safe if they didn't go mad from the concussion. When the barrage lifted, they emerged to pour a heavy fire on the attackers.

The Fifty-fourth, hoping to lessen casualties, attacked at dusk. Shaw began the approach not at regular marching pace but at the quick step, then at double-quick time, to lessen the time taken to cover the three-quarter mile of open ground. He ordered the charge at one hundred yards. Gillmore, watching the attack, saw "a compact and most destructive musketry fire" hit the regiment. Col. John J. Elwell, standing by the general, cried, "My God, our men are being slaughtered." Shaw and a few men made the top of Wagner's wall and struggled briefly on the parapet. Then the regiment fell back, leaving Shaw and 183 of 600 men lying on the field. The defeat was so swift that the supporting regiments were unable to come up quickly enough to assist the Fifty-fourth; they, too, suffered heavily.

Despite its failure, the attack, like Balaclava, was seen by some, particularly in the Northeast, as a moral triumph. More than any other action by black troops, it convinced influential Northerners that men of color had a place in the Union army. The *New York Tribune*, September 8, 1865, said that Wagner was the black man's Bunker Hill: "Nobody pretends now that the Negro won't fight." Eventually, about 180,000 men of color, representing 10 percent of Union troops, would serve, partially inspired by the example of Wagner. Why was this failure special? Colored troops had seen combat before, notably at Port Hudson and Milliken's Bend, Louisiana, but their actions did not achieve the same notoriety. An important part of the explanation is that the Fifty-fourth and the setting were both highly photogenic.

Media coverage of the Civil War was broader than in the Crimea. Reporters and artists in the field sent detailed descriptions of military movements and human interest stories to newspapers and illustrated magazines like *Harper's* and *Leslie's*. Edward L. Pierce covered Charleston and the Sea Islands for the *New York Tribune*. Photographers produced thousands of pictures that were eagerly bought by the public. Many were double images, made for the Holmes Stereoscope, which made it seem that the scene was being viewed in three dimensions. Pictures shaped how people thought about the war. When Walt Whitman imagined the end of a soldier boy who "crawls aside to some bush-clump or ferny tuft on receiving his death-shot; there, sheltering a little while, soaking roots, grass and soil with red blood," he was living the war through graphic images he had seen of corpses, often posed for dramatic effect by the photographers.

The *New York Times* said on October 20, 1862, after the September Battle of Antietam, that the sidewalks outside Matthew Brady's photographic gallery were crowded with people "chained by the strange spell that dwells in dead men's eyes." The paper added that it wished people were more appalled and less fascinated by the images. Battle was terrible in its cost but its enormous drama also made it a kind of spectacle for the public. A Tenth Massachusetts Infantry veteran of Gettysburg, Mark Nickerson, held in his *Recollections of the Civil War* (1991) that Pickett's advance on the third day "was a braver charge than the Charge of the Light Brigade." Edmund Randolph Brown, a soldier in the Twenty-seventh Indiana, said that the charge had "about it certain theatrical, as well as tragical features, well calculated to awaken popular interest and applause."

The Sea Islands provided a colorful stage for war stories. Novels of antebellum plantation life had pictured the South as an exotic place, generating romance and deep passions. Lush exotic plants gave off heady aromas and color, while Spanish moss draped the great live oaks. The white sea sand glistened like frost. Clara Barton, a nurse, described the eerie glamor of the arena in which the Fifty-fourth fought. She pictured the regiment advancing on Wagner across the glittering beach while "a long line of phosphorescent light streamed and shot along the waves ever surging on our right." She said, "The scene was grand beyond description." The civilian audience, watching the action, had a very handsome and clear view of what amounted to a morality play acted out before them.

Wagner, like ancient Troy, had elemental qualities: a fort by the sea where heroes met to compete for mighty causes. In this amphitheater, an archetypal battle was fought between the representatives of the pro-slavery power, aristocrats who had fired the first shots of the war, and on the other side, lowly African Americans, dedicated to freedom and led by some of the North's leading abolitionist families. Not only black men but women of both races were represented in the drama. The federal government decided that, as an experiment in helping blacks adapt to freedom, confiscated Sea Island plantations would be run during the war for wages by former slaves. This was called the Port Royal Experiment and attracted Northern idealists of both sexes, who came to offer management advice and basic educational skills. Among the women was Susan Walker, a famous reform advocate.

The Fifty-fourth itself was a showcase unit. Many of the men in the ranks were from free families, some distinguished. Frederick Douglass, an ex-slave and prominent abolitionist speaker, was not only crucial in promoting the regiment, but had two sons enrolled. The high literacy rate was unusual for any Civil War regiment, black or white. Cpl. James Henry Gooding, for example, was official correspondent for the *Bedford (Mass.) Mercury*. The soldiers' deportment helped the regiment's reputation. For saving the colors at Wagner, Sgt. William Carney won the Congressional Medal of Honor, one of seventeen such awards to black soldiers in the war.

The officers of the Fifty-fourth also stood out, as they were recruited largely from Boston's elite. They included Norwood Hallowell, Garth James, and, of course, Shaw. The blue-eyed, blonde-haired colonel was a handsome young man and, in a war where dashing officers like George Armstrong Custer and the Rebel raider John Hunt Morgan quickly developed romantic followings, Shaw drew popular attention. His gallant death was pictured for the mass audience in prints by Currier and Ives and other printmakers.

Shaw's gallantry convinced the social elite that their type still had the character to lead the nation. Elizabeth H. Schuyler, a family friend, said that she "never knew a hero, a Christian hero such as we read of, before." Ralph Waldo Emerson, the transcendentalist philosopher, wrote proudly of Shaw's dedication in his poem "Voluntaries": "When Duty whispers low, *Thou must,* / The youth replies, I can." But the most famous lines were penned by James Russell Lowell, a Harvard professor whose son had married Shaw's sister. "Memoriae Positum, R.G.S. (1863)" celebrates Shaw's courage: "Right in the van on the red rampart's slippery swell / With heart that beat a charge he fell / Foeward as fits a man." The sacrifice would not be in vain because "the high soul burns on to light men's feet / Where death for noble ends makes dying sweet."

In 1863 Shaw and his regiment caught national attention. Yet when *Glory,* a movie about the Fifty-fourth, appeared in 1989, David Ansen, the cultured *Newsweek* film critic wrote on December 18, "It opens our eyes to a war within a war most of us never knew about." Ansen was right. The history of black regiments had dropped largely from mainstream consciousness in the period between the war and the movie, despite the best hopes of those who supported the units. Most Americans, black as well as white, no longer knew that people of color had fought in the war, because little in popular culture addressed their story.

Nevertheless, the Fifty-fourth had not been forgotten entirely, or *Glory* would not have been made. The regiment was remembered initially by veterans and by a cultural and regional minority, the families of the New England social and intellectual elite. The quality of their literary and artistic contributions kept the story alive long enough for it be rediscovered by mainstream culture in the late twentieth century. In 1894 Emilio F. Luis, an officer in the regiment, published a good unit history, *A Brave Black Regiment.* Of more striking effect and lasting notice a memorial to Shaw and the Fifty-fourth was raised on Boston Common in 1897. Made by the internationally-distinguished sculptor, Augustus Saint-Gaudens and set in a striking public setting, the monument is visually impressive; not letting the story of the Fifty-fourth die, it gets due credit in the closing moments of *Glory.*

Saint-Gaudens wanted an equestrian statue of Shaw because, said Henry Adams in his *Education* (1918), the sculptor was obsessed by the horse as a symbol of power in the chivalric tradition. The family wanted Shaw on foot, mixed with his men, as he had been in the charge, to suggest racial solidarity. The resulting compromise was a masterpiece. It shows Shaw mounted, but horse and rider merge with the marching men who press forward toward their meeting with destiny. Some forty African Americans of different ages and backgrounds posed for the soldiers, giving the ensemble a remarkable sense of character and diversity. The piece is one of the few monuments to recognize the service of blacks in the war.

In the 1960s, stimulated by the civil rights movement, three further books on the blacks' Civil War became generally available. Dudley Taylor Cornish's 1956 study of the black regiments, *The Sable Arm,* went into paperback in 1966. Two years earlier Willie Lee Rose brilliantly

Although overshadowed after the Civil War by the story of white heroism, the bravery of Colonel Shaw and his brave black regiment was never entirely lost to sight. *Storming Fort Wagner*, chromolithograph by Kurz and Allison, 1890. Courtesy of the Library of Congress, LC-USZ62–1288.

told the story of the Port Royal Experiment in *Rehearsal for Reconstruction*. The biography of Shaw that was a key source for *Glory*, Peter Burchard's *One Gallant Rush*, came out in 1965. But the most important twentieth-century affirmation of the Fifty-fourth as useable cultural symbol was a poem by Robert Lowell, great-grand-nephew of James Russell, written in 1965 during the civil rights struggle. "For the Union Dead" returns to the Civil War to express disillusion with white America's racial hostilities, captured in the terrified faces of black children besieged on their school buses by whites opposed to integrated education.

Shaw's monument was now out of place in Boston, said Lowell, an embarrassment to white citizens: "The monument sticks like a fish bone in the city's throat." Shaw and his regiment represented a commitment to human progress no longer in vogue. The poet played off the fact that Shaw, in the bronze casting of the monument, was frozen forever in a ramrod-backed military posture, to suggest a moral uprightness lacking in modern Bostonians. "When he leads his black soldiers to death, / he cannot bend his back." In lines reminiscent of the earlier Massachusetts poets, Lowell celebrated Shaw's self-sacrifice, saying, "He rejoices in man's lovely / peculiar power to choose life and die."

Lowell's poem, placed in anthologies of American literature, has been read by thousands of students. So, through isolated but outstanding artistic efforts, Wagner escaped oblivion and was finally retrieved for a movie about the black soldiers, *Glory,* which was seen by millions, bringing the story of the black soldiers back into the mainstream of popular culture.

—◆—

Why had the black soldiers been forgotten for so long by all but a relatively few adherents of high culture? Racism is the first and obvious answer. Blacks hoped to prove through war service that they were human beings deserving of civil rights. In the American and French Revolutions a connection had been made between voluntarily bearing arms and enjoying the status of a citizen. This, rather than the pay of the mercenary, was what a volunteer fought for. As black Sgt. Henry Maxwell put it, "We want two more boxes besides the cartridge box—the ballot and the jury box."

The men of the black regiments were optimistic. Thomas Long, a private in the First South Carolina Colored, remembered that the black soldiers initially had to carry bayonets to ward off hostile white Union soldiers. But they had won respect on the battlefield. Long said, "If we hadn't become soldiers, all might have gone back as it was before," and slavery been renewed. But that could never be, "because we have showed our energy and our courage and our natural manhood." A soldier of the Fifty-fourth, wounded at Wagner and knowing he was dying, told Clara Barton he took consolation in believing that his children would be free.

They were. The war destroyed slavery. Washington retained four black regiments in the regular army, forming a positive relationship between the federal government and the black community that has served both well. But in other ways the promise of freedom was stillborn. The Port Royal Experiment was abandoned immediately after the war and the lands returned to the white planters. A freedman asked the district administrator, Gen. Oliver O. Howard, why the lands were being taken "from us who have always been true, always true to the Government!"

The answer was that the redistribution of land and wealth needed to give blacks and poor whites a real chance of bettering their situation in a highly competitive society was too radical a concept even for many friends of the freedmen to accept.

In 1871, after France's defeat by the German states, Paris made itself into a short-lived commune. The horror elicited by the red flag of communist revolution further chilled any idea of state welfare for the freedmen in the United States. After the 1876 end of Reconstruction in the South, most free basic educational and medical help for the poor was removed and blacks, reduced to peonage, steadily lost their civil rights. Northern states followed suit in this "era of good feelings" between reconciled white enemies. Susie King Taylor, a nurse and teacher in the Sea Islands, whose husband had been a sergeant in the First South Carolina, asked, "Was the war in vain? Has it brought freedom in the full sense of the word or has it made our condition more hopeless?" In 1904, Thomas Wentworth Higginson, a friend of Shaw and colonel of the First South Carolina, gave the commencement address at his alma mater, Harvard. With tears in his eyes, the old soldier pleaded with his educated white audience not to betray the colored troops. "You built Shaw's statue! Can you calmly doubt that those who marched with him should vote, like you?"

An answer came next year with the publication of *The Clansman* by Thomas Dixon Jr. An unalloyed defense of the Confederacy and the terrorism of the Ku Klux Klan, the book was filmed in 1915 by D.W. Griffith as *The Birth of a Nation*. The movie was a huge national success; President Woodrow Wilson called it "like writing history in lightning." Black soldiers appear as primates whose only desires are free food and clothing, and white women. The rape and subsequent suicide of a white girl justifies the castration and murder of a renegade black soldier by the Klan. The only good blacks in the film are house slaves loyal to their owners. Griffith's picture essentially was endorsed in the even more popular 1939 movie *Gone With the Wind*, which was based on Margaret Mitchell's 1936 bestseller.

The black experience of the Civil War has been better treated in print, but of the ninety-thousand-odd books and articles on the conflict, only a relative handful dealt with the subject prior to *Glory*. The root problem, beyond simple racism, is that the Civil War has become a hobby for many, a form of recreational literature like detective fiction. There is nothing wrong with having a leisure interest, particularly one which engages so many people with the past. But the development of a sub-genre of Civil War literature that is a discreet industry catering to the rather circumscribed tastes of a specific genre of buffs tends to stultify scholarship about what might be the most important event in U.S. history since the Revolution.

——•◦•——

Much Civil War publishing fits the pattern of other primarily escapist literature that allows us to get away from our current time and place into a more congenial setting. Consequently, it cannot deal with those nagging problems like racism, gender roles, or the huge costs of military conflict, that tend to ruffle our complacency. Following the pattern established by white Union and Confederate veterans in the 1880s and '90s of trying hard not to offend each other, many Civil War books avoid the controversial by concentrating largely on the details of white military history. Escape literature must hold out comfort to its readers by confirming their expectations. Just as the fictional detective can always be relied on to find the truth and restore order to our world, so the well-told Civil War story will once again repeat the tale of mutual gallantry in a war apparently fought to affirm all white Americans' basic worthiness. The repetition is so great that, to appear to be making a fresh contribution, we now have books about one unit on one day in one battle.

The fate of Gettysburg is a good example of how much Civil War historiography has become locked into conventional wisdom. To many at the time, including participants, Gettysburg was important but not decisive; some Rebels thought they had won. Nor was the major action on the third day known as Pickett's Charge, as his Virginia brigade was only one of several major units committed. After the war, the Virginians, who wrote some of the best-crafted initial histories, took Gettysburg as theirs and made it the high point of their tragedy, the last gallant effort of a dying cavalier civilization and the high-water mark of the Confederacy. The focus on Gettysburg as the pivotal moment distorts strategic history, slighting other battles and theaters of war, particularly the West. The city of Gettysburg naturally built on the notion to where it now has an enormous international tourist trade.

That Gettysburg was the high-water mark was firmly fixed in Civil War lore by the time that William Faulkner wrote *Intruder in the Dust* in

1948, giving us the famous image of the Southern boy for whom "it's still not yet two o'clock on that July afternoon in 1863. . . ." Before that time, all things are still possible; after that moment, when Gen. James Longstreet acquiesces in Robert E. Lee's order to advance, the Old South is gone with the wind. More recently, the theme enters Michael Shaara's 1974 Pulitzer-Prize-winning novel, *The Killer Angels,* the basis for Ted Turner's 1993 *Gettysburg,* starring Martin Sheen as Lee. Shaara follows the Virginians in casting the battle as the last act of the South's Greek tragedy. His literary license is dramatically defensible, but such a highly debatable historical scenario is not challenged often enough either by buffs or scholarly writers.

Civil War literature overall tends to deal with strategic and tactical issues rather than the causes or outcomes of the war, because the latter are complex and divisive, probing areas of regional and racial antagonism. The war has become, in historian James McPherson's words, a grand football game. In this situation, publishers risk few books that ask fresh questions or challenge the accepted narrative understanding of the war. Civil War writing often tends to be bland, ignoring huge areas that might upset the reader's equilibrium.

For example, the subject of medicine in the war, which necessarily emphasizes human suffering without glamor, generally has got minor attention. Yet twice as many soldiers died of disease than of wounds. In 1861 half the Union army was on sick call at any given time. Thousands died of "nostalgia," a psychosomatic illness traceable to homesickness and concurrent physical debilitation. The massive sickness, disproving the conceptualization of war as an abstract board game, affected what the generals could accomplish. In July 1862 one third of Lee's army was absent without permission. Many were suffering combat-related stress and could not be relied on in battle. Charles Coffin, a war correspondent, described veterans' "nerves quivering and trembling" after battle.

Soldiers took opium or alcohol or both, in the form of laudanum, to keep steady. Clara Barton, a prominent nurse, had no compunction about distributing drugs, saying, "Our men's nerves require their accustomed narcotics and a glass of whisky is a powerful friend." During battle thousands on each side "straggled" behind the lines, unable to stand the horror, and materially affected the strength at the front. Poor health affected performance at the command level. Robert E. Lee appears to have had a stroke or a minor heart attack in spring 1863. A.P. Hill suffered from venereal disease, for which he took mercury-based calomel, affecting his performance late in the war. The pain in John Bell Hood's mangled body required the heavy use of laudanum, which might help to explain his ill-conceived, even wild attacks at Atlanta in 1864. Braxton Bragg was on opium in 1863, possibly accounting in part for his erratic behavior, bordering on paranoia. Marsena R. Patrick, Provost Marshal General of the Army of the Potomac, a very responsible position encompassing all army intelligence, was frequently incapacitated by hemorrhoids and bowel pains, for which he took opium, along with electric shock treatments from the telegraph wires for rheumatism.

The war's ill effects did not end in 1865. One woman told a judge in Buffalo, New York, in 1866 that she needed a separation from her husband, who "like many of our brave and noble soldiers yielded to the demon intemperance." The wife of Joshua Chamberlain, the hero of Little Round Top at Gettysburg, considered divorcing him when he came home a distant stranger haunted by images of the dead. By 1866 it was estimated that about six thousand Union veterans, unable to adjust, were in state penitentiaries for problems ranging from alcoholism and drug addiction, to vagrancy and theft, violence and family abuse.

Until recently, little literature was devoted to the war's impact on women; yet the conflict affected them profoundly, first as wives and family members. Nathaniel Hawthorne said that many widows would "pine and wither," never knowing a full life, for each fatal shot "kills one and worse than kills the other." Women were left to raise children on inadequate pensions. Some died in the effort. Pennsylvania alone had two thousand soldiers' orphans in institutions after the war. Elizabeth Custer saw in Washington an "army of black [clad] and weary creatures who had lost their husbands or sons in the war and were working for daily bread for themselves and their children."

Some women worked by choice to aid the cause, as the war elicited from them the same patriotism and sense of release from the humdrum of peace felt by men. Charlotte L. Forten, a black woman from a prominent Philadelphia family, appears to have suffered a psychosomatic illness in 1859–1860 because she felt that her teaching career was not contributing to the great events taking place. She found purpose serving in the Port Royal Experiment, while her father fought in the Forty-third U.S. Colored Infantry. Much the same happened to Clara Barton, who worked as a nurse in the Sea Islands. She had disliked teaching and suf-

An army of black-clad and weary creatures, left to pine and wither. Confederate women mourn at the grave of Stonewall Jackson. Courtesy of the Virginia Military Institute Archives.

fered a complete breakdown in 1860. Altogether, some eighteen thousand women of both races served as nurses, called "angels of the battlefield," an extension of their nurturing role as angels of the home. A further two thousand black women served the army as laundresses and cooks.

Women, like men, paid a price for their service. Forten had to retire with damaged health. Louisa May Alcott, who was a nurse in Washington, became debilitated and lost her hair to a virus. The suffering of women was worst in the South, which by 1865 was a vast charnel house, as the journalist John T. Trowbridge observed. A Union war correspondent described the plight of one Rebel woman after the Battle of Shiloh, Tennessee. One hundred wounded were placed on her property, her horses and crops were taken. In her garden were seven new graves. A Southern girl, Emma Le Conte said her aunt Sallie miscarried in 1865 through fear of William T. Sherman's troops, sweeping through South Carolina. Although there was comparatively little documented rape, women were abused. Gen. Smith D. Atkins told Rebel women begging bread, "You women keep up this war. *We* are fighting *you.*"

Some women, demoralized or desperate, took to prostitution. A Confederate officer wrote from Chattanooga, 1863: "The war appears to have demoralized everybody and the rumor says that almost half the women in the vicinity of the army, married and unmarried, are lost to all virtue." On both sides, the abortion rate climbed in 1865 as wives sought to remove the evidence of infidelity. For the men who had been unfaithful, and their partners, venereal disease was a real possibility, with no permanent cure. This is a part of the war that is infrequently told.

⊷

Glory's effort to return the story of black soldiers to mainstream popular culture counters our tendency to downplay Civil War aspects not confined to established narrative limits. The achievement is remarkable. Possessing the power of the visual medium to fire the imagination, *Glory* tells the story with some depth and complexity, making it a wonderful starting point for viewers to begin learning about the colored regiments. At the same time, the movie is not perfect and has had its share of critics. *Glory*'s reach is curtailed by the time and content limitations inherent in film; it can't deal with the whole story or do it in full depth. Because of these basic constraints, a film should never be seen as a final authority on a subject. However, the complexity of *Glory*, a tribute to the intelligence behind the production, is worthy of serious debate. Looking at the movie suggests some of the dynamics of good film as history.

Glory has been widely praised for bringing the Fifty-fourth to the screen. At the same time, its treatment of black soldiers has been criticized, particularly in the African American community. Not only did the film create fictional characters when we have information on real individuals from black history, but the lead roles fit conventional Hollywood stereotypes. Sgt. Major Rawlins (Morgan Freeman) is the wise uncle, Thomas Searles (Andre Bruagher) the uppity educated "nigger," and Trip (Denzel Washington) the destructively angry buck.

The criticism is valid, but the problem is not so much with *Glory* per se as with film as a medium that has limited time and therefore must make points quickly and sharply, so the viewer can absorb them at first go around (unlike a reader who can turn back the page to a point not fully grasped). Typing is the fastest way to establish character. Dealing with genuine historical characters often takes too long, and real people are usually too complex to neatly convey a film's message. The movie wants to show that the regiment was a melting pot for men of various backgrounds in which black pride was formed, and so it utilizes the standard Hollywood device of the platoon to quickly achieve audience recognition. The method dates back to World War I but came into its own in the second global conflict when combat movies suggested the army functioned as an American melting pot, usually through a platoon including, let's say, a smart New York Jew, a Chicago Italian of immigrant parents, a Texas sharecropper, an intellectual who had to learn to love ordinary people, and a tough but fatherly sergeant. At one level, *Glory* simply falls within this genre.

However, the film takes the melting pot motif one step further, an important one for the audience. In the beach scene, before the regiment moves into the attack, Colonel Shaw points to the color bearer and says, "If this man should fall, who will lift the flag and carry on?" Thomas, a black man, responds, "I will." In fact, it was Gen. George C. Strong, Shaw's immediate commander, who asked the question and it was Shaw who replied. The key change enlarges the melting pot to include not just whites of different backgrounds but blacks as well, bringing Americans together. The point is underlined when Shaw and Trip, buried together in Wagner's ditch, appear to be embracing in the equality of death.

Perhaps the use of stereotyping is less justified when it is used to caricature the native Sea Island black units as a rabble in arms without character or discipline, in order to contrast them with the Fifty-fourth's high quality. James Montgomery, colonel of the Second South Carolina, is depicted as responsible for this black anarchy. The film scenario does real damage to historical accuracy. Both Montgomery and Thomas Wentworth Higginson, colonel of the First South Carolina, the first official black regiment, were disciplinarians. Higginson had great pride in the soldierly bearing of his men, who were not a rabble, and he felt they compared well with any white regiment. Sgt. Prince Rivers, who was probably the model for Rawlins, elicited this remarkable praise from Higginson: "If his education [had] reached a higher point, I see no reason why he should not command the Army of the Potomac," the major Union army in the East. In his 1869 book, *Army Life in a Black Regiment,* the colonel copied down his men's memorable sayings; ironically, to show the strength of black character in the Fifty-fourth the film uses some of the sayings in the moving campfire testimonies shared the night before the battle.

The movie uses the burning of Darien, Georgia, by Montgomery to suggest the difference between the principled Fifty-fourth and the near-banditry of the Second. But the one-dimensional explanation reminds us again that the depth of treatment is constrained by the amount an audience can be expected to absorb in a limited time. It is true that the town was burned and that the incident upset Shaw. But the reasons for the incident were complex. The burning may have been part vandalism, a product of hatred and the desire for revenge, what is called war psychosis. But it also had more calculated military motives. Montgomery, as a Kentuckian and ex-slaveholder, knew how deeply the South was wedded to its peculiar way of life. He felt that waging a hard or total war was necessary to break the people's will to defend that way. If one was gentlemanly and protected civilians, the war could last forever. Ulysses S. Grant and William T. Sherman, two senior officers who also were from the Ohio Valley and therefore familiar with plantation culture, practiced the same policy on a larger scale, fighting a hard war involving severe civilian distress.

The raising of black regiments like the Fifty-fourth was in fact part of this total war policy and taken as such by the South, which saw the presence of black soldiers as an invitation to slave revolt and the massacring of white Southern families. In retaliation the Confederacy threatened to kill or enslave officers and men, a practice not carried out officially because Lincoln promised similar retribution, but murder was committed informally. After Wagner, bodies of the Fifty-fourth were mutilated and Shaw's naked body was flung in the ditch "with his niggers." The captured wounded lay on Charleston's dock for over a day, as Rebel soldiers wouldn't help them. Although the film is not able to deal with the multifaceted complexity of this issue, it correctly suggests the perilous situation of men in black regiments and their courage in volunteering.

The movie also does a good job of depicting Shaw, played by Matthew Broderick, as a diffident leader. Some film critics wanted a more aggressive John Wayne style, which suggests that they do not always carry out the minimum of background work necessary to write an informed review. It would not take a research assistant long to find out that Shaw was indeed shy and self-deprecating, as Broderick portrays him. He wasn't sure he wanted the colonelcy. Again, the film doesn't have time to go into detail and show us that it was his mother who shamed him into it. "This decision," she said stingingly of his refusal, "has caused me the bitterest disappointment I have ever experienced." When she obtained Robert's consent, she wrote, "This is my reward for asking [for] my children not earthly honors, but souls to see the right and courage to follow it." Only by going beyond the film, to the written sources, will the interested viewer find this fascinating tribute to the emotional power of the Victorian mother as "light of the home," her children's moral steward.

That Shaw might hesitate is not surprising, as race prejudice ran high in the North. Sergeant Mulcahy, the tough Irish drill master in the movie, is a fictional creation, again a type, that works because his dislike of blacks is based on reality. Those at the bottom of the social ladder, such as recent immigrants from Ireland, felt most keenly the threat of competition from free blacks. Vicious race riots occurred in New York the same month that Wagner was fought. Sergeant Simmons of the Fifty-fourth died at Wagner without knowing that, a few days before, his nephew was beaten to death in New York by a lynch mob. Black soldiers were paid less than whites, insinuating that they were laborers rather than combat troops. They were often given the worst jobs, as we see in *Glory*, digging latrines, trenches, and graves in the Southern heat, which partly accounts for an 18 percent mortality rate, versus 6 percent for white Union troops.

The racism that ran deep in Northern society might lead us to suspect that not all the motives for recruiting blacks were idealistic. The movie does not examine the other motives, choosing instead to spend its limited screen time on the progressive moral power behind the recruiting of black soldiers. This is dramatically legitimate. But it is not the full historical story. Raising the Fifty-fourth was partly in response to the danger that trained white engineers, needed to run Massachusetts' factories, would be taken by the military draft, which would not only affect the war effort, but cut into industrial profits as well. Blacks were more dispensable than educated whites. At a cruder level, such contempt for the value of black life found expression in a Union marching song:

> In Battle's wild commotion
> I won't at all object

> If a nigger should stop a bullet
> Coming for me direct.

By highlighting some aspects of the historical record and muting others, the film plays a positive advocacy role on behalf of the black soldiers. They became a legitimate source of pride for African Americans in the 1990s, a time when the momentum of the national movement toward equality appeared to be waning and the frustration of young blacks was turning inward, making violence the leading cause of death among adolescent males. When the movie was being made some of the extras for the Fifty-fourth were recruited from the homeless on the streets of Charleston, giving them a motive for the continued fight to survive. One film recruit told Dan Rather in a *48 Hours* segment (1989) on the movie, "I never knew there was a Fifty-fourth regiment that fought in the Civil War." "I had no idea that the black soldiers made that much difference," said another black man proudly to Rather.

The film also did a public service in presenting the example of Shaw as an interesting model of commitment for young whites coming to maturity at the end of the Reagan era. During the 1980s, national leaders had advocated once again, as in Victorian England, the pursuit of private self-interest as a patriotic good in the "trickle-down" theory of economics. Also, after the turmoil of the 1960s, there had been a turning away from social involvement as a form of adolescent expression. Youth in the 1980s could appear to be passive consumers of both luxury goods and myths of American progress gained without public effort. Some critics dubbed them the "numb, dumb generation." Poet Robert Bly said that youth had lost contact with both the inner king who tells us which spiritual values to cherish and the warrior who fights for those values. These criticisms leveled at the Reagan era remind us of Dickens's and Tennyson's attacks on the Manchester school, and in both eras the example of Shaw's idealism provided an alternate model of conduct for youth, who might identify with this twenty-six year old, described in the casualty list as a student.

Glory has inspired black Civil War reenactors to continue education of the public on the role of the colored regiments. Viewed from one aspect, theirs is a worthy undertaking that promotes knowledge of history and integrates the national story. It is good that reenactors of all ethnic groups help to kindle historical interest among the larger public. But there are limits to what we can experience by dressing up for mock

Reenactors achieve a remarkable realism in recreating arms, uniforms, and formations. Reproducing the carnage and anguish of battle is more problematic. The Seventh Kentucky and Forty-ninth Indiana Infantry in action at Billie Creek Village, Rockville, Indiana, summer 1986, courtesy of Roger C. Adams.

war. Some historical reenactors tend to suggest that we can, through role playing, truly reproduce what the soldiers experienced and thus inhabit their souls, sharing their suffering and exaltation. Brian Pohanka, a reenactor in the Fifth New York, said in *USA Weekend,* June 29, 1990, that his activities supply "the guts of the Civil War." Such is not the case. Only through reading the thoughts of the soldiers themselves and the works of the historians who show the whole context of war in which they fought can we hope to come close to grasping the fullness of their experience. In particular, reenacting cannot show us the actual horror of dismemberment and death on the battlefield. By playing at fighting, we risk glamorizing battle as a weekend out, the sort of picnic civilians expected when they assembled to watch the First Battle of Bull Run in July 1861 at the start of the war.

Film also can glorify war through its mesmerizing choreography of violence. *Glory* tries hard to avoid this glamorization. At Antietam we see cannon deliberately shooting into the tree tops to bring down thousands of vicious, maiming shards on the troops sheltering in the woods.

An officer's head is hit by a solid iron shot and explodes as he leads his men into enemy fire. In the hospital scene a wide-eyed soldier whose mangled limb is being sawn off begs the surgeon not to cut any more. The fight at Wagner is depicted as a surreal purgatory of brutal hand-to-hand fighting.

Unfortunately, despite the movie's efforts, special effects in film can no more reproduce the reality of Civil War combat than can reenacting. For example, in the incident of the exploding head, the movie shows a little blood splattered on Shaw. By contrast, at the Battle of Fort Harrison, Union general Edward H. Ripley was hit in the head by a "hot steaming mass of something horrible." He thought his own face had been shot off. Opening his coat, "I threw out a mass of brains, skull, hair, and blood," a pudding of gray pulp, bone chips, and bloody mush. But the fatal mess was not his. The man next to him had been decapitated and the ruined head had been blasted into his coat.

In the film, soldiers caught in shell blasts rise in the air and fall down whole. In fact, they were blown apart. Nathaniel Southgate Shaler, a Harvard professor and Union battery commander, said in his book of war poems, *From Old Fields* (1906), that when artillery fired into a mass of infantry, the air was filled with "bits and shreds that spatter down to earth, what once were men." Nick Weekes of the Third Alabama described a round of shells hitting his unit at Chancellorsville: "An arm and shoulder fly from the man just in front, exposing his throbbing heart. Another's foot flew up and kicked him in the face as a shell struck his leg. Another, disembowelled, crawled along on all fours, his entrails trailing behind, and still another held up his tongue with his hand, a piece of shell having carried away his lower jaw."

The film misreads the misery of amputation because, in an unusually well-researched production, it makes the mistake of referencing an earlier film, *Gone With the Wind,* for its understanding of Civil War surgery. *Glory* reproduces the famous Atlanta hospital scene of a patient begging for relief as he is hacked without anesthetic. Actually, a good surgeon could remove a limb in under a minute and the patient was usually oblivious, thanks to chloroform, morphine, ether, alcohol, or shock. The real horror was that, as Charles Carleton Coffin, a Union writer put it in *The Boys of '61* (1896), the unwitting sufferer was "to wake from a dreamless sleep with a limb gone." The nerve trauma often didn't abate, leading to lifelong pain, grotesque swelling, and deformity.

In an age when most people worked manually, amputees might be reduced also to panhandling. One veteran without arms, begging aid, was told by a civilian that he deserved no better, as "he was a ——— fool for going to the war."

Glory tries to show the swelling of corpses in the Charleston heat after the failed attack on Wagner. In first-rate attention to telling detail, Rebel grave diggers have neckerchiefs over their noses and mouths to ward off the gaseous smells, deemed poisonous in this era. Reenactors, too, attempt to reproduce bloating. Journalist Tony Horwitz, in his 1998 sketch of reenactors, *Confederates in the Attic,* describes how Robert Lee Hodge does "a flawless counterfeit of the bloated corpses at Antietam and Gettysburg." Hodge undoubtedly uses as models the famous Matthew Brady photographs of bodies on those fields.

Yet, again, you have to read about the battlefield to truly picture the dead. We forget that the photographs of the dead are in pleasant soft tints of black and white. The corpses actually turned purple, green, maroon, and then black. Charles B. Haydon of the 2nd Michigan said the faces were "a smooth, dark shining mass of putridity, nearly as large as a half bushel." Thomas Meyer of the 148th Pennsylvania, on a Gettysburg burial detail, saw "faces black as charcoal," twice the normal size, with "great blisters of putrid water, some the size of a man's fist." Many wounded, he said, "were literally eaten alive by maggots." They were probably luckier than those wounded whose feet and bellies were eaten by hogs. The smell of the battlefield, not yet reproduced by special effects, was sickening. When the Rebels evacuated Wagner, a New Hampshire soldier, inspecting the works, found "bodies long unburied, heads, arms, feet (with the shoes still upon them)" lying all around. The "stench was almost unbearable."

A final criticism leveled at *Glory* is that, like many war films, it appears to uphold the myth that war is the ultimate male experience, a special right of passage that turns boys into men and without which life is incomplete. The film is in a difficult spot here, as are all of us who admire the contribution of the black regiments to the cause of proving African Americans' right to civil equality. The black soldiers were fighting to prove their manhood, important to winning civil rights. The fighting bonded blacks together in this cause, as when Trip says at the camp meeting before battle, "We men, ain't we?!" The problem is that this also seems to suggest that exposure to combat is necessarily a positive growth experience, widening one's understanding of what it is to be an adult. One middle-aged reenactor, who didn't go to Vietnam, sees mock action as a valuable substitute experience: "It's important to me because it's something I missed. What does it mean to be a man?"

Perhaps the important point to make here is that, as with most issues relating to war, the answer is complex. War can appear in retrospect to the participant as an important rite of passage into adulthood. Or it can be a shattering experience, robbing the victim of mental equilibrium. To be fair to *Glory*, it seems to suggest the latter, in that the experience of the Fifty-fourth is a rite of passage, but the cost is clearly enormous and not all will make it through. Even though Thomas, for example, has become a better man and soldier through the regiment, we finally leave him wounded on the ground in Wagner, screaming "Get the hell out of here."

<hr>

Oliver Wendell Holmes Jr. saw some of the worst fighting in the Eastern Theater. During the dreadful killing in 1864 he said, "Many a man has gone crazy since this campaign began." Holmes was severely wounded several times. Yet, looking back, he saw the experience of war as character building, saying that members of his generation were lucky that in youth their hearts were "touched with fire." He described the value of war in much the same terms as Tennyson viewed the Light Brigade. Speaking at the 1895 Harvard commencement, Holmes said prosperity had produced too much "rootless self-seeking." We should love combat over comfort, choosing the soldier's simple faith over the soul-destroying compromises and accommodations of civil life. For, "the faith is true and adorable which leads a soldier to throw away his life in obedience to a blindly accepted duty, in a cause which he little understands . . . under tactics of which he does not see the use."

The value of combat also was appreciated by Thomas Wentworth Higginson. A minister of religion, a sedentary occupation, he craved a life of action. He helped finance John Brown and refused to leave the United States when it appeared he might be arrested for treason. He commanded the First South Carolina in the Sea Islands. As if this was not dangerous enough, he took invigorating risks, such as midnight swims in a stream between the hostile lines, where he had a good chance of being shot by both sides. He never regretted his military service, saying, "Life is sweet, but it would not be sweet enough without the occasional relish of peril and the luxury of daring deeds." Higginson thought that any true man "would exchange the best year of his life for one hour at Balaclava with the 'Six Hundred.'"

Some were not so fortunate in their combat experience and postwar reaction. The humorist James Thurber's grandfather had recurring nightmares of the December 1862 Union slaughter at Fredericksburg. The anti-slavery writer Harriet Beecher Stowe had rejoiced at the start of the war that young New Englanders "embrace [the cause] as a bride, and are ready to die." But she came to know heartache when her son Fred, hit in the head at Gettysburg, grew addicted to narcotic pain relievers. He had to be institutionalized and appears to have committed suicide in 1871.

Two of the distinguished James family of Massachusetts were officers: Garth in the Fifty-fourth, Robertson in the Fifty-fifth. Neither overcame their combat trauma. Garth was restless and unsettled, moving from scheme to scheme and place to place. His life was a failure. Robertson became alcoholic. Their elder brother, William, did not serve and eventually became a distinguished psychologist. But he felt he had missed something by not going to war. He hoped that society might encourage the positive qualities elicited by the call of war without the destructiveness that had ruined his brothers. In a seminal 1910 essay, "The Moral Equivalent of War," he applauded "the military ideals of hardihood and discipline." He felt that, since the war, America's privileged youth had become spoiled and needed "to get the childishness knocked out of them, and to come back into society with healthier sympathies and soberer ideas."

Some veterans promoted football as a mock war game to build character in the next male generation. Clara Barton, a nurse as influential in America as Florence Nightingale was in Britain, thought that there should be military academies for girls as well as boys, so that young women would be trained to raise soldiers of military character, superior to the "one thousand dough heads, who had merely, without foundation—been run through 'West Point.'" William James's idea was a universal draft for peaceful public purposes, a sort of militia for community improvement, disciplined and selfless for a period of national service, building schools and roads rather than training for war. These youngsters would return to private life with a better understanding of "man's relations to the globe he lives on, and to the permanently sour and hard foundations of his higher life." Through service, character would be inculcated.

This idea became an inspiration for President John F. Kennedy's Peace

Corps. As Paul Meadows, a historian of the agency, said in his 1964 *The Peace Corps,* "In his conception of a peace army, Kennedy was inspired by the idea of redirecting to peaceful pursuits the dedication, sacrifice, selflessness, and physical fitness expressed by William James. . . ." Perhaps this is also, finally, the idea underlying *Glory.* The Fifty-fourth can provide a moral rather than a literal example of the good fight. We don't have to fight in war to lend a hand to the public good, but we do have to be willing to commit a part of ourselves. Does the movie echo James's view of character development through struggle for the public good when Shaw replies to General Strong's suggestion that the Fifty-fourth needs to rest, "There's more to fighting than rest, there's character, there's strength of heart"? The movie changes the moment of Shaw's death. In reality, he was shot through the heart as he reached the parapet and fell dead inside the fort. Broderick as Shaw is shot in the gut and lives long enough to try to force his dying body up Wagner's wall. Perhaps his effort reminds us symbolically of how much uphill work for the betterment of humanity there remains still to be done.

Of course, neither the Peace Corps nor the evocation of principled striving as a symbolic call to positive civic involvement have been entirely successful. America's most privileged don't show any particular enthusiasm for poorly remunerated public service. The students with the best grades tend to go to law school and into private medicine or business rather than embracing teaching or social work. During the Gulf War minority representatives pointed out that America's least affluent had a disproportionately high representation in the military, while the most privileged played a minor role. Patriotism in a consumer culture can come down to throwing a victory party in the wake of a successful military action. One Midwestern university student, to show his colors during the 1991 Gulf War, painted his Oldsmobile red, white, and blue. He said that other motorists got excited. "They think it's great. They say it shows initiative. They go by honking their horns and staring." James might not have approved.

Henry, the fourth James brother, also did not serve in the war, claiming a rather indefinite back injury. He retired ultimately to an English seaside village where he pursued a writing career. He wrestled with the value of war and strife. In his 1908 short story "The Jolly Corner" he asked what a man might have been like if he had fought in the war and then stayed in America to compete in the hurly-burly business struggles of the Gilded Age. His protagonist returns from Europe to the ancestral home, the now deserted Jolly Corner, in New York City. Here, he conjures up the ghost of the person he might have been. This alternative self who fought in the war is a stronger man, more forceful, attractive in the way of the powerful. But he is also morally deformed by the ravages of war and business ambition, a little repulsive. In short, the impact of war on character is complex, not simple.

<hr />

We may note that James's tale also reflects the ultimate disillusion of Shaw's class with American politics in the postwar period. The protagonist's alter ego in James's story is the sort of self-made boor that gentlemen despised. In their view, the war had not produced a better America. Despite the patricians' dedication to duty, the voters had not returned them to power, preferring men like U.S. Grant, a rough, pragmatic wager of hard war from the West. Grant's type was unintelligible to the gentleman class. He seemed crass, a creature of party rather than principle, and quite possibly corrupt.

Such self-made war heroes as Grant were fiercely loyal to the Republican Party, which they believed had saved the Union and made their careers successful, often bringing them up from obscurity to the heights of wealth and privilege. They naturally identified their good with that of the party and the nation in one symmetrical whole. They had risked their lives on countless ghastly battlefields and thought they deserved whatever rewards were available. John McDonald, a distinguished war veteran, served eighteen months in the penitentiary for his part in government corruption, appropriating public revenues for personal and party purposes. In *Secrets of the Great Whiskey Ring* (1885), he said defensively that "I always made everything subservient to party, and that all my efforts had been centralized in making the Republican party a success."

Grant was not personally involved in graft, but he overlooked corruption among his friends and he benefitted personally from some of their schemes. He finally disgusted patricians like Harvard historian Henry Adams, who at first thought Grant would be a political reformer, but ended up concluding that he was intellectually unstable, with no guiding principles or even rational process in his thought. In *The Education,* Adams said of Grant that he was "not sure that he did think."

The nadir came in 1876, Grant's last year in office and the nation's centenary. Washington was rocked by scandals, including revelations of cheating in the Indian Bureau. It was obvious by now that the attempt to change racial patterns in the South, the Reconstruction for which the black regiments had fought, was doomed to failure. Then, in June, came word that one of America's most popular military officers, Gen. George Armstrong Custer, had been defeated by Native Americans, losing his life and much of his command on the Little Bighorn River. Like Balaclava and Wagner, Little Bighorn was an encounter of little military significance that reflected poor judgment at the command level. And like them, it became a cause célèbre.

FIVE

+‡+

Bearers of Burdens

Although most people don't know much about U.S. military operations in the last quarter of the nineteenth century, two famous cavalry regiments caught the public eye at the time and have remained in
our collective imagination since. These units were the Seventh U.S. Cavalry and the volunteer Rough Riders. They came to attention partly because they were led by colorful, newsworthy individuals, George
Armstrong Custer and Theodore Roosevelt, but they stayed in mind because they played symbolic roles for society. This chapter will suggest
that these men in blue shirts have been the bearers of cultural burdens,
first to carry their civilization's values to far hills, and then to bear the
guilt of their mission. Finally, at the end of the twentieth century, another
potential burden could be seen, that of adapting to constant change,
coping with the promises and pitfalls of technological transition. Because these symbolic uses have seemed more obvious in the case of the
Seventh, this unit has stayed more sharply in public focus; over time, the
seeming relevance of the Rough Riders has diminished until their depiction has drifted almost into caricature. We will offer some reasons for
the difference in longevity of public interest in the two regiments.

On June 25, 1876, Bvt. Maj. Gen. George Armstrong Custer and five
troops of the Seventh Cavalry died to the man, facing Sioux and Cheyenne hostiles on the rolling ridges overlooking the Little Bighorn River in
southern Montana. Like the Light Brigade and Fort Wagner, the military
defeat involved questionable judgment and was probably avoidable. The
battle was of minimal military significance, not hindering the army's ability
to destroy Native American power. And if, as some writers claim, it rep-

resented the high point of native resistance to white invasion, it was a pyrrhic victory with no discernible strategic or even tactical gain. Total defeat followed.

Yet, the Custer battle won notoriety from the start and continues to occupy a solid place in the popular imagination. Most Americans know who Custer was. The battle has been the subject of at least nine hundred paintings, as well as numerous books and films. In the 1960s Custer was featured as a cardboard cut-out hero on cereal boxes, alongside Robin Hood and King Arthur. The *New York Times,* in a Sunday feature article on October 27, 1991, noted the continuing popular interest in, and debate surrounding, the battle: "Fascination with the battle has inspired a legion of hobbyists" who chew over all the known details of the engagement and stage elaborate reenactments.

———⋄⋅⋘———

Why should this battle be remembered, more so than, say, the 1866 massacre of Capt. William Fetterman's command outside Fort Phil Kearny? Why not celebrate army victories such as Custer's 1868 defeat of Cheyenne braves on the Washita River? The answers are complex. We can begin by noting that the Little Bighorn came in 1876, America's centennial year, and thus appeared to have special symbolic import. But it would not have been so noticed had not Custer been a prominent public figure, what today we would call a media personality. He had a cultivated charisma that he shared with his regiment, building on the romance attached to the mounted figure since the Middle Ages.

Custer's exploits were followed by an eager public just as Frank Sinatra's were in the 1940s and '50s or Princess Diana's in the 1980s and '90s. Custer began shaping a distinct and striking persona as soon as he left West Point in 1861 to fight in the Union army. He had golden hair, good looks described as "Nordic," a buoyant personality, and a taste for horseplay, involving practical jokes such as nailing a box over a sleeping man to make him believe he had been buried alive. The general neither drank nor smoked during his mature years. His good, clean, boyish demeanor made Custer a popular figure. He added to his stature by a very real taste for fighting, an aggressiveness that in the Civil War made him stand out among Union generals often made too cautious by the strength of defensive firepower they faced in the invasion of the South. By late 1863 Custer was a leading hero, an equivalent of the twentieth-century pinup, his portrait on the covers of national magazines such as *Harper's Weekly*, which in March 1864 showed the general, sword in hand, leading a massed cavalry charge.

Custer dressed the part of the swashbuckling hero. Col. Theodore Lyman, of Gen. George Meade's staff, noted in 1863 that Custer "looks like a circus rider gone mad!" He wore a braided hussar, or European light-cavalry tunic, in black velvet trimmed with gold lace, tight trousers, and high boots. His hair was worn in long coiffed ringlets. At times he also sported a velvet sailor suit with a red necktie. Like Robert E. Lee, he knew how to prick a horse to make it balk dramatically, and he used the trick as he passed the reviewing stand, leading off the Grand Review of the Army of the Potomac in Washington, May of 1865. He grasped the publicity value of the new mass-produced visual images, photographs. He gave pictures of himself to friends and influential public figures. To help win the heart of Elizabeth Bacon, he gave her a large, hand-tinted portrait of himself. His likeness, along with that of successful actors such as Frances Kemble, crowded shop windows and could be found on handkerchiefs, mugs, and other keepsakes.

Custer's concern with symbols and special gestures was not entirely self-seeking. He recognized the importance of élan to unit morale and hence also to performance in the field. Like the men in the ill-fated Light Brigade, Custer had a deep faith in the potency of light cavalry—he called one of his hunting dogs Cardigan after the leader of the charge at Balaclava—and he tried to instill an aggressive fighting spirit in his troopers. His Civil War brigades sported red neckties to give them a sense of elite status; these emblems were cherished and worn proudly at reunions long after the general's death. Whenever possible, Custer had the regimental band play to invigorate the men in battle, adopting the jaunty "Garry Owen" as his marching song. After one 1874 scout into Dakota's Black Hills he had the command pause to dust off and brush up before marching sprightly into Fort Abraham Lincoln to the strains of the band. Of course, not everyone was impressed. Trumpeter Theodore Evert wrote mockingly in his diary, "It was a Grrrrrand Entree." But the style worked with many soldiers and much of the public.

As a consequence Custer was remembered when more successful Indian fighters were not. For example, few people have heard of Gen. George Crook, a seasoned western soldier, because he had a gruff manner and seedy appearance, campaigning in badly-frayed brown corduroy trousers, a plain brown wool shirt, and an old felt hat. He avoided the press and the public spotlight. His aide, Col. John G. Bourke, wrote, "He was singularly averse to the least semblance of notoriety," having the shyness and modesty of a girl. His fame suffered accordingly.

Although the dominance of Custer's image has somewhat narrowed the focus of interest in the history of Plains warfare, it has also kept alive in our collective cultural conversation the issues raised during the period. After his death Custer's legendary stature in the popular imagination was further embellished by numerous artists and authors, including the general's widow, Elizabeth Bacon Custer, and the army scout turned impresario, William F. Cody. Both wanted to make money but each sincerely believed also in Custer's greatness. Left with a small army pension and wanting to remain close to the memory of the man who had been at the center of her existence, Libbie Custer devoted a long life to burnishing her husband's image. She idealized their past together in works like her 1885 *Boots and Saddles*.

Buffalo Bill fought a small skirmish in 1876 in which he claimed to have taken the first scalp in revenge of Custer. He incorporated the bloody retaliation into his "Wild West Show," begun in 1883, and soon went to a full-scale reenactment of Custer's death, an impressive production that briefly even featured Chief Sitting Bull and some of his warriors. The show was wildly popular, touring America and Europe, with a special performance for Queen Victoria. It fixed in the public mind the image of the battle as a gallant last stand and encouraged that blurring between entertainment fiction and documentary history with which we are familiar today. Cody insisted his show was an accurate reenactment and it came to be accepted as an educational experience, although Cody had little actual evidence for his colorful version in which he played Custer, dying at the last amidst the bodies of his gallant veterans. In 1893 leading journalist Brick Pomeroy was quoted in the performance program as saying that Cody's show had "more of real life, of genuine interest, of positive education" than any imaginary work like *Romeo and Juliet* and should be renamed "Wild West Reality."

In fact, much of the course of the Little Bighorn battle is still in doubt and large parts of the traditional version, although touted as absolutely authentic, are as imaginative as Shakespeare's plays and perform the same cultural role, fulfilling the emotional needs of the audience. From the first, creative assumptions were made that cannot be proven. A good example is the work of Walt Whitman, a famous poet who helped to immortalize the fight. Like Custer, Whitman understood the power of the modern media, exemplified in photographs and cheap print. Whitman would stand on Broadway, in his carefully cultivated costume as the democratic poet, giving out pictures of himself to prospective buyers of his works. Whitman was steeped in popular culture and accepted the Custer persona in its entirety.

As a poet, Whitman was searching for an episode that could serve as the basis for an American epic to show the nation's coming of age as a vital component of Western culture. He had hoped to find the material in the Civil War, but the conflict had proved too big, complex, and messy, filled with ambivalence, loose endings, and too much blood, muck, and excrement. It couldn't be honed into a crystal saga; the real war, said Whitman, would never get in the books. It was too deep, too shocking, too enormous in its suffering.

Custer's death offered a more focused, contained event for epic narrative, a battle between clear opposites: the cavalry representing Christian civilization and progress, the Native Americans a way of life colorful and romantic, but primitive and necessarily doomed to extinction. In a contest of primal forces Custer stood at the center, a Christian hero much like Count Roland, who died fighting at Roncevaux in 778, the true knight exemplifying the ethic of sacrifice in a profound cause. Such an example of sacrifice seemed much needed in 1876, a celebratory centennial year marred by revelations of corruption in business and government. Custer had testified before Congress about graft in the Indian Bureau and was applauded by the public as an example of soldierly integrity versus the looser ethics visible among civilians.

Custer and the Seventh, then, carry the symbolic burden of advancing civilization and, at the same time, of atoning with their deaths for the sins of a nation distracted from its civilizing mission by material obsession. In "A Death Sonnet for Custer," written shortly after the battle, Whitman imagines that Custer, "After many battles," dies true to his soldierly faith and "yields up thyself." Here is a parallel to the martyrdom of Christ and also to the dying Roland who, in the epic *The Song of*

Roland, yields up to God his mailed glove, token of his knighthood, in recognition of soldierly duty fulfilled. Whitman notes that this symbolism links the Little Bighorn to earlier sagas of the Anglo-Saxon peoples:

> Continues yet the old, old legend of our race,
> The loftiest of life upheld by death,
> The ancient banner perfectly maintain'd,
> O lesson opportune, O how I welcome thee!

Implicit in the sacrificial version of the event is the assumption that it could not have been an embarrassing blunder that destroyed the command. There must have been an ambush, a cunning surprise, "the Indian ambuscade, the craft, the fatal environment," in Whitman's words, that led to the death stand.

As with Roland's betrayal by Ganelon, there must also be a whiff of treachery to explain the hero's death. In this case some critics laid the betrayal at the feet of Maj. Marcus Reno and Capt. Frederick W. Benteen, officers of Custer's command who did not like Custer and did not aid him at the end.

The *New York Herald,* July 12, 1876, picking up on the epic theme, compared the Little Bighorn to the stand of Leonidas and his Spartans against the Persians at Thermopylae in 480 B.C. Closer to the moment, the Light Brigade offered a parallel example of sacrifice, not in consummation of a blunder, but in "the utter consecration of one's life to his duty, the sublimest thing a man can do." Always in these mythic versions of the event, the soldiers without exception die well; in Whitman's words, "The cavalry companies fighting to the last in sternest heroism."

A vivid visualization of this theme was "Custer's Last Rally," a grand eleven by twenty-two foot painting produced by John Mulvany in 1881 that shows Custer in the center of a ring of troopers, each man grim and dauntless. Custer, long-haired, and in a distinctive costume made of buckskin, wields a sword, the legendary weapon of the chivalric hero. Actually, Custer had his hair cropped for the campaign, he wore an army gray jumper, and the sabers were left in storage as useless in battle. No matter. The impression left was of a gallant band of heroes.

On initially viewing Mulvany's work, Whitman "sat for over an hour before the picture, completely absorbed in the first view." In the *New York Tribune,* August 15, 1881, he said it captured the western saga,

The 1904 edition of the F. Otto Becker print shows the traditional view of Custer's death, with a long-haired and sword-wielding general going down last "in sternest heroism." Courtesy of the Anheuser-Busch Corporate Archives, St. Louis, Missouri.

matching herculean figures of Sioux warriors against stoic soldiers, "wringing out every cent of pay before they sell their lives." The poet found nothing like it "in Homer, in Shakespeare; more grim and sublime than either, all native, all our own and all a fact." This was the archetypal version of the Custer painting, realized also in the popular works of Cassilly Adams and Otto Becker, who was commissioned in 1896 by Anheuser-Busch, the Saint Louis brewery, to produce a version for its outlets. In all, over one million copies were printed, many to hang in bars, restaurants, and train terminals.

The idea of Custer and the Seventh as sacrificial heroes, dying to protect and advance civilization, has had a durable life. In 1942 Warner Brothers made *They Died with Their Boots On,* starring Errol Flynn and Olivia de Havilland. Here, George and Libbie know the general is going to die, turning poor judgement into a willing act of self-sacrifice. Custer says that an overwhelming force of braves is making for Gen. Alfred Terry's infantry and he must come between them. In an aside to an immigrant English officer, "Queen's Own" Butler, a fictional character created to link Custer to the Light Brigade and remind Americans in 1942 that they were about to fight alongside the British, Custer says, "It's Terry or us. What chance does his infantry have against thousands of Indians?" The storyline works for the movie, but it involves two historical distortions. First, the tribes were in a defensive posture and were not making for Terry. Second, infantry long-range rifle fire, backed by artillery, was more effective against hostiles than the less powerful carbine fire of cavalry. Terry would have had a much better chance than Custer.

The theme of the burden of sacrifice worked well in 1942. The Japanese had just bombed Pearl Harbor and the outnumbered regular army was being asked to fight without aid in the Philippines to slow the Japanese advance and buy time for America to raise a volunteer army. De Havilland swoons at the final parting, which students in film classes now find funny, but it represented a real situation in 1942. Army wives had to cope with the sacrifice of their men, while young boys, about to fight for democracy, desperately needed models of manly fortitude like Flynn's Custer.

The movie uses the traditional notion of an ambush to explain Custer's end, forming a snug parallel to the Japanese surprise attack at Pearl Harbor. All the soldiers fight to the end, with Custer dying last, an assumption that has continued to be made even by eminent scholars like Stephen E. Ambrose who, in his 1975 *Crazy Horse and Custer,* said the general could well have been the last soldier alive. The idea links Custer's death to that of other legendary heroes, including Davy Crockett, who die last as the greatest warriors. But there is no evidence for this, nor for the idea that every man died tough. And there was no ambush. These are creative embellishments, but they come out of a kernel of truth: the men of the Seventh died doing their duty. This cardinal fact helped to keep the sacrificial version alive. Although less popular than it used to be, the traditional story continues to offer an example of selflessness to a materialistic culture. Custer's Last Stand is particularly popular with Americans who feel that respect for national heroes has been eroded by political correctness, although the issue is not just left- versus right-wing. Charlton Heston, for example, considered a conservative spokesman, refused to play Custer, whom he saw as an incompetent egotist.

An interesting feature of the film is that Custer is portrayed as a friend of the Native Americans and bears the burden of trying to obtain justice for them. His death makes Congress acknowledge past wrongs and give fair treatment. Gen. Phil Sheridan says sympathetically to Libbie, "Your soldier won his last fight after all." The theme of reconciliation worked well in 1942, because the Japanese were proclaiming an East Asia Co-Prosperity Sphere aimed at bringing Asian peoples to their support and undermining Western colonial power, and so Hollywood needed to suggest a positive attitude toward native peoples. But, in actuality, while Custer did respect some Indian traits and opposed cheating the natives, his death did not win better treatment for the tribes. Rather, it reinforced Sheridan's actual hard-war policy and his belief that "the good Indian" was usually a dead one.

———•◦•———

The idea of Custer's sympathy for the Native Americans suggests a further positive symbolism attached to the deaths of the Seventh; they represented the vanishing of an earlier America for both natives and whites. The last western fight would come at Wounded Knee in 1890, the same year as the frontier was declared officially closed. Ironically, the soldiers who subdued the West often had more in common with the warriors than with the politicians and railroad executives whose interests they furthered. The frontier cavalry troop as much as the tribal village belonged to a vanishing way of life.

The officer corps, with its ethic of duty and modest pay, stood outside the acquisitive spirit of the age with its accent on material success. Soldiers were poor, life on the frontier was hard, the food bad, the amenities few. Some turned to alcohol to assuage boredom and the pain of old wounds and rough marches. But, at its best, the life was carefree and harked back to a simpler America. Libbie Custer caught the spirit when she said in *Following the Guidon* (1890), "The most contented people I ever knew lived in the very heart of the great American desert." Unlike the eastern businessman, she said, the soldier knew "no carking care." Using a popular concept of the westerner, she depicted the cavalry as descendants of the knights errant, devoted to chivalric ideals of an earlier and less crass age. Ironically, by their actions, the soldiers inevitably advanced the modern improvements they questioned. On June 20, 1926, the *Boston Globe* said that Mrs. Custer could see fields of plenty thanks to her husband who had fertilized the West with the blood of progress—progress that also made the plains garrisons redundant.

The Little Bighorn as the end of an era for red and white people has had its appeal. The theme permeates the 1968 movie *Custer of the West,* in which the general, played by Robert Shaw, angrily rejects the use of an armored train that would turn war from a noble contest between champions into a mechanized slaughter and destroy the important role of individual striving in the frontier saga. This fictional episode is based on the fact that Custer did reject the use of a battery of Gatling guns in his last campaign, but only because they were unreliable and would slow him down, rather than a yearning for a pre-industrial tournament. The armored train, nevertheless, symbolizes the technology and organizational skills that doom the free spirit of the open West and also, ominously, look forward to the orchestrated slaughters of World War I.

Not everyone who knew Custer admired him or regretted his death. Some officers in the regiment resented his nepotism and favoritism. He was often depicted as hypocritical. Despite his clean-cut image, he had gonorrhea, contracted in 1859. He was felt to be ruthless toward infractions of discipline in his subordinates, but cavalier about obeying his superiors' commands. Lt. Charles Larned of the Seventh said that Custer was a martinet, "selfishly indifferent to others, and ruthlessly determined to make himself conspicuous at all hazards." On two occasions Custer failed to aid small parties of troopers cut off by warriors, a betrayal of the Western military code that others held against him. Captain Benteen said, "I'm only too proud to say that I despised him."

The more negative views of Custer fueled a further major symbolism of the Last Stand, namely that it was a deserved penance for white expansionism and Custer's personal role in the mistreatment of the original possessors of the land. Thus, the cavalryman came to bear the sacrificial burden not of advancing civilization but of murdering the first Americans. The concept gained ground in the twentieth century as Western colonialism came under sustained attack and was captured in the succinct phrase "Custer died for your sins" and in the popular post-Vietnam bumper sticker "Custer had it coming."

The obvious focal point for a depiction of Custer as a counter-hero is the Washita River. In November 1868 Custer attacked a Cheyenne village on the Washita in a winter offensive that achieved complete surprise and tactical success. A graphic recreation of the episode occurs in the 1970 movie *Little Big Man,* based on the novel by Thomas Berger. Here the natives are peaceful, living in tune with nature, and Custer sanctions an unworthy massacre of the friendlies. He not only has the captured ponies butchered to no purpose, but condones the murder of women and children. The scene is a clear reference to My Lai, then prominent in the public mind. Arthur Penn, director of the film, said, "Although I am focusing on history, I believe that the film is contemporary because . . . history does repeat itself."

The change in perspective from the nineteenth century is understandable. Previously, the extinction of the Native American had been seen as a necessary adjunct to progress. Social Darwinism theorized that inferior peoples would have to be shuffled off the board to make way for improvement. By the third quarter of the twentieth century, particularly after the Nazi holocaust, the attitude was unacceptable. We were better able to appreciate, thanks to the efforts of anthropologists and folklorists, that cultures cannot be judged entirely by their technological status. And we were very much aware of the costs to the formerly colonized peoples of the Western military presence.

At the same time, the movie depiction of the Washita is an exaggeration. The camp was that of Black Kettle's band, which had been raiding in Kansas, killing settlers. With the approach of winter, the chiefs sought a truce, but withdrew from negotiation when told they would have to surrender at risk. Thus, the Native Americans were not simply peaceful friendlies. Custer did order the destruction of nine hundred ponies, but did so to undercut the braves' offensive potential. And when he heard that his Osage scouts were shooting women and children he intervened to stop the killing.

The actual massacre that inspired the Washita movie sequence happened in 1864 when Col. John Chivington, with two regiments of volunteers, not disciplined regulars, attacked peaceful Cheyenne at Sand Creek, Colorado. Non-combatants were deliberately killed and mutilated, along with the warriors. Ears and sexual parts were cut off; the bellies of pregnant women were ripped open. In a scene that almost mirrors an episode at My Lai, Cpl. Amos Miksch recalled the fate of a boy trying to crawl from a body-filled trench: "I saw a major in the 3d regiment take out his pistol and blow off the top of his head." This killing ground became the climax of another 1970 movie, *Soldier Blue,* which detailed the affair without adequately explaining why it happened.

Movies of this period were highly colored by anger against the devastation in Vietnam. In *Little Big Man* the reminiscences of Jack Crabb, an old scout played by Dustin Hoffman, are used to suggest the corruption, immorality, and squalor attendant upon the white invasion of native cultures. The tribes are depicted as largely harmless. Thus, the film reverses earlier stereotypes. Custer is played by Richard Mulligan as vain and insensitive. He destroys the command by belief in his infallibility, the sanctity of a "Custer decision." This Custer has utter contempt for humanity, including the settler and the Indian.

The problem with this reversal of earlier stereotypes in the light of the Vietnam War is that it was no more balanced. Ironically, Custer's own egotism, embellished by those writers and artists who made him the central figure in the Plains saga, made him such a target. Custer did show bad judgement at times, especially at the Little Bighorn, but he was no fool or sadistic madman. He was not an "Indian hater." He respected the Native American way of life; his subordinates complained that he spent more free time with the native scouts than with his soldiers. He admired the warriors' skill in light-cavalry tactics, saying, "Surely no race of men could display more wonderful skill." And he was glad when a courageous brave escaped the cavalry's guns, noting that "for once the Indian had eluded the white man."

The fact is that any war between radically different cultures not sharing a common social and military etiquette will be vicious, no matter how much individual bravery and courtesy may be shown. And neither side is innocent. Both combatants in the Plains warfare showed magnificent heroism and occasional compassion, but both were also guilty of great cruelty. Mutual misunderstanding and hostility produced vengefulness. Lt. William Drew, at Platte Bridge Station, Wyoming, recorded that Indians had tortured a trooper to death in a revolting manner. "Our boys swore that if they ever got hold of an Indian they would cut him to pieces." And they did.

To acknowledge the cruelty shown by both sides is not to deny that Native Americans have a point when accusing whites of ethnocentricity in dealing with Plains warfare. One reason why Whitman's hope that the

Little Bighorn would become America's epic has failed is that we now acknowledge the tribes as Americans. Americans killing Americans can't be the national saga. Tribal leaders have worked to change the name of the battlefield from "Custer's Last Stand" to the "Little Bighorn." They have pointed out that the tour of the site is structured almost entirely from the Seventh's point of view. And, ironically, although the park is on a Crow Reservation, few of the many monuments recognize the warriors.

Yet, despite continuing mutual anger, there has been progress in the way we view the era. The benefit of the critical pieces that appeared during Vietnam and the Civil Rights struggle is that they offset earlier adulatory pieces and began the search for better-balanced syntheses. A good example of this emerging genre is Thomas Goodrich's fair-minded 1997 work, *Scalp Dance: Indian Warfare on the High Plains.*

If the end of Custer and his men no longer appears quite satisfactory as either a token of the white struggle to civilize the West or as the cross of guilt borne by those who destroyed native culture, it now symbolizes a further burden, that of adapting to constant technological change. To comprehend this burden requires a little exploration of what probably happened on the Little Bighorn.

All accounts agree that Custer was overconfident as he approached the river. General Terry had told him to use his discretion but, if he found a large force of hostiles, to wait for reinforcements. Custer, who had boasted he would cut loose from Terry, decided to attack immediately, probably both to get all the glory for the Seventh and also to stop the hostiles from escaping. The general discounted the significance of scouts' reports that he faced perhaps four thousand braves with his seven hundred troopers. His error has encouraged the myth of Custer's contempt for Native Americans. But his actions actually reflected an understanding of enemy tactics.

Usually facing superior numbers and firepower, the braves adopted a hit-and-run policy, relying on surprise to inflict casualties and then breaking off the engagement before it became impossible to escape. Custer's fear that the quarry would elude him in the endless rolling ridges and valleys led him to attack without a full reconnaissance and to violate another basic military precept: he divided his command in the face of superior enemy forces. Fearing an escape south, he sent Captain Benteen with three troops, about 125 men, to cut off exit from the river valley. He then further divided his command, sending Major Reno with three more companies, probably 140 men, to cross the river and attack the encampment from the southern end. Custer, with the remaining five troops, around 285 men, would move further north and, Reno assumed, then cross the river at the northern head of the village and assist him by taking the braves in rear.

Reno was met by charging warriors and formed a dismounted skirmish line. He was driven back to the timberline skirting the river and then, in danger of being surrounded, ordered an every-man-for-himself dash to safety on the high bluffs across the river. There he formed a defensive perimeter where he was joined by Benteen, returning from his futile patrol to the south. Efforts to move north toward Custer's position met fierce opposition. In the meantime, what had happened to the rest of the Seventh? Conventional wisdom says that Custer rode north and came down to the river at Medicine Tail Coulee, intending to cross to the aid of Reno, but was driven back by overwhelming forces and died hard on Custer Ridge.

Native American sources do not suggest a stiff fight at the coulee. Yet the standard scenario was unchallenged by whites until the mid 1980s. In 1983 a range fire destroyed the thick grass covering the battlefield and provoked an archaeological dig. Beginning in 1984 Richard Allan Fox Jr. and other scholars excavated the site. Using the forensic evidence provided by shell cases, they plotted the course of the fight. Their conclusions were presented in the 1993 book *Archaeology, History, and Custer's Last Battle*, which was made into a good documentary film in 1995. The lack of cartridges suggested that Custer had met little resistance at Medicine Tail Coulee and had turned back voluntarily. Indeed, cartridge cases proved that the cavalry had touched the river again much further north before stopping and putting out a skirmish line to form a defensive perimeter on the heights above the river.

The best explanation for this evidence, which fits with Native American accounts, previously largely ignored, is that Custer had seen the noncombatants streaming north from the village and himself moved farther north in pursuit. He wanted to capture the families to force the braves to surrender. But there were too many for him to surround and so he sent back word for Benteen to join him before moving into action. Unaware that Benteen was fighting for his life, he waited too long. The enemy, using the cover of the long grass, infiltrated the perimeter created by his skirmish line. By the time the threat was realized, the braves were present in great force, a panic ensued among Custer's troopers, and the skirmish line collapsed. The lack of government shell cases as compared to Native American cartridges suggests that the end came quickly, with many soldiers putting up little resistance. Such a conclusion fits with the fact that only about forty braves were killed in the whole battle. Toward the end, the surviving cavalry bunched together, meaning that they had lost tactical control of the position and, in clumps, provided a clear and immobile target. Ironically, Mulvany's and other paintings, rather than showing a prolonged and gallant last stand, show a fatal herding of lost men.

The archaeological findings fit with other historical evidence. Surviving officers, viewing the bodies next day, saw a fatal collapse of the perimeter skirmish line. Benteen said, "It was a rout, a panic," as "there was no line formed." Lt. Luther Hare agreed: "the men were struck with terror and did not fight well." Enemy accounts described white suicides, soldiers running, failing to use their weapons, and firing wildly as though drunk, all indications of terror and panic. Two Moons said, "They acted and shot their guns like something was wrong with them. They surely had too much of that whiskey."

The soldiers were not drunk. Many were exhausted, as Custer's forced march had robbed them of sleep. Fatigue helped induce morale-destroying fear. Crucial in this breakdown were the revolutionary technological changes and related tactical reforms taking place in conventional armies. Muzzle-loading muskets had been replaced by fast-firing, long-range, breach loaders, so potent that soldiers no longer needed to stand shoulder-to-shoulder to cover a field of fire; indeed, to crowd was lethal, as enemy firepower would decimate a compact mass. So, the battlefield spread out into a thin skirmish line. U.S. cavalry tactics, adopted in 1874, only two years before the Custer fight, decreed that men would now fight in squads of four, each soldier five yards apart, with a space of fifteen yards between squads.

The emotional dynamics of the new tactics were little understood, suggesting that technology changes faster than our ability to grasp its human implications. The point was made by Col. Ardant Du Picq, a French regular and contemporary of Custer, in his 1870 work, *Battle Studies*. He warned that as soldiers spread out the loss of shoulder contact would mean less of the sustaining sense of comradeship. Officers also would have less contact with, and control of, individual men, meaning that the soldier could feel isolated and succumb to fear. It was therefore essential that the members of a squad know and trust each other because "four brave men who do not know each other will not dare attack a lion." If dispirited the men "will gather into small groups and become confused." This appears to be what happened to the Seventh.

Because the phenomenon was new, the need for the familiarity of a buddy system to guarantee unit cohesion was not understood in the U.S. Army. The first four men to dismount were detailed into a squad, often with no prior experience of working together. The situation was exacerbated by high personnel turnover and a raw recruit pool. Many men were immigrants (50 percent between 1865–1874) without good English or shared American cultural values to provide social cement. Poor food and harsh conditions of service led to much sickness, nostalgia, and desertion. Between 1866 and 1867 alone, 512 men deserted the Seventh. Sixty men who fought on June 25, 1876, had been in the regiment a month or less, so that unit cohesion was weak.

Du Picq noted a further factor. The conventional soldier increasingly expected to fight at a comforting long range provided by high-powered weapons. Should a primitive warrior, used to killing with short-range weapons, manage to close, his more "civilized" opponent could be overcome by horror and suffer a paralysis of the motor functions. "In modern battle," said Du Picq, "which is delivered with combatants so far apart, man has come to have a horror of man." Native American pictures of the Custer fight show warriors with spears and clubs killing soldiers who appear frozen, unable to use their Springfield carbines.

A similar failure to understand the dynamics of their technology cost the British army its worst defeat at the hands of native forces. In 1879, three years after the Bighorn, a Zulu Impi overran a British contingent at Isandhlwana, South Africa, partly because the fast-fire Martini-Henri rifles used ammunition faster than it could be replenished through the cumbersome resupply system. Facing Zulu spears with only bayonets, many soldiers' morale collapsed and the perimeter skirmish line disintegrated into small bunches of men who were then overwhelmed. Their defeat is the subject of the 1979 movie *Zulu Dawn*. A small contingent of men at Rorke's Drift, who kept their heads and used their modern firepower to effect, survived the Zulu onslaught, as shown in the 1964 film *Zulu*.

The burden of technological change is one that we share as we enter the twenty-first century, and it is no coincidence that the interest in technological factors at the Little Bighorn comes at this time. Not only does today's military have to adjust to massive hardware changes inconceivable a hundred years ago, but our whole society must cope with constant technical evolution. Before we have fully digested the impact of television on how we think and act, the computer has vastly increased the pace of the post-print revolution. What this will mean cannot be assessed yet, but the prevalence of Y2K fears at the end of 1999 suggested a widespread emotional unease regarding our lack of knowledge about the full ramifications of the technology that now drives our lives. Fox and his associates have been attacked for deducing too much from the incidence of shell-case distribution, but the notoriety surrounding their work indicates that Little Bighorn will remain among the useable historical events we can reexamine to articulate our changing generational concerns.

The transitional nature of this fin de siècle period is even more clear in the case of the Spanish-American War. Unfortunately, its potential to teach lessons for our period has been neglected recently in popular culture. In 1898 most Americans saw the troops fighting in Cuba and the Philippines as heroic standard-bearers of white civilization. Yet, today, few people know much about the troops or the conflict. Most don't know precisely where it was fought, nor do they understand the event's implications for twentieth-century history. What remains in the popular imagination is an image of the buoyant, boyish "Teddy" Roosevelt leading his Rough Riders up San Juan Hill. When "Bo" Gritz, a Reagan-era mercenary, was asked why he felt personally obliged to launch searches for American prisoners of war allegedly still held in Asia, he replied, "because both Teddy Roosevelt and John Wayne are dead." Covers of books about the war often show a toothy Roosevelt grinning out from under his Rough Rider slouch hat.

To a degree, our concept of Roosevelt is a caricature, one partly of his own making, as he affected a noisy, rambunctious stage presence; in fact, he was a nuanced politician who advocated conservation, campaign finance reform, and progressive taxation. He was not a bad amateur soldier either, although he played no key role militarily. His part in the war is remembered for two reasons. First, he wrote one of the few good books about the campaign in Cuba, *The Rough Riders,* published in 1902. Second, gifted as a communicator, Roosevelt also was a talented self-promoter. He understood the power of the media and he used it. He is sometimes credited with inventing the press conference, twice weekly meetings held in his barber's shop.

Although the Rough Riders were only on active operations for four months, they garnered most of the publicity. As commentator Frederic Paxon put it, Roosevelt was the only man in the war who "caught the public ear" and "placed himself in the line for political promotion." Finley Peter Dunne, through his comic creation Mr. Dooley, suggested that TR's book should be retitled *Alone in Cubia,* an "Account iv the Desthruction iv Spanish Power in th' Ant Hills, as it fell from the lips of Teddy Rosenfelt an' was took down by his Own Hands." The pacifist lawyer Ernest Crosby lampooned Roosevelt's publicity-seeking antics in his 1902 novel *Captain Jinks, Hero.*

It is a tribute to Roosevelt's forceful personality and great political influence that, when the government authorized the creation of three volunteer cavalry regiments, he got second-in-command of the only one made operational. As the colonel, Leonard Wood, was often on detached service, TR frequently led the unit. Looking at the war partly through the writing of Roosevelt as an articulate participant in events helps us see the transitional nature of the conflict.

The war was transitional in almost every way. It looked back to the internal frontier period, but also forward to America's international role in the next century. The frontier had closed officially eight years previously, and there was great nostalgia for the adventure of the West. TR was among those who promoted dude ranching as a way of sampling the experience. At the same time, the campaigns against Spain's colonies comprised the first major U.S. overseas war and foreshadowed the twentieth-century role of the U.S. as a superpower and the world's policeman. Thus, while Americans thought the war would recapture for them the virtues of a simpler age, it actually set them firmly on the road away from the past into a future century of mounting complexity.

The war generated a chivalric revival, with visions of knightly encounters on fields of glory. But war sentiment also was inspired by a cluster of ideas known loosely as Social Darwinism. Rooted in the past, the ideas also fueled modern Western colonialism and would reach a horrifying extreme in the racist ideology of Nazi Germany. Evolutionists suggested that nature was constantly evolving and all life was in a struggle for existence, the survivors being those best adapted to their environment. Social observers applied this concept to human societies, seeing a pattern of "the survival of the fittest" among competing peoples and ethnic groups. The advanced nations had the best chance of survival, but they had to guard against the physical and moral flabbiness created by their own wealth. Periodically, they must engage in fighting to preserve their muscle tone. Alfred Thayer Mahan, America's leading naval strategist, noted in 1894 that the Roman Empire crumbled when "the strong masculine impulse" was eroded by the "worship of comfort." TR warned that only through strife could a nation win greatness, for an idle rich nation "is an easy prey for any people which still retain those most valuable of qualities, the martial virtues."

In the struggle for survival, weaker branches of the species, including the Native Americans, would go to the wall. Like Whitman, Roosevelt believed they would become extinct. Others might be salvaged through the benevolent guardianship of the advanced races; overseeing "little brown brothers" was "the white man's burden." Rudyard Kipling, poet of the British Empire, enthusiastically endorsed America's acquisition of colonial possessions, and Roosevelt noted that British military observers took a family pride in U.S. victories.

Although condescension to weaker peoples seemed appropriate in 1898, the white burden would end in anti-colonial wars of liberation during the second half of the twentieth century. From one perspective, French Indo-China, later called Vietnam, followed this pattern. Expansionism also would bring the U.S. into conflict finally with Japan, an Asian nation with its own sense of ethnic superiority and imperial agenda. The moral burdens of that conflict, Pearl Harbor and the atom bombs, continue to weigh on both nations. The path to the Pacific armageddon has not been dealt with well in American popular culture, because the trail of memory is cut short by the overwhelming image of Japanese treachery in December 1941, at Pearl Harbor, but the road runs back to 1898.

White America's sense of ethnic superiority in 1898 also heightened the problem of race at home for the coming twentieth century. Northern and Southern whites wished to complete their reconciliation and bury the hurt of the Civil War, but at the expense of African American rights.

An ex-Confederate, Gen. Joseph Wheeler, was appointed to head the cavalry brigade in Cuba, while the role of black soldiers in the war would be slighted.

America had strong economic and humane motives for war. The Cuban insurgency, begun in 1895, interrupted sugar production, in which Americans had large financial interests. The Philippines, as the *Chicago Times-Herald* pointed out, were the "gateway of the vast and undeveloped markets of the Orient," and their development was being held back by the dead hand of Spain. Guerrilla war in the Spanish colonies, like all unconventional wars in which there are no rules, became ugly, with atrocities on both sides. American opinion sided with those fighting for their freedom, particularly after the Spanish reconcentrated civilians in camps in order to isolate and destroy the guerrillas left behind, a policy that was militarily effective but produced great suffering among the displaced.

At the same time, legitimate American concerns were exploited by the tabloids, then called the "yellow press," trading upon popular prejudice against Hispanics. The media manipulation of public opinion, partly to boost sales, led to enormous popular pressure on the government for war. Although many journalists would later change their minds, they initially romanticized the Cuban and Filipino guerrillas. Much exposure was given to the remarks of American mercenary Frederick Funston, who, in *Harper's Weekly,* March 5, 1898, likened the courage of Cuban insurrectionists to that of the Light Brigade and hoped somebody would write a Tennyson-style poem about them. The Spanish became what we now call the "villains du jour," and the press invented outrages to add to some real cruelties. One story, building on popular belief in Hispanic decadence, depicted Cuban and even American women being strip-searched by Spanish customs officials. The power of the press to create and direct public sentiment, revealed in 1898, has increased greatly since then as communications vehicles have become faster and more sophisticated, with newsreel, radio, television, and the web. As then, this power can be both positive and negative in effect.

When an American battleship, the *Maine,* blew up in Havana Harbor on February 15, 1898, the press immediately jumped to the conclusion that the Spanish were responsible. The ship's captain, Charles D. Sigsbee, pleaded that judgement be suspended until the facts were known. But neither he, nor other influential Americans who were appalled by the public furor, such as former president Grover Cleveland and author

Mark Twain, could sway the tide of opinion. A trend was set in motion toward defining support of a war policy as the only legitimate patriotic position. The *Journal of Commerce* was moved to deplore "The artificial patriotism being carefully worked up," including "this remarkable fashion of hanging the flag over every schoolhouse." When a Kansas shopkeeper closed his store to protest the declaration of war on April 15, 1898, his premises were mobbed. Mass media was creating mass public expression.

———◆———

Although it was popularly assumed that the Spanish would be thrashed easily, the armed services bore the burden of fighting with a potpourri of old and new equipment, trying to adjust traditional military precepts to the changing nature of war. The public believed at the time, and many textbooks still affirm, that the American battle fleet was state of the art, thanks in large part to the efforts of TR as assistant secretary of the Navy. In fact, although the navy had embarked on an ambitious program of building huge "dreadnought" battleships, much of the force was outdated. Clumsy, unseaworthy monitors, firing smoothbore shells akin to those used in the Civil War, were still in service during the war.

Commodore George Dewey, heading the Asiatic Squadron, easily defeated the catastrophically obsolete Spanish Pacific fleet in the Battle of Manila Bay, May 1, 1898, but the margin of victory hid the fact that not one of Dewey's ships was fully armored, indispensable in an engagement with a first-rate fleet. The press, in love with the new technology, liked to suggest that this was an advanced war of machine on machine, a sanitized mechanical contest beyond the blood and gore of past human butcheries. Today we often embrace the abstract concept of war as a technological board game. The *New York World,* on May 4, 1898, announced Dewey's "splendid mastery of the engines of destruction under his control." The captain of the *Brooklyn* was reported by *Harper's Weekly,* June 4, 1898, as saying that his ship was so advanced the crew was almost irrelevant: "It was my simple duty to push the button and their work was done." Frederic Remington, who had covered the simpler cowboy West, had an almost religious awe of those who controlled the complex new technology. Writing in *Harper's Weekly,* May 14, 1898, he said, "I believe they love this bewildering power which they control. Its problems entrance them; but it simply stuns me."

Although it remains common to lavishly praise the marvels of robotic technology, human effort was needed then as now. Consequently, battle remained bloody. In action, temperatures in the engine rooms of the big ships reached two hundred degrees Fahrenheit. Each time the main batteries fired, hot ash and scalding water splashed the stokers in the boiler rooms. An engine man on an American battleship recalled that "it meant sure death if the Olympia got a shot through her anywhere in our vicinity." Manila Bay was, he said, "the longest day I ever lived."

Just as we, who live in the dawning days of the computer revolution, are beneficiaries of its assets but victims of its crudities, the military labored with adjusting to a technology both ancient and modern in its transitional nature. Although the main batteries on the U.S. fleet's capital ships fired smokeless powder, the secondary complement fired the older black powder that put out huge smoke clouds. On the destroyer *Foote*, one officer could be heard shouting at another, "Take your damned smoke out of my way." A little experience dictated that the fire from secondary batteries had to be discontinued in a major action.

American naval battle tactics, like European, were retrogressive. Despite the development of effective torpedoes that could destroy a capital ship in minutes, orthodoxy held that the battleship was invulnerable. The big ships went into battle in a straight line that made them wonderful targets, close together as they would have been in the great age of wooden sailing ships a century before. Had the Spanish used their fast torpedo boats to dart around the American line, launching torpedoes and then pulling off, they could have won a devastating victory. But, themselves captives of past practice, they placed their small ships instead in the main battle line, guaranteeing their annihilation.

The dreadnoughts, like our own highly expensive superweapons, were impressive symbols of power for the taxpayer, but were becoming too expensive to lose and hence of limited practical value, risked only under the most ideal conditions. Adm. William T. Sampson, commanding the Atlantic Squadron, refused the army's request to help destroy the batteries defending Santiago, Cuba, through a close-in naval bombardment. When the city surrendered, it was found that many of the cannon that had daunted Sampson were antique eighteenth-century brass smoothbores fired by a flintlock mechanism. Thus did the military struggle to adjust to the politics of a military technology meant to dazzle and overawe, but which denied that successful war, ultimately, was still about the brutal business of dismembering one's opponents at great personal risk.

As with any new technology, there was a tendency to overstate the potency of the modern weaponry. The Spanish did not contest the American landing in Cuba, at Daiquiri, because they feared the impact of the navy's big guns on any shore defense. But experience elsewhere showed that naval bombardment was largely ineffective. Because of excessive Spanish caution, the unopposed landing took place among the shrieks and laughter of American troops, like "the bathers in the surf at Coney Island on a hot Sunday." Yet the navy had only one quarter of the boats needed for an expeditious assault and, as no reconnaissance was made, nobody knew that a beach landing was impracticable, so the boats had to tie up at Daiquiri's dock like fishermen coming home. Roosevelt said correctly that "Five hundred resolute men could have prevented the disembarkation." After observing early operations in Cuba, Major Batsan of the Ninth Cavalry wrote home to his wife: "It is a good thing we are not at war with England or Germany or France, for we would not last a week."

The army's adjustment to modern war was more painful than the navy's. The regulars, essentially a frontier police force, numbered only twenty-eight thousand men, with a further one hundred thousand in the National Guard. Many state governors refused to let the Guard be federalized, voicing a traditional fear that doing so would leave the people naked to a central tyranny. So volunteer units had to be raised from scratch. Many of their officers were incompetent and the men ill-disciplined, seeing the war as a lark. Their slackness upped the death rate, as camps were filthy and badly policed, breeding typhoid and dysentery.

Again suggesting the transitional nature of the episode, there were only enough modern Danish-pattern Krag-Jörgensen rifles to equip the regulars; most volunteers had to take old Springfields, which gave off a puff of black-powder smoke, revealing the rifleman's position. A lack of tropical kit forced most men to fight in sweltering blue wool. Transportation and equipment of all kinds, including shoes and underwear, were wanting. Equipment given to the states for storage had rotted through neglect. The food was appalling, often consisting of the same salt pork and hardtack rations issued in the Civil War. Roosevelt noted from camp in Tampa, Florida, that there were no fresh meats or vegetables and the preserved beef was largely spoiled, "stringy and tasteless." Regular army

A time of technological transition. American artillery in Cuba, firing obsolete black-powder cartridges, tries to locate the Spanish enemy through the dense mist of its own battery smoke. Courtesy of the National Archives, NWCS Still Picture Reference Number: 1 1 1–SC-94437.

rules prevented the purchase of fresh foods locally. "I, of course, paid no heed to the regulations," he added. Less well-connected officers couldn't make their own arrangements, and their men suffered accordingly. In Cuba, the expeditionary force had less than a dozen ambulances and lacked hospital supplies of all kinds, including artificial lighting for night surgery.

The secretary of war, Russell Alger, and his army bureau chiefs were scapegoated for the chaos. But it was not entirely their fault. America had not envisioned fighting a major war or built an army for that purpose. These pains of a major power struggling to be born were inevitable. There was no general staff along British or German lines to supervise mobilization and coordinate operations. And the public had demanded an accountability meant to produce efficiency, but which in fact hamstrung the service in endless petty rules and reporting formulae.

When they got to Cuba, the Americans found that some of their armaments worked well, but others were obsolete, requiring a constant pattern of adjustment and improvisation. The Spanish, like most Western armies, had non-recoiling artillery pieces firing smokeless rounds. American guns still recoiled, bounding back after every shot and having to be resighted by gunners exposed to enemy rapid-fire. The guns also used black powder, making a perfect target for counter-battery fire. The guns could be kept in action only briefly and then had to be relocated for safety. American journalist Richard Harding Davis said the guns came up at a gallop and went back three minutes later just as fast. Although the Maxim machine gun, a fast-fire, water-cooled weapon, delivering 500 rounds per minute, was now standard in European armies, the Americans had only the old Gatlings, hot and likely to jam, firing black powder, and restricted to 380 rounds. Other experimental pieces, such as a dynamite gun that lobbed explosive charges, produced some initial terror, but little real damage.

Lack of battle practice showed up. The American column marching to assault the defenses of Santiago at San Juan didn't understand how the Spanish were shelling them with pinpoint accuracy, despite jungle tree cover. It turned out that a tethered balloon, used by the Signal Corps for observation and floating above the marching men, was providing an excellent range marker. Effective aerial reconnaissance would have to wait until World War I. No ground reconnaissance had been made of the Spanish position, and the troops found barbed wire in their path that had to be hacked at with bayonets, as the wire cutters had been left onboard ship. Fortunately, the Spanish were demoralized and, with equal ineptitude, had dug their trenches too close to the top of San Juan and Kettle Hill, so that they overshot the Americans struggling below.

<hr />

Americans, whose last serious exposure to war was a half century ago, held many romantic notions about the nature of combat. Roosevelt expected that individual character would be crucial. In the American gentleman tradition, he hoped to combine the best chivalric elements, college sportsmen from the Ivy League, with veteran westerners, cowboys and lawmen (Rough Riders had originally referred to Pony Express couriers). Such men, he believed, would be "soldiers ready made, as far as concerned their capacity as individual fighters." Desired qualities included "hardihood and a thirst for adventure" and abstinence from drinking, casual sex, and heavy tobacco use. TR was proud that in the officers' mess he never heard "a foul story or a foul word." Good examples of the ideal were Dudley Dean, "perhaps the best quarterback who ever played on a Harvard Eleven," and Bucky O'Neill, "a famous sheriff throughout the West."

Roosevelt carefully cultivated an image of how good soldiers should appear. In blue blouses, brown gaiter trousers, and slouch hats, "They looked exactly as a body of cow-boy cavalry should look." TR told Elizabeth Custer, "Your husband is one of my heroes," because they both believed in the offensive power of light cavalry. He assumed that his men would use their mounts in Cuba to gallop up and "hit their adversaries with their horses," before despatching them with sabers and pistols. Such notions reflected a common ignorance of modern war in which even a moderate rifleman could hit a rider at seven hundred yards. In action, the Rough Riders were not allowed to use their horses or sabers to save their lives.

The reality of active operations forced many adjustments in perspective. TR found the men went drinking and whoring when the occasion offered. They also had a high need for tobacco. Everyone became filthy; one officer said his own stench kept him from sleeping. By the end of the Cuban campaign, officers and men were in rags. The dirt and demoralization bred disease. TR was shocked to learn that strapping college athletes succumbed to yellow fever and malaria just like anyone else.

Roosevelt found that he didn't dare let men take wounded comrades to the rear because they failed to return, even though neglecting casualties exposed them to land crabs and vultures that attacked wounds and eyes. The treatment of the injured was a far cry from the ritual last rites performed in boot camp when the first volunteers to die had been buried with full military honors. Most distressing, modern combat lacked manly individual encounters. Advanced long-range, fast-fire weapons put down a blanket of unaimed fire that claimed victims indiscriminately. TR wrote, "it was peculiarly hard to be exposed to the fire of an unseen foe, and to see men dropping from it." Rather than being, as commonly believed, a neutral force compatible with traditional values, technology changes our cultural as well as our physical environments, and we perennially have to readjust our precepts to accommodate it. Staying close to the ground proved a much better tactic than butting up against the enemy.

On the advance from Daiquiri, the Rough Riders blundered into the rearguard of the retreating Spanish at Las Guásimas. In the confused fighting, Capt. Allyn K. Capron and Hamilton Fish, a wealthy collegian, were killed, two good men taken at random, further rattling TR's view of the appropriate destiny for heroes. The colonel confessed that for most of the action he could see neither the Spanish nor the men of the black Tenth Cavalry who came to the rescue.

The empty, isolated nature of the battlefield induced terror. Roosevelt admitted that in battle there was "a good deal of panic and confusion in the rear" of the lines. One reporter saw men "flying panic-stricken" and concluded correctly that any person "can only bear a certain amount of danger." Such lessons about the reality of combat, learned painfully by those who served in 1898, did not enter mainstream consciousness and have had to be relearned by each generation that goes to fight, mainly because of one fact. Starting in 1898 Americans have done all their fighting overseas, so that most people have no direct exposure to war and retain an innocence about its nature. Even when veterans have tried to write truthfully about what combat was like, they have tended to produce shock but not belief.

When he returned home, Roosevelt continued to be reminded of war's reality by the later deaths of men injured on campaign and by the calls for help of veterans too weak to work or widows left in need. In *The Rough Riders* he wrote about his experiences with a candor that often matches or even surpasses the realism of Stephen Crane's contemporary novel, *The Red Badge of Courage* (1895). But the romance of men adventuring in war also reasserted itself in his work, so that heroic notions came to coexist uneasily in his writings with stark portraits of the confusion, disorganization, and blind destruction that marked the actuality of campaigning. We would expect this of a book written in a transitional period when advanced technology was just beginning to assert its role on the battlefield.

———◆———

Given the interesting features of the 1898 conflict, why does it receive so little popular attention? Partly because, unlike the Custer battlefield, it has not attracted the attention of reenactors and politically visible ethnic groups. The action took place outside the Continental U.S., in Cuba, a country now at odds with the U.S., and the Philippines, which are physically remote, so that on-site popular recreations of events are virtually impossible. Also, Americans during and after the war showed a great deal less respect for the Hispanic foe than the Cheyenne and Sioux warriors of the Plains warfare, which has diminished popular interest in the military narrative of the conflict. Cubans and Filipinos show increasing concern about the results and implications of the struggle but, unlike Native Americans, they have no influence upon the internal American cultural dialogue. U.S. Hispanic citizens seem little engaged by the war to date; if they do recognize the dynamics of the conflict, it may receive more popular attention.

Further, as an expression of nostalgia for the vanishing West, the fates of Butch Cassidy or the Wild Bunch offer much crisper material for drama. The war saw Americans struggling to understand and adapt to the promises and pitfalls of new technologies, but the *Titanic* sinking, occurring not long after in the new century, offers a sharper paradigm for that burden and has been used as such many times, the last movie example appearing in 1998.

As a predictor of future combat, the war proved in some ways a poor medium for prophecy, even though *Atlantic* magazine saw it as portentous, coming at the dawn of a new century "like a sign and a promise." For example, the relatively short duration and low cost of the war misled Americans into concluding that future wars would be over quickly. Modern high-powered weapons seemed to bring immediate, decisive results. The British drew a similar conclusion from their one-sided 1898 victory over poorly-armed native forces at Omdurman in the Sudan. Even though the Dutch South-African farmer-militia kept up sustained fighting much longer in the Boer War of 1899 to 1902, the British still believed in a swift, mobile war, because much of their time was spent chasing mounted Boer commandos across the wide-open veldt. Hence, at the onset of World War I in 1914, they expected to be home for Christmas.

Because subsequent wars didn't follow their shape, the 1898 campaigns have been neglected. But they are worth remembering as proof that military events don't tend to repeat themselves and that preparing to fight the last war is not often wise. The American military leaders who have correctly counseled against making future predictions based on the swift and one-sided victory in the Gulf War of 1991 could point to Santiago and Omdurman in support of their position.

Many Americans saw the 1898 war as the first step toward a twentieth-century colonial empire. But their descendants have proved hostile to traditional colonialism, associating it with European decadence. Hence, they have little interest in returning to the war for precedent or inspiration. America's later imperialism has been cultural and economic, led by legions of Big Macs and Cokes rather than marines. When America does intervene militarily on the ground, the goal is usually to withdraw as quickly as possible, to take but not to hold territory. Increasingly, the U.S. tries to win war from the air, with no territorial involvement at all.

A disturbing aura of racism clings to Western imperialism, which has produced some later discomfort with the Spanish-American War ethos and a tendency to wish it forgotten. U.S. troops condescended to their Cuban and Filipino allies, treating them largely as pack bearers and calling them "niggers," "gooks," or "greasers." In the Philippines, the U.S. reneged on a promise of independence, partly through fear that Germany or Japan would step into the major-power vacuum. The broken promise provoked the American-Filipino War of 1898–1902 in which about 1,000 Americans and 220,000 Filipinos died.

In this second war, the U.S. resorted to the same anti-guerrilla measures as the Spanish, reconcentrating population and creating free-fire zones. In a war without perimeters, the killing of civilians became frequent and casual. Both sides tortured captives. In retaliation for the mutilation of an American soldier, Gen. Lloyd Wheaton ordered a town burned and all the inhabitants killed. The American-Filipino War looked forward to the mutual racist savagery exhibited in the Pacific during World War II and in Vietnam. The lesson about the nastiness inevitable in an unconventional war between alien ethnic groups was not learned, because the actuality was mainly kept from the public, and popular drama largely avoided the issue. So, the burden of slaughter and guilt had to be borne again by each new generation. A few popular writers, notably David Howard Bain in his 1984 return to the Philippines, *Sitting in Darkness,* have explored the implications of the American-Filipino War for later U.S. interventions in the developing world, but their work has not been widely influential.

Ironically, Filipino protests against the American occupation were used to suggest the people's unfitness for freedom. The *New York Times* said they were ingrates and that to grant self-government "would be to give a dynamite cartridge to a baby." A related assumption of African American racial inferiority, prominent in white thinking at the turn of the century, has also embarrassed remembrance. TR's attitude is representative. The Rough Riders were brigaded with two regular regiments, the white First and the black Tenth. The Tenth helped get Roosevelt's outfit out of a mess at Las Guásimas and played at least an equal role in taking San Juan. TR said at the time that he "could not expect to have better men beside him in a hard fight."

However, in his later book, he shaded his comments to fit dominant white stereotypes of black character as unfit for civil rights. The Tenth were now "smoked Yankees" who had animal courage but not moral fiber and became helpless without their white officers. He claimed that he had to order them forward at San Juan at the point of his revolver; under his paternalistic handling, they "flashed their white teeth at each other, as they broke into broad grins, and I had no more trouble with them." Roosevelt distorted badly. George Kennan, who carefully studied black performance, wrote, "It is the testimony of all who saw them under fire that they fought with the utmost courage, coolness, and determination." Roosevelt had reversed the fact that members of the Tenth were regulars who had been bloodied on the western frontier, while he was the inexperienced amateur from Washington.

Finally, the dominant image of Roosevelt himself crimps creative interpretation of the war. Although his book was nuanced and often insightful, his boyish persona imprinted on the face of the war still overshadows his ideas and overpowers our ability to think originally about the topic, particularly as no other artist left a popularly competitive vision of the conflict. The contributions of both Frederic Remington, the western artist who drew the war, and Stephen Crane, who reported it, are overshadowed by their earlier work.

———◆———

TNT's 1997 *Rough Riders,* a rehash of the Cuban campaign based largely but loosely on TR's book, illustrates the difficulties associated with popular drama. *TV Guide* called the broadcast a "gripping cable film," but it failed to draw intelligently upon the complexity of events and Roosevelt's reactions to them. TR was played by Tom Berenger as the predictably boyish, exuberant adventurer, and the film relied heavily on conventional stereotypes for its underpinning themes. Not based on extensive research, this is a "feel good" movie, purveying patriotic platitudes to gain audience acceptance of a weak script. The film begins with the myth of American innocence, suggesting that U.S. motivation was entirely altruistic and the issue was simply freedom. A fictional protagonist, Henry Nash, says that the Cubans "just wanted to be left alone—breathe free like we done. Them folks in Spain, the Old World, wouldn't let 'em." His simple idea is followed by a collage of images suggesting Spanish depravity; the strip-search story is reproduced without editorial contradiction.

Having set up a conflict between innocence and evil, the movie cannot deal complexly with the racial issues of the war. The Cuban insurgents are background figures led by an anomalous American CIA-style officer, suggesting they are incapable of independent action. The depiction of the Spanish is colored by negative stereotyping of Hispanic intelligence; in a fictional insertion, the Spaniards have to be shown how to operate their artillery by German advisors. The same treatment is given African Americans. Following TR's postwar, politically-inspired view of black dependency, the regulars of the Tenth are placed directly under the amateur Roosevelt's command. Adding insult to injury, the film is dedicated to "the American citizen soldier" who "never let us down," further slighting the black and white regulars' major contribution to the war, and continuing the American myth of amateur superiority.

Another myth left unchallenged is that of inevitable American technological superiority, which TR had critiqued in his book, pointing to the obsolescence of much American equipment. Consequently, the movie cannot deal creatively with the issue of a people and an army caught in a time of huge technical change and instead projects a sense of assurance not felt by participants at the time. In a reversal of reality, the American artillery silences the Spanish. The myth of combat as a series of heroic individual encounters continues, with antagonists picking out personal targets at close to point-blank range. Film often returns to earlier film for authentication, in the belief that the familiar visual image is more plausible than the researched written word. In this case, Spanish behavior is copied from Hollywood's World War II depiction of the Japanese in films like *Bataan* (1943), monkey-like figures who treacherously snipe from trees. Every sniper is, of course, seen and shot by a Rough Rider.

The movie misses the opportunity to suggest dramatically the chilling reality of anonymous death by unaimed fire, which so impressed Roosevelt. When Bucky O'Neill is shot fatally after boasting that "There ain't a Spanish bullet made that can kill me," the scene is not treated ironically as a comment on the delusion of individual invulnerability in modern war, but as inspirational, driving the boys of O'Neill's company to become men by avenging their military father, a theme borrowed from the death of John Wayne as Sergeant Stryker in *Sands of Iwo Jima* (1949).

The film does suggest some of the less tangible impulses toward war provided by the knight's quest for adventure. Collegians quote the speech of Shakespeare's Henry V on the eve of Agincourt. But the movie isn't quite sure what to do with these anomalies, gentlemen caught in an action film, any more than it can suggest the full scope of TR's character as a man trying to combine the lives of thought and action. The problem peaks with Gary Busey who, playing the part of Gen. Joseph Wheeler, was apparently unable to envision how an aristocratic Southerner might actually have conducted himself. Latching onto the fact that Wheeler was for a time delirious with fever, Busey opts to career around the jungle hee-hawing like a demented Gabby Hayes.

The film does capture, or more accurately mirror, contemporary technological America's sentimental nostalgia for an earlier and seemingly simpler era, the rural world of the vanishing frontier. The western theme is emphasized by concentrating on O'Neil, Plains Indians who train the men for irregular warfare, and the fictional Nash, a stagecoach robber turned patriotic American. Elmer Bernstein's musical score connects us to his theme for *The Big Country* (1958), underlining the western motif. The film languishes in homage to the American West without explaining its importance to us. In a flash forward, Nash, now a middle-aged millionaire, visits the western graves of O'Neill and his old stage-robbing buddy to thank them for making him what he is. It is difficult to see how this scenario can symbolically explain modern America and its wealth, or the results that proponents of the war expected from the conflict. Berenger, as TR, weeps after the taking of San Juan and says, "It'll never be the same again." But what won't be? Is the film trying to say that America's victory has actually destroyed its own innocence? If so, it doesn't say it clearly.

The real TR had other things on his mind than nostalgia. The assault on Santiago cost 10 percent of American effectives, a heavy loss, and brought home the true character of modern war. The Americans held to their position on San Juan precariously. Had the Spanish not been starving and despairing, they could have driven the Americans into retreat and possibly a rout. TR cabled almost hysterically to Washington for reinforcements, asking "for Heaven's sake to send us every regiment," as "we are within measurable distance of a terrible military disaster." The significant losses made commanding general William R. Shafter fear, as many of his successors in later small wars have, that the public would be upset. In military historian Walter Millis's words, he feared that America "was no longer accustomed to hear of heavy losses and would judge them accordingly."

Although the Spanish high command would shortly lose its nerve and give up Santiago, their troops for a time continued to put a good fire into the American position. The American artillery went beyond the infantry lines to engage them, a risky tactic even against small Native American groups, but positively reckless against modern, massed rifle fire. The British pulled off the same tactic against the warriors at Omdurman in the same year, but a similar attempt in 1899 against well-organized Boer commandos at Colenso put all their guns out of action. Clearly, the old methods of war have to give way to the new. By 1914 it would not even be safe to stay above ground.

A good filmmaker or dramatist has much to work with in this time of paradoxes, poised on the line between two centuries, trying to assimilate past ways of acting to new roles and technologies with their implications for war and society. An inkling of what can be achieved is suggested by the provocative 1979 Australian movie *Breaker Morant*, starring Edward Woodward. The film takes a little-known episode in the Boer War, the court-martial of three officers for war crimes, to explore how the changing nature of military technology and tactics in unconventional fighting affected the ethics of war. Credit is due TNT for bringing the war in Cuba to the television audience, but the network muffed the chance to do something similarly original and stimulating with it.

Roosevelt was not offered the opportunity to fight in World War I because, facing major conventional opponents, the U.S. could not afford amateurism. The transition to professionalism was complete. TR's pride was hurt, but worse was to come. In 1918, his son Quentin, among the millions of youths struggling on the Western Front, burned in his aircraft. His father, who had witnessed violent death, understood the horror of this. But he remained wedded to his generation's faith in strenuous conflict as a maker of individuals and nations. He wrote gamely of the innocents dying in France, "Only those are fit to live who do not fear to die; . . . Both life and death are parts of the same great adventure." We turn to look now at how the experience of war in the twentieth century has been treated in our popular culture.

SIX

✛

Innocents at War

The people who endured World War I entered it with romantic and often naive notions about the reality of modern combat fought with high-powered advanced weaponry. A century of costly conflicts followed. Yet, as we exited the millennium, a large sector of the American public appeared as innocent of the nature of war as when the bloodshed began. Despite the praise for realism of treatment extended by critics to such movies as Steven Spielberg's *Saving Private Ryan*, Hollywood has not done all it might in helping to educate the public about the full nature of combat in modern war. Media protestations to the contrary, American innocence of war was not ended by the terrorist attacks of September 11, 2001. Our discussion will suggest that, in the final analysis, innocence may be a disturbing phenomenon for a democracy, which relies on the understanding of its citizens to help shape approaches to public policy.

The United States took part in both World Wars and after 1945 played a primary role in fighting actions aimed at containing communism, leading to Korea and the ten-year involvement in Vietnam. Since the Soviet collapse, the U.S., sometimes with UN or NATO allies, undertook military interventions in trouble spots around the globe. Many of the soldiers sent to fight in these wars were innocents, adolescents with little exposure to the nature of life or war. They came back with experience of combat. But many of those who remained at home stayed largely in a state of innocence or ignorance about the reality of military action. Complacency was shaken somewhat by the legacy of the atom bombs, the concern in the Cold War over potential nuclear devastation, and by the collective trauma engendered by the failed war in Vietnam. But, as a new century began, willful misunderstanding of the devastating effects of military action appeared to be again in vogue.

The resistance to grasping the destructive side of war probably has several sources. First, Americans in the twentieth century fought all their battles overseas. Almost alone among the world's major nations, America's fields and factories were not attacked. Consequently, a majority of Americans had no firsthand exposure to the reality of battle; the same is true even of a majority of veterans, who never fired a shot in anger. Combat veterans who have tried to speak about their experience candidly have met a poor reception overall. When Norman Mailer tried to give a realistic depiction of Pacific War fighting in *The Naked and the Dead* (1948), he received some critical acclaim, but he was also accused of being emotionally perverted. The problem here is the association of human depravity not with war itself, but with the participant who speaks about it in what is called the "kill the messenger" syndrome. Some popular writers and filmmakers, partly through ignorance and partly with an eye to audience comfort level, have tended to not deal with the full picture of war, but to reinforce popular conceptions of adventure and heroism. Thus, the minority of citizens who try to study war in depth, serious military history devotees and concerned voters, have not been best served.

In addition, the majority of people reject candid dialogue about war partly through a universal human desire to avoid confronting nastiness in life. The cult of innocence as a defining aspect of American character exacerbates this inclination. The veneration of youth, developed early on the frontier as a means of setting the strengths of the New World off from the age and seeming decadence of the Old, has left some citizens with the notion that innocence, a state of purity maintained by a lack of knowledge about matters deemed unseemly, is a virtue. Put another way, it is commonly supposed that some things are best not talked about, including the detailed nature of slaughter and the less savory aspects of foreign policy, such as covert operations or alliances with authoritarian states. Whether a nation at the height of its world power can avoid frank discussions of war without serious consequences is a question yet to be answered.

<hr />

It is hard to believe, in the sharp light of hindsight, that the belligerents could have embraced war enthusiastically in 1914. By its end in 1918, the Great War had cost 8.5 million soldiers dead and a further 21 million wounded. Influenza took off a further 22 million civilian and military souls by 1920, many previously weakened by malnutrition and stress caused by war and rationing. The conflict cost the participants an estimated $232 billion. Yet, at the start of the debacle, crowds cheered in all of Europe's major cities. Bert Hall, an American in Paris, watching soldiers marching to war, wept tears of joy and wrote, "There never was a thrill like the early days of August, 1914."

People were profoundly innocent about what the combination of mass mobilization and long-range, quick-firing weapons might produce on the field of glory. The novelist H.G. Wells, one of the less belligerent writers, nevertheless in his 1909 novel, *Tono-Bungay,* compared favorably the symbol of the austere and beautiful naval "destroyer, stark and swift, irrelevant to most human interests," with the crass civilian life of England, where "the realities are greedy trade, base profit-seeking, bold advertisement." The idea of war as a tonic for the ills of peace was about to reach fruition.

War would overcome the selfish individualism of modern culture. Lt. Malcolm Graham White, who went from Cambridge University into the Rifle Brigade and died in 1916, was as challenged as William James by the lack of public dedication in peacetime. Only war, he said, seemed to produce idealism. Thousands who felt "it was not 'up to them' to live for their country in peace time" now believe "it is absolutely their duty to die for it in war time and fling their lives away with heroism." He concluded, "It is apparently easier to fight for one's country than to devote one's leisure to social problems."

Such a person was Rupert Brooke, a gifted but uninspired young man who drifted aimlessly until the war sparked his idealism. Now it was magnificent to be young and alive: "Now, God be thanked Who has matched us with His hour, / And caught our youth, and wakened us from sleeping, / With hand made sure, clear eye, and sharpened power." (Brooke died of blood poisoning on the way to the front.)

Inevitably, among all this exuberant romanticism, knighthood was again in flower. Chivalric language described battle. The romantic writer Arthur Machen was sure that at the pivotal Battle of Mons, where the marksmanship of the British army helped stop the German advance on Paris, "St. George had brought his Agincourt Bowmen to help the English." Lawrence E. Jones, of the East Surrey regiment, leading his men into an attack, recited Michael Dayton's romantic poem "The Battle of Agincourt." His colonel, waiting for zero hour, mentally made up a regimental polo team, that most knightly of mounted sports. Those who died in such attacks, said the poet Edmund John in November 1914, would meet in Heaven, where "kings and knights of the old chivalry / Now hail thee at the last."

They look so worn in their campaign photographs that it is easy to forget how young and innocent many of the soldiers were, going straight from school to the army. The favorite play of some was still J.M. Barrie's 1904 juvenile fantasy, *Peter Pan*, about a boy who refuses to grow up, but fights pirates and Indians, encouraged by his helpmeet and surrogate mother, Wendy. Barrie was a romantic who idolized such popular figures as Capt. Robert Falcon Scott, who pluckily if ineptly lost his life with other members of his expedition party returning from the South Pole. Rupert Brooke, who saw Barrie's play three times, always "laughed and wept." Another devotee was Julian Grenfell, also a privileged but bored young man who found purpose in the war, saying, "I adore war. It is like a big picnic." He was killed in 1914.

The Peter Pan craze even reached Ireland, where republicans took advantage of Britain's difficulties to wage a guerrilla war of liberation, which became ugly on both sides. Michael Collins, an able terrorist and the subject of a thoughtful 1996 film by Neil Jordan, was a Barrie devotee. He actually thought that peace might be concluded if Peter Pan fans could sit down and negotiate. "I wonder who on the enemy side appreciates & loves Peter Pan? Shall we find a bridge that way?" Other IRA gunmen had an adolescent romantic side, too. Michael O'Suilleabhain had hated "the bondage of learning" in school and was deeply proud of his twin holsters with Smith & Wesson revolvers. He postured as a cowboy, that latter-day knight, and admired equally rakish figures among the enemy Auxiliaries, particularly one whose "holsters swung far below his waistbelt and were strapped half way down his thighs, in cowboy parlance, tied low."

Such romanticism couldn't fully survive the violence in Ireland, which prematurely jaded and aged Collins, or the carnage in the trenches of France. By 1914 firepower had made the conventional infantry advance almost impossible. In 1800 an infantry battalion could fire two thousand rounds per minute; a century later it was twenty thousand. A typical example was the Somme, a British offensive begun on July 1, 1916, to take pressure off the French. The high command, certain that an artillery bombardment would destroy enemy resistance, ordered the troops to walk across no man's land and keep their alignment. The result was that the troops strolled into a storm of machine-gun fire. By day's end the British had lost sixty thousand men. A Northumberland Fusilier wrote, "I could see away to my left and right, long lines of men. Then I heard the 'patter, patter' of machine guns in the distance. By the time I'd gone another ten yards there seemed to be only a few men left around me." Historian A.J.P. Taylor feels that, for the British, "Idealism perished on the Somme."

More soldiers died in the Second than in the First World War, but the Great War seemed particularly horrible because of the shock to innocence caused by the first use of such weapons as poison gas, flame throwers, and high-explosive barrages that disintegrated bodies (we get dog tags from this war as an attempt to identify the chunks of flesh that remained). Endurance was made harder by the static nature of trench warfare. The natural human instinct to take action when in danger could not be accommodated under shell fire; soldiers had to sit there and take it. War trauma led to breakdowns, appropriately called "shell shock," and to deep bitterness. Soldier-poet Wilfred Owen wrote in his poem "Dulce at Decorum Est," after observing the effects of gas on his men,

> If you could hear, at every jolt, the blood
> Come gurgling from the froth-corrupted lungs,
> . . . .
> My friend, you would not tell with such high zest
> To children ardent for some desperate glory,
> The old Lie: Dulce et decorum est
> Pro patria mori.
> [It is fitting and proper / to die for one's country.]

Most of these boys could not see an honorable way out. Owen was killed urging his men forward under fire just a few days before the armistice. Siegfried Sassoon, a decorated infantry officer, denounced the war in writing, hoping that his court-martial and execution for treason would dramatize his protest. They put him in a mental home instead.

Many civilians shared the soldiers' pain. Cynthia Elcho, who lost two brothers, cried, "Oh why was I born for this time? Before one is thirty to have known more dead than living people." For others on the homefront, however, the romance of the crusade continued. Poet John Masefield, writing a book on the disastrous 1916 Gallipoli campaign, used chapter headings from *The Song of Roland* and described the troops as happy warriors who "went like kings in a pageant to their imminent death." The equally popular writer, Henry Newbolt, continued to see the mud-covered Tommies as "all the Company of the High Order of Knighthood," reborn in khaki.

Some of the thoughtful survivors came to see themselves as a Lost Generation, blighted in their youth and offered up for sacrifice by their elders. They produced a remarkable literary outflow: Richard Aldington's *Death of a Hero* (1929) about a young officer who commits suicide to end the misery; Robert Graves's *Good-bye to All That* (1929) detailing the end of idealism; Ford Madox Ford's *Parade's End* (1924–1926) assaulting homefront and army brass callousness; and Sassoon's *Memoirs of an Infantry Officer* (1930) about his personal struggle. Similar works on the Continent included Erich Maria Remarque's *All Quiet on the Western Front* (1928), chronicling the waste of German youth.

Not all Germans agreed with Remarque's anti-war stance. The victors were perhaps more debilitated than the losers, many of whom itched for a rematch. Ernst Jünger, a trench veteran, in *Storm of Steel* (1929) asserted that war had defined his generation and they would continue to wage it. Adolf Hitler agreed. He would harness the tools of modern war, the application of management techniques and technology, to the liquidation of those he held responsible for Germany's defeat and Europe's ills.

In Britain many people didn't want to remember the war or listen to the veterans. They'd had enough of gloom and they patronized escape stories like P.C. Wren's *Beau Geste,* published in 1924 and filmed in 1926; the tale follows three British boys, Peter Pans, who seek adventure in the French Foreign Legion. Steadily, however, the Lost Generation view gained support, especially after the Second World War, which completed Britain's decline as a world power and the retreat from empire. British Great War film has a bleak mood, with such critical pieces as *King and Country* (1964), about a mentally simple boy shot for leaving the front; *Oh! What a Lovely War* (1969), Richard Attenborough's musical saga of a devastated generation; *Ryan's Daughter* (1970), David Lean's taut story of the star-crossed love between a shell-shocked British officer and an Irish girl, set during the guerrilla war; *A Month in the Country* (1987), based on J.R. Carr's story of two British soldiers who go on a crusade and return damned; and finally *Behind the Lines* (1997), about the agony of Sassoon and Owen in a mental hospital.

The American experience differed from the European, principally because it was shorter and somewhat atypical of the war as a whole. As late as July 1918 only nine U.S. divisions were at the front, and they encountered an exhausted opponent. Early American books on the war tended to be adventure stories, depicting combat as fraternity or bunkhouse horseplay. E. Streeter's *"Dere Mable": Love Letters of a Rookie* (1918) took a typically jaunty approach to the war:

> But this cannot go on for long,
> Cause Uncle Sam is coming strong.·
> And when we charge the German line
> We'll chuck the damn thing in the Rhine.

Americans at the front attacked with an early-war recklessness that increased their casualties, and some new arrivals didn't want the fighting to end until they tasted blood. The flier Eddie Rickenbacker noted of his squadron: "Not content with the collapse of the enemy forces the pilots wanted to humiliate them further with flights deep within their country where they might strafe airplane hangars and retreating troops for the last time."

This is not to say that service was a picnic for American combat troops. 53,500 were killed and a further 320,710 were wounded, some crippled physically or mentally for life. Historian William Manchester's father took a wound in the right arm that reduced it to the bone, "with a claw of clenched fingers at the end." The suffering produced some graphic writing, such as Dalton Trumbo's 1939 story of a totally emasculated soldier, *Johnny Got His Gun.*

But most of American society was untouched by the war, and for many veterans it remained a bit of a lark, a time of intense companionship and freedom from routine. Deaths were light compared to, say, 1.5 million each for the Germans and French. When the American Legion sponsored a return to France in 1927 the *Literary Digest* noted on October 15, 1927, "It was difficult for the French to understand the holiday gaiety—the almost carnival spirit—of the former dough boys in their war pilgrimage to scenes and mementoes which are invested with a sad sacredness in the French mind."

Literary critics have suggested that some American Lost Generation writers were less upset by the war than by domestic social concerns. The persona of the combat-damaged veteran was a vehicle for expressing other complaints, some individual. John Dos Passos's *Three Soldiers* (1921) uses the military as a stalking horse for the allegedly oppressive American capitalist society that treats the worker, like the soldier, as a pawn. Judith Fetterley charges, in *The Resisting Reader* (1977), that Ernest Hemingway's *A Farewell to Arms* (1929) is more an attack on women than on war. Lt. Frederic Henry easily leaves the Italian front behind. It is a woman who embitters him, the nurse Catherine Barkley, who thoughtlessly dies in childbirth. Kenneth S. Lynn agrees, saying that Hemingway only saw a little combat, which he enjoyed. He used the image of the wounded soldier to pursue other hurts.

Much the same may be said of William Faulkner's *Soldier's Pay* (1926). Faulkner saw no combat, even though he sometimes posed as a mysteriously wounded flier. Rejected in love, he joined the Royal Flying Corps and trained in Canada. But the war ended before he could see action, adding to his disgruntlement against a society that had disappointed him and, in the "roaring twenties," was abandoning traditional mores. In *Soldier's Pay* veterans at a dance "feel provincial: finding that a certain conventional state of behavior has become inexplicably obsolete over night." Girls who had loved them in uniform now go for younger men. Donald Mahon, the protagonist, a scarred and dying fighter pilot, is rejected by his fiancée and by the townspeople who wish he would die to stop reminding them of the war. The noble white male is unappreciated.

A self-pitying element is present also in Faulkner's later story "All the Dead Pilots" (1934), which reflects resentment at aging, the betrayal of youth and innocence. Veterans with thickening waistlines, saddled with families and commuter rides to work, envy the dead soldiers who are still, in photographs, "lean, hard, in their brass-and-leather martial harness."

America has produced little good film about World War I, with the exception of the 1930 version of Remarque's book, and Stanley Kubrick's 1957 *Paths of Glory,* a bleak story of French soldiers shot by lot for alleged mutiny. This post-Korea study of the futility of war and the powerlessness of individuals was not typical of film in an era that, in the afterglow of World War II, was normally celebratory in tone. *The Lost Battalion* (2001), an Arts and Entertainment Network's made-for-TV movie, fails to be effective. In the movie, a command blunder leaves the

U.S. 308th isolated behind the main lines in the Argonne Forest, October 2–8, 1918. Uncertain of its message when dealing with fruitless butchery, yet televising in a time of heightened American nationalism, it is determined to criticize the callousness of the high command and the futility of war, while at the same time delivering a conventional and predictable paean of praise to the heroic qualities of the American fighting man, and the army as a showcase for the American social melting pot. The end of the movie might double as a recruiting film.

—◆◆—

A minority of the public, often the college educated, who grew up in the 1960s, continue to engage seriously with the Great War, largely through the British experience. They have patronized British turn-of-the-century drama on PBS's *Masterpiece Theatre*. The British recur to the Edwardian period as the time when things started to go wrong for them. Democracy and prosperity were growing, but the First World War and its aftermath stultified progress. Major problems remain unresolved, such as the divisive effect of the class system. Two PBS presentations that look at this pivotal era are the costume soap opera, *Upstairs, Downstairs,* about the Edwardian class system in a London townhouse, which began airing in 1974; and Vera Brittain's *Testament of Youth,* a powerful Lost Generation memoir written in 1933 and filmed by the BBC in 1979. Both have had great success in America, where *Upstairs, Downstairs* enjoys periodic reruns and *Testament* was reissued in VHS by A & E Television Networks in 1998.

This minority American intellectual interest in Edwardian Britain is sparked by the parallel between the damage to optimism done by the Great War in Britain and by the Vietnam War in America. A coterie of Americans seek in the British experience prior models to explain their own loss of certainty. At the Commonwealth Cemetery in France, someone in the 1920s wrote in the visitors' book, "So ended the golden age." In America, Tom Engelhardt has called the post-Vietnam era "the end of victory culture," meaning a loss of faith by a sector of the public in America's goodness and mission. Significantly, in Britain the most popular character in *Upstairs, Downstairs* was Rose, the maid struggling with the class system, but in America it was James, the son who is sent to war, comes back emotionally wounded, and commits suicide. It is the aftermath of a bad war that fascinates the American audience, including some who are uneasy that they didn't fight in Vietnam, but sense they could have been like James if they had. Simon Williams, who played James, was amazed during an American tour to find fans reaching out to touch him to make sure he had remained alive.

It is not surprising that Americans still troubled by Vietnam should find parallels in Europe's earlier trial by fire. Both have been defined as "bad wars," which are seen as leaving lingering psychological damage, today called post-traumatic stress disorder (PTSD). We now understand a good deal about this condition, thanks to the Vietnam veterans' willingness to discuss their feelings. But many people would be surprised to know that the problem was widely understood in the 1920s. Some excellent pioneering studies were done in that decade, including some so far unequaled work on the problems of Civil War veterans. The disconnect in our knowledge came after World War II, which was supposed to be a good war; conventional wisdom at the time, expressed in, say, the army documentary movie *Let There Be Light* (1946), said that veterans should get over combat trauma in six to eight weeks.

Understanding of mental wounds was so widespread in the 1920s that it entered popular fiction. Lord Peter Wimsey, Dorothy Sayers's fictional detective, is a war veteran who suffers mild PTSD, as do some of his acquaintances. Sayers's characterization is not surprising, as she had edited the 1919 volume of *Oxford Poetry* with Sassoon, and knew the condition first-hand. In "The Unsolved Puzzle of the Man with No Face," a character explains to Wimsey why the murderer might be a vet: "Here we've been and had a war, what has left hundreds o' men in what you might call a state of unstable equilibrium. They've seen their friends blown up or shot to pieces. They've been through five years of 'orrors and bloodshed, and it's given 'em what you might call a twist in the mind towards 'orrors." He goes on to say that "they may seem to forget it and go along as peaceable as anybody to all outward appearance, but it's all artificial, if you get my meaning. Then, one day something 'appens to upset them—they 'as words with the wife, or the weather's extra hot, as it is today—and something goes pop inside their brains. . . ." His is not a bad description of acute PTSD.

In both conflicts, the veterans' depression was partly induced by the sense of having fought in a futile, even misguided cause. Wilfred Owen wrote, "My subject is war and the pity of war." This made the deaths of comrades hauntingly unforgettable. Charles Hamilton Sorely, a British officer, would "see millions of the mouthless dead / Across your dreams in pale battalions go," just as Vietnam vets feel the presence of lost comrades and seek communion with them at the memorial wall in Washington. The sense of futile waste led relatives of the missing in action during both wars to feel particular emotional pain about loved ones left to wander perpetually in an alien battlescape. Anxiety about missing soldiers led thousands to seek contact with their lost ones through spiritual mediums in the 1920s and has partially fueled the MIA campaign in America.

The pain of fighting in a bad war was increased by a sense that the suffering was unevenly distributed. Grunts were shocked at being "in country" one day and in "the world" shortly after, where life went on as usual. Similarly, British Tommies, soon after given leave from the trenches, were in "Blighty" (Britain), where, as one commented, "you would not know there was any war." The gulf in experience between soldier and civilian came to be symbolized by the issue of army language. A Great War soldier commented that when on leave there was a danger of saying at breakfast, "Goddamit, Ma, where in hell's the butter?" Tim O'Brien, a grunt, said he offended the innocence of his hometown girl when he talked about the "shit" in Vietnam.

After both wars, society overall appeared eager to move on from the experience. British captain William Gerhardie observed bitterly, "The war, it is agreed by all, is a bore." The title of one of Great War veteran Ford Maddox Ford's books, *No More Parades* (1925), is precisely what upset many Vietnam vets. In both cases veterans felt that the public didn't want to share the knowledge of what the war had been like. The Vietnam-era poem "KEEP MUM!," written by veteran Norma J. Griffiths in 1986, is remarkably like the bleakly honest writing of the Great War poets. She says that the soldier must be taught to fight and kill, "'E's doin' a duty / Wot mus' be done." Blood will run, but that is because there is "honor and glory / wot must be won." And if he has questions,

> Tell 'im it's freedom.
> Tell 'im we've won.
> But 'bout the horror,
> keep mum, keep mum.

Some of both generations felt so alienated they wished they hadn't survived, and Vietnam veterans suffered a high suicide rate. Ford's protagonist, Christopher Tietjens, sometimes wished he had died at the front. The strain of carrying on led to alcohol and drug addiction in both eras, as well as to family abuse. The red poppy, which grew in the British sector in France, became a symbol of war's bloodshed and is still given out on veterans' days. But the flower also produces opium, the morphine of forgetfulness, and was understood in this context by the war poets.

The sense of alienation was partly generational in both wars. Youth felt their generation was sacrificed by older people who did not have to share their suffering and betrayed by national leaders who did not appear to have viable political goals realizable through military means. Both eras have witnessed a legacy of cynicism about the quality of political life.

The likeness between these wars is clear in the parallel story of two books, Vera Brittain's *Testament* and Lynda Van Devanter's 1983 memoir of army nursing in Vietnam, *Home Before Morning*. Brittain was in many ways a classic model for the later '60s generation. A strong and able woman, she rejected the traditional female role, serving as a frontline nurse and then getting a degree from Oxford University. At the start of the war, her ideas were typically naive. Like J.M. Barrie, she admired Captain Scott and expected men to act like knights. Bored by school, she embraced the excitement of mobilization and supported her brother Edward in his desire to join up. She was disgusted when her father tried to stop the boy, saying the older man had no notion of honor.

Here is an interesting point, for Vera later said the older generation had sacrificed youth, shifting the burden of what happened onto them. Yet in her family's case, youth embraced its own destiny, leading to the question of how far young people can blame others for actions that, if taken when of age, are perhaps their own civic and moral responsibility? At what age is innocence no longer an excuse for actions? There is possibly something a little bit disingenuous among some members of both war generations who suggested they didn't have adult choice in what they did.

At any rate, Edward went, along with Roland Leighton, Vera's innocent boyfriend. Roland wanted a Viking funeral if he was killed, on a burning ship, but his death was less romantic. Mending trench wire, he was shot through the base of the spine and died pumped full of morphine. The lack of his body for burial haunted Vera. After his death she volunteered as a nurse. Neither she nor Edward could communicate what the front was like to their parents, who grumbled about rationing, poor servants, Vera's language, and smoking in public. By 1918 Vera had also lost her brother and all her male friends, changing her life. She felt her generation was picked out by a dark fate, growing up unaware,

> While, imminent and fierce outside the door,
>   Watching a generation grow to flower,
> The fate that held our youth within its power
>   Waited its hour.

Vera suffered the divided feelings typical of a so-called bad war. Even though she hated killing, at Oxford she was shocked that younger students knew nothing about the war and laughed at her pride in service. Her dilemma was that to endorse the fighting was to approve a dubious cause, but to reject it was to make the sacrifice meaningless. Depressed and stressed, she began to feel monstrous, a witch with a beard. Over time, she fought through her pain and became so influential an opponent of international aggression that Hitler slated her for execution if he conquered Britain.

Lynda Van Devanter, too, went to war full of idealism. She would crusade for freedom and democracy, "part of a generation of Americans who were 'chosen' to change the world." In Vietnam she experienced the same effects of modern weaponry on humanity as had Brittain: boys badly burned or mutilated. She came to doubt that American values could be imposed by force, as Brittain had questioned what gains to civilization could compensate for war's huge costs.

When Van Devanter came home, she encountered the refusal of civilians to lose their innocence about war. Her family refused to look at her slides, taken in the operating room. "I had learned my lesson quickly. Vietnam would never be socially acceptable." She felt an experience gap, symbolized in language. At dinner, her mother reprimanded her for saying "pass the fucking salt."

Like World War I soldiers, Van Devanter came to feel comfortable only at the front. At home she was embarrassed by materialism and missed the selflessness of Vietnam. At the same time, she began to doubt the war and became a protester, but was shocked when some peace ad-

vocates rejected as an establishment hoax the concepts of duty and valor.
Like Brittain, she suffered the emotional stress of divided feelings, at one
time imagining that she was getting smaller and would disappear. She, too,
felt picked out by fate, saying that "Vietnam has set us apart from others."
For a while, she felt "like an empty shell. Nothing has meaning."

But she fought through this period and became a leading veterans'
advocate, helping others to lead healthy lives. Her story is remarkably
similar to Vera Brittain's. Like the earlier British nurse, she tried to ratio-
nalize her feelings about the war and not just suppress them: ". . . my
feelings about the war will never go away. I don't want them to. For if I
forget entirely, I may be passively willing to see it happen again." And
like Brittain, she wrote poetry to express her sense of war's cost. "TV
WARS—First Blood Part II" was written in 1990, as America prepared
for the Gulf War; in the poem Van Devanter pictures a white-haired
woman standing on the dock as a troopship prepares to take her grandson to the Gulf. The woman says, "I'm proud of my grandson / He has
to go / To protect our interest." But, adds the poet: "Dear lady, / Your
interest just left on that ship."

Writing of a bad war, both Robert Graves and Wilfred Owen saw their
job as warning coming generations about the destructive nature of combat. They didn't succeed. Philip Caputo, who fought in Vietnam, admitted, "I had read all the serious books to come out of the World Wars, and
Wilfred Owen's poetry about the Western Front. And yet, I had learned
nothing." What had happened was that World War II had intervened,
giving a much more positive view of combat and war's value. Some post-
1945 movies and books, such as James Jones's *The Thin Red Line* (1960),
did try to deal with the war's dark side, but the general tone of works on
World War II, particularly Hollywood movies, was celebratory.

The positive tone was not necessarily inappropriate, given the achievements in World War II. But the '60s generation was misled about what a
war in Asia, against an enemy of an alien ethnic background, would be
like. The film that most inspired the Vietnam generation as youngsters
was *Sands of Iwo Jima* (1949), in which John Wayne played the seasoned Sergeant Stryker who turns the boys of his platoon into men. He
was every adolescent male's dream of a father figure. But the film misled
by suggesting that only the Japanese enemy was capable of brutality or

evil; we unfailingly fought fair. In Vietnam the soldiers would find out what their real fathers who fought in the Pacific already knew; the potential for good and bad is in all humanity.

The strong positive tone of works about World War II built on real achievements. During the Great Depression, the viability of capitalism, even democracy itself, had seemed in question. Major nations turned to authoritarian leaders to bring stability, but they also threatened world peace through their expansionist demands. The peacetime draft of 1940 met with muted hostility. Yet, after Pearl Harbor, the nation rallied and became the major military presence in the Western European and Pacific Theaters of war. America's industrial output was phenomenal, equipping not only U.S. forces, but giving huge material assistance to the Allies also. The nation emerged victorious and prosperous, the GNP rising from $97 billion in 1940 to $190 billion in 1944. America was the unchallenged leader of the Free World. All this had been accomplished at relatively modest cost. America alone of the major Allies was not a battleground, and American losses of 800,000 killed and wounded, though painful in themselves, were minimal compared to, say, 5.6 million dead for Germany.

The story of success is at the base of the current "Good War" myth, which dominates American popular thinking about the war. According to this myth, Americans in World War II were united in a just cause in which all participated fully. There were no internal divisions, people knew their roles and carried them out, all were brave, honorable, and true to both patriotic and family values. The problem with this myth is not that it is untrue, but that it doesn't tell the whole story. Despite the current claim that Americans understood the Nazi menace and confronted it head on, the U.S. did not declare war on Germany; it was Hitler who declared war to support his Japanese ally, thus bringing America into the European conflict. Although America was relatively united, race was a divisive issue. American forces were segregated, as was American society, which nearly led to protest marches on Washington. Black service personnel were badly treated, particularly in the southern states, for trying to insist on their civil rights.

The war brought social dislocation, and mothers who worked in war industries were blamed for a rash of juvenile delinquency. Burnam Ledford, a young man during the war, said that "some of our children had troubles in those years, and I always felt like it was the war and the unsettled times that caused it." Despite the myth of chastity, Victory Girls gave free sex to boys in uniform and 75 percent of GIs admitted to having sex overseas, most of it casual. At one point in the Italian campaign, venereal disease was the leading cause of U.S. military disability.

There was unselfishness on the home front, but the black market also flourished. Labor fought for more money at home while the boys fought overseas, and big corporations made huge profits from massive preferential government contracts, driving smaller firms out of business. In 1945, only 34 percent of Americans said they had made any sacrifice at all. Many civilians refused to lose their innocence by looking at the human costs of the war. Residents of Pasadena asked that mutilated veterans at the plastic surgery facility be kept on the hospital grounds as their deformities upset the public. The government created widespread outrage when it released pictures of dead marines on Tarawa. "If the marines could stand the dying, you'd think the public could at least stand reading about it," commented one bitter fighting man.

The nature of combat had not changed that much since the First World War. Despite the popular image of blitzkrieg, sanitized lightning war between sleek fighting machines, much of the fighting in the Pacific, Italy, and France replicated the brutal inching forward of 1914–1918. Predictably, psychological wounds were the largest single category in World War II, and many didn't heal. Twenty-five percent of World War II casualties still in veterans' hospitals in 1990 had mental wounds. In 1992 a woman recalled of her brother who had fought in the Pacific: "We never understood him when he came back from the war. He left as this bright, energetic eighteen-year-old and returned languid and somewhat of an alcoholic. He got married, then quickly divorced, and died of cirrhosis of the liver at thirty-four. I never knew what happened to him over there to make him so sad."

The war elicited both nobility and brutality. Charles Hinds, a trooper with Gen. George S. Patton, recalled that artillery units in North Africa used peaceful Arab caravans for target practice. Veteran and novelist Mitchell Goodman was haunted by the memory of an army jeep driving into Italian citizens who didn't jump aside in time. GIs became adept at "liberating" the property of enemy and friendly civilians, that is, stealing it.

Despite the myth that education was better in the 1940s than today, and people had greater character and fiber, the rejection rate of military inductees for mental or physical inadequacy shocked the nation. In 1940–1941, it was 50 percent. Many boys were out of condition, leading to the charge that they were spoiled by "momism," an accusation at odds with the claim that women were also neglecting their families. David L. Cohn, who was involved with GI orientation, argued in 1947 that many soldiers had been the victims of rote education, so they couldn't think critically. A majority could neither define democracy nor fascism and could not place China, a major ally, on the map. Philip Wylie, a writer with the Office of War Information, was so disillusioned that in 1942 he published *Generation of Vipers,* accusing youth of thoughtlessness, materialism, conformity, and mindless addiction to fads, sex obsession, and alcohol and drug abuse.

A note of hysteria pervades such hand-wringing over declining standards in any era. Simply put, the World War II generation was no different from any other. Yet the myth of uniqueness is getting stronger as the last of the generation leave the stage of history and America faces a new century full of uncertainties, complexities, and global challenges. World War II appears to many as a golden age when issues were clearer, Americans were sure and confident. Matthew Modine, star of a highly overdrawn film portrait of air warfare, *Memphis Belle* (1990), said in publicity releases that the war generation had a commitment lacking today, a debatable statement if it implies that Americans today would not fight for national survival.

Jonathan Alter, in *Newsweek,* May 23, 1994, made the equally debatable assertion that the war generation's achievements far surpass any of Bill Clinton's generation. Henry Hyde, senior house manager in the 1999 impeachment proceedings, somehow felt a presidential conviction was needed to "keep faith" with those who fell in the 1944 D-Day invasion of France. News anchor Tom Brokaw has taken the veneration to its extreme, claiming in his 1998 best-seller, *The Greatest Generation,* that "this is the greatest generation any society has ever produced," quite a claim when you consider, say, the generation that produced Jesus Christ or even the U.S. Founding Fathers. Brokaw says the facts bear him out, but so all-embracing a statement cannot be tested and is not intended to be: it is meant to be accepted emotionally, on faith.

It is good to respect the achievements of the war generation. But problems arise when our view of history diverges significantly from reality. First, we get a distorted view of history and of our place in the past, which is dangerous for our understanding of our role in the world today. Historian Stephen J. Ambrose repeatedly calls the 1940s youth "the generation that saved the world for democracy." Full marks to Ambrose for engaging in an important public dialogue, but he distorts in order to flatter. What about contributions by America's allies? The British Empire and Commonwealth were in the war since 1939, over two years before the U.S. How about the resistance movements in the occupied countries? We need to remember also that ten million Chinese and twenty million Russians died in the Allied cause, even though their countries were not democratic.

When we project an event as a "good" war, we can no longer view it objectively in relation to other conflicts. For example, in May 2001 it came to light that Sen. Bob Kerrey in 1969 took part in a Navy SEAL special operation in which civilians were killed. One SEAL and a villager said that the deaths were by execution; other veterans said they were accidental. The media made much of the incident and it was even said that Kerrey, to all appearances an honorable and decent man, should give back his Bronze Star. Kerrey handled the criticism with restraint, only allowing himself to remark that, if the incident had happened in World War II rather than the Vietnam War, it would not have led to such a grilling. He was correct. Indeed, our mistaken idea that there are good and bad wars so distorts our perspective that many people do not even grasp that such incidents occurred in Europe and the Pacific during World War II.

Second, when we insist that our society peaked in the past, we blunt our youth's initiative. We cannot expect them to strive upward when they can only be second-best to their ancestors. Third, the "Good War" myth distorts the full nature of modern war and what military involvement is likely to mean in the immediate future. It has revivified the seductive notion, just as on the eve of World War I, that war can be fun, uniting and diverting us from tedium. It suggests that right and wrong in war can be absolutely clear-cut, and that evil can be punished through surgical strikes delivered by advanced weapons systems. As combat veteran Paul Fussell has pointed out in *Thank God for the Atomic Bomb* (1988), the dangerous implication of World War II was that, because we fought incarnate evil in Nazism, we could think ourselves purely good. Our self-image is wrong, he says, as we were not pure, only less evil than our enemy. We shot and tortured prisoners, committed rape, and in our rage inflicted unnecessary destruction. The danger is in coming to believe they are justified by an innocence of evil. Thus, in 2002, the Pentagon developed plans for unilateral nuclear strikes against potential enemies, a strategy that would appall us if used by others, but which is seemingly justified by our virtuous intentions.

———

Because of myth, we have a distorted popular view of what the war was like and, consequently, how it should best be depicted. To make the point, I would like to compare two creative pieces, made twenty years apart. The first is Steven Spielberg's *Saving Private Ryan* (1998), said to be the most authentic World War II movie made to date. Stephen Ambrose, who was a consultant on the production, said it recreated the Omaha Beach landing better than anything in print. Film critic Leonard Maltin gave it high marks as a complex examination of men at war. Spielberg said he didn't want to shoot a "Hollywood gung-ho Rambo kind of extravaganza."

The combat footage at the start of the movie is accurate, with men vomiting and crying for their mothers, receiving ghastly wounds from unaimed fire, body parts strewn amidst seeming chaos. But, as we move inland, we also leave reality. The combat becomes artificial, with the Germans missing aim and falling down like toy soldiers. Contrary to actuality, the Germans, not the Americans, have armor and plenty of ammunition; the GIs are reduced to homemade bombs. In the last battle, visibility is perfect, but no friendly planes appear until the final stage, even though the Allies had total air superiority.

The basic plot, sending a platoon behind enemy lines to find one man when thousands are dying, is not credible, something close to sentimental nonsense. The final reaction of the platoon, disobeying their orders to bring in Ryan, is unlikely, as is Ryan's refusal to go home. The men stay in a highly dangerous position that jeopardizes their mission. Spielberg here dismisses a dilemma faced by soldiers so great that it caused breakdowns. They had incompatible obligations: to die if necessary for their country but to live if possible for their families. The film dodges the problem by somehow having the suicidal defense of a bridge as the route home. The moviemakers did not understand that riflemen resented their interminable frontline service and felt they bore too much of the burden of sacrifice; they wanted to leave. It is not widely understood that the

American army, unlike others, allowed no rotation out of the combat infantry to less dangerous positions. The one in twelve men assigned to a rifle company stayed until he was wounded, dead, or cracked up. Suggesting that they would have indulged in suicidal heroics under these conditions insults the men's intelligence.

Private Ryan, in explaining to the platoon the importance of holding the bridge, shows a grasp of strategy impossible for the common soldier, who could see little of the larger picture. Similarly, Captain Miller's neat stratagems for beating the Germans imply a rational, chessboard quality to combat that it never had. The climactic battle is an Alamo-style Last Stand filled with superheroes. Spielberg and his fans have confused realistic special effects at the start of the movie with an accurate depiction of the totality of combat, which we do not get in *Private Ryan*.

The second work seems less realistic, to the point that some critics label it science fiction. Kurt Vonnegut's *Slaughterhouse-Five* was published in 1969 and filmed in 1972. As publication coincided with the peak of U.S. involvement in Southeast Asia, the book is sometimes associated with the Vietnam War. And no doubt Vonnegut had current American bombing in mind as he wrote, but the book is an important contribution to World War II literature.

The comic style of the work tends to put off students of the war. Nevertheless, it is about a serious event, the fire-bombing of Dresden by the U.S. and British air forces, February 13–14, 1945, producing in the medieval city center an inferno burning at one thousand degrees Fahrenheit and killing upwards of one hundred thousand civilians. The attack remains an enigma, as Dresden had little military significance. Although a communications hub, the city was clogged with refugees fleeing the advancing Russians, and so could not be used effectively by the enemy military. Anyway, the city was in the Soviet zone of operations, so we had no business there.

Why then was Dresden bombed? Perhaps it was to demonstrate our air power to the Soviets in case they doubted our postwar strength. More likely, the raid was a product of war psychosis, rage at the instigators of the conflict. The British were exacting revenge for the blitzing of their cities. The Americans, too, by this time, were angry at the Nazis. The desire to punish became more intense as concentration camps were opened. Canadian author James Barque charges that the U.S. and France deliberately abused thousands of German POWs in retaliation for Nazi

The shattered battlefield environment, suggestive of a moonscape. The Abbey of Monte Cassino, Italy, following Allied bombing in World War II. Picture by combat artist Tom Craig, courtesy of Army Art Collection, U.S. Army Center of Military History.

brutality. The Germans certainly reaped the whirlwind. By 1945, along with Dresden, cities like Hanover and Cologne were reduced to moonscapes by bombs more powerful than could have been envisaged even as recently as 1940. A GI said that the damage to Aachen was "more incredible than the wildest Dali landscape."

To deal with Dresden, Vonnegut uses humor, making his protagonist, Billy Pilgrim, an inept chaplain's assistant whose subsequent career takes him into bland suburban living as an optometrist and to fantasy life on the planet Tralfamador with a porno queen, Montana Wildhack. Humor is used, first, so that the book will be read and not rejected because of its disturbing, controversial theme. Laughter brings down defenses, as John Dryden and Voltaire appreciated in their eras. By contrast, David Irving's scholarly study, *The Destruction of Dresden* (1963), is far less known and Irving has been accused lately of neo-fascism.

Humor also keeps post-traumatic stress under control for the individual survivor and enables the subject to talk publicly. Vonnegut was a POW in Dresden during the bombing and largely suppressed the memory, saying "there was a complete blank" where it should have been. To bring it back entirely would probably have caused a severe emotional setback. Many veterans cannot discuss their worst experiences at all. Vonnegut applies humor to PTSD, with its inevitable flashbacks, in order to cope. Given that Billy has to periodically go back to hell in Dresden, he also speeds forward to heaven in Wildhack's arms, balancing nightmare fantasy with sexual fantasy.

The participant in war has to laugh at the random absurdities of combat or be broken by them. Death in war is arbitrary and irrational, taking the good and the bad, the experienced and the rookie alike. The most decent of the Americans in the book, Edgar Derby, is shot for looting, although he is actually just admiring a piece of porcelain like one at home. Vonnegut notes that nobody in war is morally clean. Allied fire bombing boiled alive schoolgirls sheltering in a water tank. But their brothers might have skinned Jews and gypsies for lampshades. Nobody should claim complete innocence.

Vonnegut's humor is also intended to bring the fighting man down to size; he is not the mythological figure of popular legend. There is a key exchange early in the book, when the author tells a war buddy and his wife that he is planning a Dresden story. The wife reacts angrily, saying he will mislead her children into thinking war is glamorous: "You'll pretend you were men instead of babies, and you'll be played in the movies by Frank Sinatra and John Wayne." Vonnegut took the point. His subtitle is "The Children's Crusade," a medieval military debacle, and Billy is drawn as a preposterous figure resembling a pink flamingo. Heroics are put down. Col. Wild Bob, from Cody, Wyoming, a Custer figure who says he will take care of the men, dies early of exposure. The platoon is not the magnificent group of *Sands*. Paul Lazarro, for example, is a vicious smalltime thief obsessed with revenge. Vonnegut describes himself as a self-trained and inadequate army scout who gets lost and is captured in the Battle of the Bulge. Obviously, Vonnegut exaggerates to make his point. But his portrait of innocents at war acts as an antidote to the romanticizing of life at the front.

The book's seminal contribution is its graphic depiction of the power of aerial warfare and the cost to those on the ground. Bombing is neither clinical nor sanitized, and it is not economical of lives. The ability to deliver massive destruction from the skies was a major development of World War II, including, finally, the dropping of the war-winning atom bombs on Japan. Since then the air arm has had an increasingly large place in America's military deployments.

—◦◦◦—

The advocacy of unrestrained air power dates from the 1920s when enthusiasts from several nations, including Billy Mitchell of the U.S., argued that planes alone could bring decisive results without messy ground action. At first, the threat posed to noncombatants provoked moral qualms. The U.S. condemned Axis area bombing of civilian targets in Spain, the Low Countries, and China. But poor British bombsights and weakly protected aircraft drove the RAF to inaccurate and largely indiscriminate night bombing. The U.S. finally followed suit in Europe and never tried precision bombing against Japan, where civilians in cities were a target from the start.

Irrespective of the common belief advanced by the media and some political and military figures, the potency of air power as a tool that can win war without significant ground action is still in question. The official U.S. Strategic Bombing Survey of 1946 suggested that air attack could not break the will of a people to fight. Morale went up under bombing in all belligerent countries. Targeting specific assets, such as oil refineries, could be successful, but indiscriminate attacks on industry met only moderate success; Germany's industrial output was rising at the end of hostilities. It is doubtful that the horrific losses to Japan, where sixty-one cities were attacked, destroying 40 percent of their surface area and killing seven hundred thousand, could have ended the war without further action such as the atom bombs. The renewed use of these dooms-day weapons has proved unpalatable to date, although their use has been advocated by a minority in the United States during every subse-quent war, including the aftermath of September 11, 2001.

Despite the questions, it was tempting to rely on the air fleet after World War II, as it was relatively cheap and more popular than a large conscript army. Although Korea was an all-arms operation, air power in both ground support and strategic assault roles was important. Attacks on the North, to dissuade the leadership from its aggressive policy, reached World War II levels in 1950–1953, leveling most major buildings in the north-central provinces, and driving much of the population underground.

Air power was equally central in Vietnam. During World War II, the U.S. dropped two million tons of bombs in all theaters. From 1965–1973, eight million tons fell on Indochina. In just two years, 1968–1969, South Vietnam suffered one and a half times the tonnage dropped on Germany. It was estimated that there were twenty-one million bomb craters in South Vietnam, in addition to one third of the tropical forests and six million acres of farm land being rendered unusable by air-deliv-ered weapons. Although the U.S. deployed huge ground forces, their mission was technically defensive, to protect against enemy aggression, with only limited offensive search and destroy opportunities. Air power was intended to interdict the enemy's offensive capability. But the extent to which airborne close support effectively handicapped the Viet Cong or strategic bombing seriously hindered North Vietnam's support efforts is still argued.

Support for air power as the first line of military action has increased since Vietnam. It was paramount in the 1991 Gulf War. No less an inter-national military authority than John Keegan has asserted that the 1999 NATO operations in Yugoslavia prove that a lasting victory can be won from the air alone, a doubtful claim, because lasting solutions always require a ground presence to sort out the post-action situation. And at a recent symposium on air power organized by the Air Force Association, a slide proclaimed, "It's no myth . . . the American Way of War."

A number of factors continue to make the primary use of air power a popular option. Unchallenged command of the skies, unleashing massive destruction on the earth below, gives a sense of godlike omnipotence. Americans can see themselves as administering retributive justice from the heavens on groveling evil opponents. Thus, during the bombing campaign in Afghanistan, John Barry, writing in *Newsweek,* December 10, 2001, bragged, "To many Taliban, the Americans must have seemed like creatures from another planet: out there somewhere, in the sky or across the horizon, powerful beyond comprehension." Barry's analysis ignores the crucial role of Northern Alliance ground forces in what was not conceived as a unilateral airborne offensive but a combined arms operation. Also, he repeats the myth, prevalent in the earlier Gulf War, that American bombing is so pinpoint accurate that errors are rare. In fact, much of the air assault was imprecise carpet bombing carried out by B-52s, causing huge physical damage and significant civilian casualties.

Air assault distances us from the suffering below, so that this method of warfare can appear more humane and less troubling to the senses than ground attack. Many villages were attacked from the air in Vietnam with significant civilian casualties, but no aircrew was ever tried for war crimes. The film shot by attacking aircraft does not disclose the human carnage caused by their weapons, but makes it appear that only inanimate objects have been eliminated. A missile is an even more morally sterilized weapon. Thus, President Clinton, who avoided service in Vietnam as an immoral war, authorized the launching of a cruise missile on average every third day of his presidency. We have reached the logical conclusion of the extension of the battlefield and the distancing of the enemy's humanity by long-range weapons, which began in the late nineteenth century. In high-tech war, the flesh and blood nature of the opponent has been receding steadily from the screen.

This removal of the human dimension of killing has been aided by the euphemizing of language. Bombs are not dropped, hardware is delivered. A target is not destroyed, it is neutralized. A region is not depopulated, it is sanitized. Civilians are not killed, collateral damage is incurred. The distancing saves us from the discomfort of seeing the real casualties of war. But that is also the problem with it. David Ross, a medic in Vietnam, 1965–1967, had the misfortune to see the bombing from ground level. He had to assist in the amputation of a child's leg, damaged by a bomb. The mother had been killed in the same raid. "I wondered how people would feel in Pittsburgh," he recalled, "if the Vietnamese came over in B-52s and bombed them." Timothy McVeigh, the Oklahoma City terrorist, was in part motivated by the airborne slaughter of Iraqis in the Gulf, which offended his sense of honor, and made him think that the destructive nature of wholesale bombing must be brought home to the American government and people.

The euphemizing of war reached a new stage with the Yugoslav operations, analyzed by Bob Shacochis in *Harper's Magazine,* December 1999. He maintained that part of America's self-perception as virtuous innocents was the belief that, even though we have used force to pursue our national interests, we have no enemies. We do not fight other peoples but only evil leaders who have transgressed against universal values and must be chastised. Thus, the bombing in Yugoslavia became "humane intervention." The problem, of course, is that, as the military knows, bombing can help to achieve humane ends, but it can never be humane in itself. Euphemizing killing as a "new military humanism" is not helpful to soldiers who must carry out the missions and who are isolated from a culture that does not want to share with them the moral burden of acknowledging the human cost.

Writers on national defense, and the media, have misled the public by not addressing in depth the problem of defining military targets in the modern post-industrial environment. The front line of air attack has changed to include civilians who staff a country's infrastructure. For example, with the importance to national life of electricity and communications networks, power stations or television studios may be legitimate targets. But we should be told and should accept responsibility for the fact that these facilities are staffed by noncombatants who will be killed. In the last century, sixty-two million civilians versus forty-three million soldiers were killed in war. The media (with the honorable exception of PBS) have largely failed to point out also that intensive bombing has left hundreds of thousands of unexploded bombs from Iraq to Kosovo, for which the United States takes little responsibility.

The drive to emphasize air power has been boosted by the public refusal to accept friendly casualties. In World War II massive firepower was used to pulverize the ground ahead of advancing troops, at huge cost to the human and physical environment, but in an attempt to eliminate any opposition. The body bags returning from Vietnam shocked the public, and since then the use of overwhelming force has accelerated.

Thus, in the 1990 invasion of Panama the excessive use of force on the part of a military terrified of adverse public reaction to U.S. casualties resulted in a high rate of civilian deaths.

Even minimal friendly casualties now appear to be unacceptable as the price for being a world power. When an American pilot was downed in Bosnia, June 1995, his rescue, hailed as a major victory, became a national measure of success. Even though pilot error appeared to be responsible for the incident, the airman was showcased in *Time* and *Newsweek*, whose banner headline read, on June 19, 1995, "An American Hero," alongside the claim that "It was the stuff of which legends are made." When three American soldiers were captured during the 1999 war with Yugoslavia, the public was outraged that they might have been roughed up, and demanded their immediate release, even though we were bombing Belgrade at the time. Our self-perception of innocence of intent to do harm was such that we did not think that our enemy should be angry with us or even retaliate by taking prisoners.

The potential domestic political costs of even one casualty are now perceived to be so great that, in the Yugoslav campaign, President Clinton refused to commit any ground troops, and pilots were ordered not to fly below fifteen thousand feet in order to avoid all anti-aircraft fire. A post-battle air force report showed that the high flights had led to inaccurate strikes. Of 744 alleged hits, only 58 could be confirmed. Inaccurate high-altitude bombing inevitably increased the risk to civilians. Lt. Col. Paul Brygider commented that the public would much rather see foreign civilians harmed than accept any U.S. military casualties.

Although it was popular after 9/11 to say that American attitudes had changed irrevocably, some basic political imperatives remained un-altered. In the "war on terror" in Afghanistan, the U.S. again resorted to a strategy of high-level bombing, leaving the bulk of ground action to the ill-equipped and unstable Northern Alliance, with limited U.S. and U.K. special forces assistance. Even this minor level of ground commitment led an ABC news report to caution, on September 17, 2001, that any ground involvement was "potentially dangerous." The vast legions of the U.S. regular army appear at this time to be as unusable due to the potential costs of casualties as were the Dreadnought battleships of World War I, which could be risked in battle rarely due to fear of public disapproval of losses. Bill Maher, of the television satirical show *Politically Incorrect,* was led to remark in the first week of October 2001 that perhaps the suicide bombers had more courage than the U.S., launching cruise missiles on Afghanistan from two thousand miles away. His perhaps inopportune remark led to public denunciation of Maher for seeming lack of patriotism.

The danger in the dynamic of arm's-length airborne warfare for America's global credibility was spelled out in *The Washington Quarterly*, Autumn 1998, by John A. Gentry, an American officer who has worked within NATO. He argues that the U.S. "presents a schizophrenic posture to the world" because "we crow about being the world's only superpower and claim the perquisites of that status, including the world's obeisance under the threat of sanctions," but we radiate fear about our people being hurt. The upshot is that Americans appear "like international bullies who throw our technological weight around while lacking the moral courage of our purported convictions."

Ultimately, the problem with overwhelming reliance on air power is that its effectiveness remains in doubt. Despite the media showcasing of "smart bombs" during the 1991 Gulf War, indiscriminate carpet bombing predominated and 90 percent of bombs missed their immediate target, the same percentage as in World War II. *Newsweek* reporters John Barry and Evan Thomas, after analyzing the huge number of misses in Yugoslavia, concluded on May 15, 2000, "The surgical strike remains a mirage." The problems are summarized by Robert A. Pape in *Bombing to Win* (1996). First, we define our opponents as evil leaders to be removed, but "decapitation strategies" do not work from the air. Second, "punishment strategies," aimed at turning civilians against a regime through bombing attacks, backfire because citizen support of the state goes up under air attack. Only strikes on specific military targets can be effective, but they often have to be carried out at low levels to work and so carry mutual risk, often politically unacceptable. Third, and most important, without troops on the ground to control the post-battle scenario, military gains are difficult to translate into political outcomes. Air assault can make immediate military gains but only a ground presence can control the postwar situation. We can instance here the problems of ethnic division in the Balkans that remained intractable after a successful bombing campaign, and an argument can be made that the start of the NATO air assault actually speeded up the pace of ethnic cleansing rather than impeded it. The case for the superior humanity and ultimate long-term efficiency of air power remains to be proven.

Of any Americans, the Vietnam combat veterans who witnessed the power of modern weaponry in Southeast Asia currently have the most exposure to war and the least hold on the national myth of innocence. At the same time, perhaps no event in American history has been so subject to mythical reconfiguration in popular thought as the Vietnam War. By the end of the conflict, America's sense of virtue had been rent. Domestic and world opinion was disturbed by the unleashing of enormous military power on small Asian countries. Vets and civilians turned against the war, leading to violent confrontations with authority, culminating in the shooting of student protesters at Kent State University, Ohio, May 4, 1970. The war on the ground was ugly on both sides, including atrocities. The most shocking for American self-esteem was the massacre at My Lai village, March 16, 1968.

The painful scenario was played out against a backdrop of the African American struggle for equal rights and concern about the fairness of the draft, which appeared to unjustly target the blue-collar class. America's sense of national innocence was badly soiled. The damage was caught in three film images: in one, a little girl, seared with napalm, runs crying toward the camera; in a second, a U.S. major explains why "It became necessary to destroy the town [of Ben Tre] to save it;" and in the third, a Saigon policeman, Gen. Nguyen Ngoc Loan, shoots a prisoner in the head before a television camera.

Peter Marin, a writer and poet, saw this time of anguish as an opportunity to rethink the value of war as a tool of diplomacy. But he already sensed in the mid 1970s that such was not happening. Molders of popular opinion redefined the war early on to see Americans as victims of an Asian "quagmire." The war became not just a failed military event, but a disease on the body of American pride and innocence, a syndrome to be kicked, as President Bush said in 1991.

One thing to be kicked was the recognition of defeat. The popular history of the war was rewritten to where Mark M. Woodruff, in *Unheralded Victory* (2000), asserted that the U.S. won in the field. The Military Book Club, February 2000, said the book showed "How the U.S. Won the War in Vietnam." The core argument is actually an old one, that the military could have won, but were hamstrung by a public that fell victim to Hanoi propaganda and liberal media distortions. Weak politicians didn't dare give the military full scope to win, so they fought the war with one hand tied, a stab-in-the-back theory similar to that espoused in Germany after World War I.

In fact, there was an enormous military commitment to the war. Over 3.5 million American men and women served in Vietnam. Roughly 40 percent of army and 50 percent of marine corps divisions, along with 50 percent of the air force's bombers, saw service at some time. Despite this buildup, the enemy was not defeated. Film has assisted in the role reversals that suggest defeat was political, not military. In the *Rambo* movies of the 1980s, the superhero is a jungle-wise fighter who outwits the enemy, aliens in their own environment. Rambo is let down by incompetent and corrupt politicians, the real villains. Coleco Industries made a Rambo doll because, the company said, the character "has the potential to become a new American hero."

A myth persists also that the war effort was undermined by civilian loss of the will to fight, caused by biased media coverage. Yet, as late as 1968, 61 percent of Americans saw themselves as hawks and 70 percent favored continued bombing of the North. The liberalism of the media, particularly at the editorial level, was exaggerated. Ron Kovic, a disabled veteran who opposed the war, was refused airtime on a television talk show because the producer said it was not "tasteful at all to let the people of L.A. see a crippled kid on a Sunday morning." Kovic said some vets wouldn't speak out through fear of abuse. "After one of the TV shows a cameraman called me a commie traitor to my face."

When television did air negative stories, such as CBS's coverage of the burning of Cam Ne village, the network was deluged with angry calls saying the show was obscene and unpatriotic. So, studio heads tended to avoid the controversial. When, in 1971, one hundred Vietnam Veterans Against the War testified about atrocities, the media ignored them. Such neglect has led to a gap in popular recollection of the war's full character. Tim O'Brien, a vet and writer, noted in the *New York Times Magazine*, October 2, 1994, that when he talks about My Lai to students, he gets "dull stares, a sort of puzzlement, disbelief." He concludes, "Evil has no place, it seems, in our national mythology." Rather, "we erase it" and "take pride in America the White Knight, America the Lone Ranger, America's sleek laser-guided weaponry beating up on Saddam and his legion of devils." Tom Englehardt, a student of popular culture in the Cold War, agrees in *The End of Victory Culture* (1995), noting that after Vietnam, America rebuilt a cult of "childlike innocence."

For example, unfavorable reporters have been barred from war zones and media releases have been controlled to ensure "favorable objectivity."

Again, commercial entertainment has helped to recast the war. In 1978's *The Deer Hunter* American prisoners are forced to play Russian Roulette, reversing the earlier televised image of the Viet Cong (VC) as victims. The movie has civilians in Saigon also sponsor the game, suggesting that all Vietnamese are vile and not worthy of America's support. In the November 1988 issue of the popular comic book *The 'Nam* the photojournalist who put the execution picture on "the front page of every newspaper in the States!" is the villain, while General Loan is portrayed as a patriot filled with righteous indignation at the evil VC prisoner.

Much public expression of grief about the losses in the war has been channeled in an ethnocentric direction. From 1965 to 1975 America lost roughly 58,000 killed and 153,000 wounded, cause for real sadness. But, in the same period, the Army of the Republic of Vietnam (ARVN) lost around 200,000 and the enemy as many as 1 million with a further civilian loss of 450,000. There are perhaps 1 million war widows in Vietnam and 879,000 orphans. To put this in perspective, U.S. losses were about the same as in American coal mines between 1870 and World War I, and considerably lower than the domestic gun deaths during the Vietnam era. Yet many Americans think of themselves as the chief sufferers. Richard Corliss commented in *Time,* January 26, 1987, that "the nearly 1 million Vietnamese casualties are deemed trivial compared with America's loss of innocence."

In addition to war deaths Vietnam has suffered enormous environmental destruction. Unexploded munitions in one province alone have killed 747 and wounded 449. It is estimated that 6 million unexploded pieces of ordnance remain in Cambodia. The effects of Agent Orange on American veterans has caused significant public concern, but there is little thought about the much greater impact on the Vietnamese who remained in the poisoned landscape. U.S. planes dumped 18 million gallons of herbicides over 6 million acres. Vietnamese health officials believe that the chemicals have caused 400,000 cases of death or debilitation and 500,000 birth defects in children.

Concern over the missing in action shows a similar public inability to recognize the mutuality of pain and loss. In 1976 President Gerald Ford opposed Vietnam's entry to the UN, saying that country had failed "to provide full accounting for all Americans missing in action." Such "brutal and inhumane treatment of the families" of U.S. MIAs "lacked the commitments of peace and humanitarianism necessary for membership in the United Nations." His stance is revealing in several ways. First, the U.S. offered no reciprocity, denying to the Vietnamese an equal human right "to know." Second, Ford betrayed a remarkable innocence about what happens to bodies in combat. How could anyone account for flesh atomized by mortar rounds, smashed in plane crashes, eaten by animals, rotted by heat and humidity? Refusal to look candidly at the nature of combat continued to hamper the American worldview.

Unrealistic hopes for the survival of MIAs were encouraged and exploited by Hollywood. In such movies as *Uncommon Valor* (1983) and *Missing in Action* (1984) daring American teams go back to find GIs trapped in the horrors of Asia, perhaps the ultimate symbolism buried in the MIA issue. No American must be left in the impure "other." Critics panned these productions, but they sold well. One happy viewer said, "We got to win the Vietnam War." The blurring between the entertainment and political/military worlds is symptomatic of what has happened to much public perception of the war. When, in 1982, James "Bo" Gritz, a retired special forces freelancer, decided to stage an unauthorized raid on Laos to rescue alleged U.S. POWs, Clint Eastwood, a movie actor and close friend of Ronald Reagan, was chosen to tell the president. Reagan, who had starred in *Prisoner of War* (1954) as a victim of communists in the Korean War, was so excited he said that if POWs were found, he would start World War III to get them out. The raid fizzled, but the idea that Americans were still victims of Asian cruelty remained potent.

Some documentary filmmakers have attempted to portray the war complexly, looking at issues as they affected both sides. PBS has taken the lead. *Frontline,* the PBS news show, ran *Remember My Lai,* a 1989 Yorkshire Television examination of the effects of the massacre on all the participants. In 1998 PBS also aired *Regret to Inform,* a remarkable examination by Barbara Sonneborn, a war widow, of how women on both sides have coped with the loss of husbands. In January 2000 *Frontline* presented "Bombies," a report on the undetonated U.S. anti-personnel bombs dropped on Laos during the Vietnam War and which so far have caused over twenty thousand postwar casualties.

It is appropriate that the widow of a combat soldier should make *Regret to Inform,* for the combat veterans have had the most trouble discarding the memory of, and responsibility for, their role in the war. Many have striven against romanticizing the experience. Tim O'Brien insists that in Vietnam he learned that good and evil are in all people, not just the enemy. "For all my education, all my fine liberal values, I now felt a deep coldness inside me, something dark and beyond reason. It's a hard thing to admit, even to myself, but I was capable of evil."

His realization does not fit well with the popular perception of American innocence, in which the potential for evil is defined as outside, foreign. Not surprisingly, given their alien insight, a 1995 study found that vets rated themselves as "very happy/satisfied" less than half as often as civilians, and "very unhappy/unsatisfied" six times as frequently. Vets not only bear the self-imposed guilt for the violence they committed but, when the dominant organs of social expression deny any collective responsibility for the carnage of war, they pick up the tab for the whole culture. It is popular, for example, to say that excesses occurred because the average age of grunts was low, about nineteen, versus twenty-six in World War II, and that teenagers lack self-discipline. Edward Doyle and Stephen Weiss in their 1984 study, *A Collision of Cultures,* assert that "The United States fought the war with teen-agers and paid a price for this immaturity." But it was not teenagers who wrote the military policies implemented in Vietnam.

The media's denial of more general responsibility began early in the war. The *National Observer,* November 1969, said that "It is not the system" that accounted for My Lai, but "individual responsibility [that] must be fixed." Francis Ford Copolla, in *Apocalypse Now* (1979), also portrayed extreme carnage as the result of individual moral slippage, of soldiers going mad in the jungle environment. A black vet commented, "By making us look insane, the people who made the movie were somehow relieving themselves of what they asked us to do over there. But we were not insane. We were not ignorant, we knew what we were doing."

The sense of being outcast partly explains veteran instability and unwellness. Robert Rawls, who was in Vietnam 1969–1970, says, "I sit by myself and I just think. You try to talk to somebody about it, they think you're out of your mind or you're freaked out." Feeling scapegoated helps us understand the spitting myth. Many vets believe they were spit upon by war protestors when they returned home. But sociologist Jerry Lembcke, who investigated every possible instance, reported in *The Spitting Image* (1998) that none could be verified. It appears that the vets have crystallized their general sense of being lepers into this one mythical image of rejection.

They also say they didn't get a parade, but what they often mean is that they didn't get a continuing public dialogue on their experience. If I am correct, then tying a ribbon to a tree and throwing a parade will not substitute for the veterans' need for support in continuing to process their experience through mature public discussion. Not surprisingly, we have the psychosomatic Gulf War Syndrome affecting veterans who witnessed the 1991 slaughter in the desert, even though they got to parade on their arrival home.

One of the vets who tried to spark a dialogue on the broader implications of Vietnam is Oliver Stone, director of *Platoon* in 1986. It is indicative of the movie industry's nervousness about serious debate on the war that Stone couldn't get a sponsor for ten years and his film was finally financed abroad. Some reviews were positive. *Time*, January 26, 1987, called it "Vietnam As It Really Was." But there was also hostility. The *Cincinnati Enquirer*, February 26, 1987, labeled it poisonous. Stone's point that a whole society shapes what its military does aroused anger. His platoon is a social microcosm, as the ship was for Herman Melville.

Stone takes a key symbol of American goodness, John Wayne's Sergeant Stryker (the film has repeated references to Wayne's signature line in *Sands*, "lock and load") and bifurcates him. The result is Sergeant Elias, a good soldier who wants to fight by ethical rules, and Staff Sergeant Barnes, a warrior who has left behind restraint in the desire to win and sanctions murder to achieve his goals. Barnes is not merely an individual psychopath. He and Elias represent the division of America against itself. For Stone, Barnes is a recognizable type: the young soldier Taylor says of him, "Barnes was our Ahab," in a direct reference to Melville's *Moby Dick* (1851), a link reinforced by Barnes having a lightning-shaped battle scar, just as Ahab was disfigured by lightning. His outer deformity reflects an inner one, produced by pain and rage. Ahab is obsessed by pursuit of the white whale that has injured him, the American in a relentless war with nature. Barnes is also obsessed by the regenerative power of violence. But his demon is not the white whale—it is the red menace, the specter of communism. Stone asked U.S. society to consider where this obsession might take us. In one instance the road leads to My Lai and to the court-martial of Lt. William L. Calley Jr. for his role there.

The events of March 16, 1968, are well documented. Three companies of Task Force Baker launched a search-and-destroy mission into Son My Village, a collection of four hamlets north of Quang Ngai City. The target was the 4th VC Local Force battalion, believed to be based there. C Company, under Capt. Ernest Medina, spearheaded the attack with a heliborne assault on My Lai-4 hamlet. Encountering no resistance at the landing zone, Medina ordered his men into the hamlets.

As they advanced, some villagers ran away and were shot down, standard procedure with fleeing peasants, who could be VC. Second Platoon, led by Lt. Steven K. Brooks, swept through the northern half of the village, tossing grenades, burning buildings, killing occupants and livestock. Some women were raped. The platoon then headed north to Binh Tay hamlet and repeated the procedure.

Meanwhile, First Platoon, under Lt. Calley, moved through the southern half of My Lai-4 with the same tactics. Some inhabitants were killed as they emerged from houses, others were rounded up and shot in a drainage ditch. Some 450–500 people died. Vignettes included a girl being raped and then killed by an M-16 rifle fired into her vagina; two boys shot while trying to shield each other; mothers with babies fired on; a child crawling out of the drainage ditch being tossed back in and killed.

At first the army said that this was a successful operation with about ninety VC eliminated (the official Peers Commission inquiry later estimated that only 3–4 of the victims could be VC). Only after the *Cleveland Plain Dealer* published photographer Ron Haeberle's pictures did the authorities act. Eighty-five percent of civilians who responded to the pictures protested their publication, some calling it unpatriotic. One mother felt they violated her family's innocence: "How can I explain these pictures to my children?" When the *Washington Star* also published pictures of dead women, the reader response was similar; one reader said it was unseemly that the women were shown unclothed.

In trying to understand My Lai, we shouldn't condone it or relieve individuals of responsibility for their actions. But we ought to seek the larger patterns of causation regarding such incidents in war. Some authors have dismissed the massacre as the work of a few weak junior officers. Calley's character, in particular, is questioned. Journalist Seymour M. Hersh, in one of the first studies, *My Lai 4* (1970), noted that Calley was a college dropout from an emotionally cold family. He allegedly drifted before entering the army. Hersh implied he was a poor soldier. A man who knew him in Officer Candidate School described "a kid trying to play war." James S. Olsen and Randy Roberts, in the later *My Lai* (1998), describe Calley as pudgy, pasty, weak-chinned, with "gerbil-like" eyes. He was "a poor excuse for an officer," derided by his platoon and called "shithead" by his superior, Medina. The problem with this view of Calley is that his record doesn't reveal abnormality or unusual incompetence, while his interviews and trial testimony suggest intelligence, sensitivity, and a willingness to take personal responsibility.

The grunts also are belittled as below average in intelligence and immature, aged eighteen to twenty-two. An army psychologist noted, "Terrified and furious teenagers by the tens of thousands have only to twitch their index fingers and what was a quiet village is suddenly a slaughter-house." Whatever the truth of this assertion, responsibility goes beyond the individuals. Military studies conducted in World War II found that less than 20 percent of men in a rifle platoon fired their weapons. There were many reasons, but one was a natural and moral revulsion against killing one's own kind. To overcome instinctive resistance, the Cold War army had soldiers train not with bull's-eye targets but pop-up human figures. The result was that the firing rate in Vietnam was 90 percent. Moreover, because of conventional army wisdom since World War II that weight of fire saved friendly lives, each platoon carried a huge arsenal of M16s, capable of one thousand rounds per minute, M60 machine guns, and M79 grenade launchers, even rocket launchers, pump shotguns, and other weapons. Young soldiers were ferociously armed and trained by intention.

Another immediate explanation for the killings was that Charlie Company had taken casualties from unseen enemies recently and frustration was running high, a volatility exacerbated by officers who didn't enforce rules protecting civilians and even encouraged their abuse. The Peers Commission, which investigated My Lai, found that Lt. Col. Frank Baker had given illegal orders to burn the village and kill the livestock. Medina also appears to have implied that he wanted everyone eliminated. Again, however, responsibility must go further. Generals and politicians wanted a high body count and sanctioned pressing the limits to obtain it. The media and much of the public accepted body count as a measure of success. Villages were routinely destroyed from the air in a climate that sanctioned massive retaliation.

The essential point regarding responsibility is made in a movie about

A problem of mutual racial incomprehension. Field artist Augustine Acuña captures the psychic distance between grunt and peasant in his 1966 painting *Roundup and Questioning of Villagers*. Courtesy of Army Art Collection, U.S. Army Center of Military History.

the British Empire which bears closely on the Vietnam War. In *Breaker Morant* (1979) three Australian officers are tried for shooting prisoners during the Boer War of 1899–1902. The defending officer, Maj. J.F. Thomas, says that it is hypocritical at one time and place to reprimand officers for "burdening the column with prisoners," and "at another time, and another place, haul them up as murderers for obeying orders." Responsibility must be shared at all levels.

If the soldiers loathed the Vietnamese as Orientals and abused them accordingly, the mutual racist incomprehension fueling their animosity was deep in both Western and Eastern cultures, making atrocity inevitable and not the fault of a few individuals. Lance Cpl. Kenneth Campbell wrote, "we were taught to hate these people. They were gooks, slants, dinks, they were Orientals, inferior to us." The culture, through its teachers, journalists, and filmmakers, had failed both to educate the soldiers about Vietnam and to suggest that cultural difference should not be equated with inferiority. A typical grunt said he despised the peasants, "who defecated in public, whose food was dirtier than anything in our garbage cans back home."

The most crucial point about this innocence of Vietnam's different history and manners was that it assumed Vietnam was a cultural vacuum that the communists were trying to fill. Instead, the U.S. would insert American-style democracy into the blank space. Thomas Bailey, an army intelligence officer, said in retrospect, "We were really trying to define them in our terms without beginning to see what their terms were at all."

The danger of ignoring cultural difference and trying to impose a simple formula on a complex world was seen, at the start of America's Indochinese involvement, by British novelist Graham Greene, who in 1955 published *The Quiet American*. His protagonist is Alden Pyle, an American intelligence officer, educated to believe that the West is in a worldwide struggle with monolithic evil. Ignoring Vietnam's political dynamics, Pyle blindly chooses a General Thé to be Vietnam's George Washington. Thé is, in fact, a corrupt warlord with no comprehension of American-style democracy. Pyle's naivete gets himself and many innocents killed. The narrator comments, "God save us always from the innocent and the good."

Calley was an innocent when he went to Vietnam, and he initially thought after My Lai that he had done nothing wrong. He later realized that he had dehumanized Vietnamese adults and children into an abstracted evil. This was largely the result of how communism had been portrayed in schools and theaters. Calley said that throughout his education it had been drilled into him that communism, never clearly defined, was bad. The students were told only that it was a disease to be stamped out. Military indoctrination reinforced the pattern. At his trial, Calley said, the army instructors "didn't give it a race, they didn't give it a sex, they didn't give it an age"; it was simply "my enemy out there."

Calley's perception was correct. In school movies of the 1950s, a red octopus of communism oozed across continents to ensnare the world. In the television show *I Led Three Lives* hard-to-detect communist agents were shown infiltrating everything from U.S. schools to outer space. In commercial film, learning that your child had polio was better than finding out he or she had become a communist. Most of the infected died tragically of the red disease.

Associating the unintelligible Vietnamese, without recognizable Western traits, and the identity-less communist menace was easy. An army major, imagining the red blob spreading on the map, told reporter Martha Gellhorn in 1966 that if the U.S. didn't win in Vietnam, "the west coast of America is open to invasion." The idea that, from a Vietnamese point of view, theirs could be a struggle for national integrity and not international expansionism, did not enter his thinking. His Vietnamese opponents were not a people but part of a monolithic international conspiracy. On this point, Calley said, "We weren't in My Lai to kill human beings really. We were there to kill *ideology* that is carried by—I don't know. Pawns. Blobs. Pieces of flesh, and I wasn't in My Lai to destroy intelligent men. I was there to destroy an intangible idea."

Once the Vietnamese had been denied a separate third-party identity occupying a viable middle ground, and were therefore either American-style democrats or communist dupes, a lethal dilemma arose. How could you let the dupes live? Calley stated the problem precisely. If you asked a girl which she preferred for her country, democracy or communism, and she said communism, "Then what was I to do? Kill her?" Given his education, the choice to kill seemed reasonable. Calley drew an analogy to Mary Shelley's 1818 story *Frankenstein*. Here, a creature, molded by its creator, wants to do good, but destroys a village when the people turn against him. American soldiers might be the monster, thought Calley, but their nation was Dr. Frankenstein, ultimately responsible, because, "The people of the United States did create the United States Army."

The point has been further developed by M. Scott Peck, a psychologist and student of the concept of evil. In *People of the Lie* (1983) he posited that My Lai was neither an aberration nor unpredictable. Evil, he says, is not always of an obvious, direct kind. It can come from arrogance and complacency, innocence in fact. He charges that we were too lazy and too narcissistic to learn about Asian communism or nationalism, with the result that we became "unwitting villains," destroying what we didn't understand. He estimates that 90 percent of American soldiers and civilians had no knowledge of Vietnamese history or culture.

—◆—

The atrocities committed by both sides in Vietnam are not aberrations but pieces of a broader pattern in world military history. Whenever good becomes separated entirely from evil, and evil is posited as being an outside force so unspeakable it cannot be allowed to continue, then atrocities will happen. Anthropologists like Lawrence H. Keeley have suggested

The ban on the ungodly. Colonial militia destroy a Native American village, along with its inhabitants. From an early woodcut.

that evidence as far back as we can go in prerecorded time shows that the treatment of alien societies, "nonstate groups" who follow different "tribal" mores, has often been ruthless. Some primitive peoples waged total wars of extinction. Later examples in the Ancient Period would be the Greek sacking of Troy and Julius Caesar's Roman massacre of the Bituriges who were defined as barbarians, beyond the pale.

War to the knife is seen clearly in the Old Testament biblical "ban," which Jehovah placed on those individuals or societies so offensive to Him that they had to be annihilated, including women and children. Biblical scholar Susan Niditch comments in *War in the Hebrew Bible* (1993) that under the ban, "a sharp line is drawn between us and them, between clean and unclean, between those worthy of salvation and those deserving elimination." The idea was adopted by Christians and used to justify ferocity against heretics and infidels.

Oliver Cromwell's slaughter of the Irish, and Puritan extermination of warlike Indian tribes, were in this tradition. Puritan divine Cotton Mather, in his 1689 sermon "Souldiers Counselled and Comforted," tried to ease the consciences of Massachusetts militia about wholesale slaughter by suggesting that New England represented the Children of Israel in the Wilderness, and the Indians were the Amalek, deserving to be banned and totally destroyed. The attitude survived in Hollywood movies prior to Vietnam. In *Northwest Passage* (1940), set in 1759 during the French and Indian War, Spencer Tracy as Robert Rogers reminds his American rangers, "Now, we're under orders to wipe out this town, so see that you do it."

When Calley was under arrest, he received sympathetic letters from veterans of previous wars, suggesting that such incidents as My Lai were bound to happen. A Spanish-American War veteran told about abuse of Filipinos. In his support, historians know that in the Philippine Insurrection, towns were burned, civilians raped, tortured, and killed. In one operation on the island of Jolo as many as six hundred natives died. In the Pacific Theater during World War II mutual racism led to ferocity on both sides. An army lieutenant wrote to Calley, "I was witness to many incidents similar to the one you're being held for." Another confessed, "I was given the order to seal a cave where a mother and her eleven or twelve children holed up. This took place in 1944 on the island of Ie Shima." A veteran of the European battlefield said, "My fellow soldiers and I did on occasion kill enemy soldiers [POWs], civilians, and children." A retired marine acknowledged, "I was in two operations in Korea where women and children were killed." Information on one such incident, at the town of No Gun Ri, July 26, 1950, is only now coming to light.

The ultimate point is this. Wars have been fought and will continue to be so whenever diplomatic strategies for resolving international disputes fail. The U.S. has been no worse and, at times, considerably more humane than other nations, in waging war. But wars are inherently destructive of the human and environmental fabric. Ultimately, killing cannot be sanitized in the eye of history and it should not be distanced from our immediate focus. When we must put our soldiers and enemy peoples at risk, we should understand fully what is about to take place.

Consequently, our popular understanding of war must be sophisticated and comprehensive, complex and not simple. To either ignore or euphemize what we ask the military to do, avoiding our share of responsibility in order to ensure our emotional comfort and prolong our innocence, is wrong. To present fighting as popular escapist entertainment, to package conflict like a mini series, as some of the networks did in the

1991 Gulf War, is particularly inappropriate. If we must exercise force, we should sanction it with gravitas and in full knowledge of the likely results for all involved. We can achieve this only if the organs of popular education—teachers, writers, and filmmakers—accurately depict all of battle. Many of the public are avid readers and viewers of military history. They deserve the most complete picture possible.

In the wake of the September 11, 2001, terrorist attacks, both the Washington administration and the media had a significant opportunity to educate the public about the nature of violence in a global context. The results were patchy. This is not to deny the resolution with which the administration developed and carried out a policy to attack terror, the courage of those who fought the damage on September 11 or have served the country since, as well as the decency and compassion of the American people whose sense of national pride and concern for the suffering in New York have been manifest. What is in doubt is whether to date we have been as well-served intellectually as we have been emotionally by our leaders and organs of mass communication.

It was popular after September 11 to say that America had lost its innocence (once again), but President George W. Bush and the media were quick to put that innocence back in place. Rather than discussing the complex economic, political, and religious causes of antagonism toward the U.S. in the technologically less-developed nations, Bush chose to bolster public naivete by simply evoking a war of good against evil, a struggle to save civilization from barbarism. Thus we need seek no deeper for answers than the emotionally (but not intellectually) satisfying explanation that we are hated for our virtue, a simple diagnosis that the president reinforced by declaring that other nations must either be for us (good) or against us (wicked). There was no complex middle ground. Much of the mainstream media accepted the president's rhetoric, even comparing him favorably to Britain's war leader, Winston Churchill, particularly when Bush reiterated such stern sentiments as "we are resolved" and "we will prevail."

The Churchill analogy was part of a media rush to compare the post September 11 situation to Wold War II, the historical era of greatest current interest. Dan Rather said on CBS, October 7, 2001, that the circumstances "can only be described as a world war." Henry Kissinger made the inevitable Pearl Harbor analogy, and was outbid by Robert Kogan, who declared in the *Washington Post,* September 12, 2001, that September 11 was "more awful than Pearl Harbor." Actually, the comparison was a poor one. In 1941, a major international power, Japan, made a conventional military assault on an opponent with which it was vying for territorial power in the Pacific, delivering a formal declaration of war as part of the proceedings. In 2001 terrorists with no state sanction committed a criminal act with no tangible expectations of conventional military or political advantage. The only connection between the two events was that both hurt.

Tom Brokaw, writing in *TV Guide,* December 22, 2001, felt that there had been a sudden "call to greatness" akin to that of 1941. Looking at a youthful New York firefighter, he was sure that "we are in good hands" with youngsters who would replicate the deeds of Brokaw's "Greatest Generation." What the analogy scrupulously ignored was that the resolute commander in chief, George W. Bush, along with lieutenants such as Colin Powell, was a member not of a great but a naughty generation, the one from the nasty 1960s. Another popular World War II reference, if equally clumsy, was to the Axis Powers (Germany, Italy, and Japan). In his 2002 State of the Union Address, President Bush refurbished this as the Axis of Evil, composed of Iran, Iraq, and North Korea. The concept caused deep unease among America's allies abroad and made State Department analysts squirm, as the three evil states are not allied and only one, Iran, has proven connections to terrorism. But the concept played well in domestic opinion polls.

Media commentators saw in the purchase and prominent display of U.S. flags an upsurge of patriotism akin to that following Pearl Harbor. The extent to which this represented a real commitment to a wartime sense of stringent sacrifice might have been questioned, however, when the flags became part of Halloween, Thanksgiving, and Christmas designer displays. The media didn't probe whether the display of bunting was entirely meaningful: would the war spirit stand up to significant U.S. casualties or fiscal damage by the military bill upon Social Security and Medicare? Donald Rumsfeld, secretary of defense, to date has consistently refused to discuss with journalists the daily costs of the military campaign, perhaps in itself an admission of concern about the depth of public resolve to sacrifice long-term.

Although the first President Bush said in the Gulf War of 1991 that we had kicked the Vietnam syndrome, his son's administration appeared less certain. The myth that the Vietnam War was lost through candid press coverage and subsequent negative public reaction continues to dictate policy and actions. Immediately after October 7, 2001, when the bombing campaign began, the Pentagon bought up all high-definition satellite photographs of the Afghan region to stop the media from seeing the full civilian damage. After much criticism, the Pentagon disbanded in March 2002 the short-lived Office of Strategic Influence, which had been created to feed disinformation (also referred to primly as "falsehoods") to the foreign press. So great is the determination to avoid candor, reported David Samuels in *Harper's,* January 2002, that Rumsfeld has even refused to let civilian historians at military institutions discuss with journalists the 1980s Soviet military operations in Afghanistan.

The media appear to have largely acquiesced in the idea that tough investigative reporting is unpatriotic in time of war. In Afghanistan, no U.S. television journalist appeared closer than fifty miles to the front lines. Pentagon bulletins were repeated at face value. For example, the media accepted a military report that during mop-up operations special forces had killed one hundred Al Qaeda for only one U.S. soldier slightly injured in the shin. Anyone with military understanding should know that the losses in a firefight could not be so disproportionate. Only later was it revealed through non-U.S. media sources that the dead were Northern Alliance negotiators killed by error. Some media heads have allegedly issued orders to slant the news to reduce public sympathy for overseas suffering. The *Washington Post* reported, October 31, 2001, that CNN chair Walter Isaacson had ordered his staff to balance images of civilian devastation in Afghan cities with reminders of Taliban evil. Ray Glenn, the copydesk chief of the *Panama City (Fla.) News Herald,* allegedly told his staff during October to write no stories that led with civilian casualties.

In any national emergency, there will be an inevitable question of the need for heightened security versus a concern for individual rights. The media has done a relatively good job of covering this complex subject, including noting worldwide disapproval of U.S. violations of the Geneva Convention protocols on treatment of POWs, and debating the civil rights issues raised by the potential trial of non-U.S. citizens by military tribunals. President Bush's December 1, 2001, executive order keeping sixty-eight thousand pages of President Reagan's papers sealed, under the dubious pretext of post-9/11 national security, received less coverage. Despite the damage done to the writing of recent history, the media seemed more fascinated by the woes of historians Stephen J. Ambrose, Doris Kearns Goodwin, and Michael A. Bellesiles, each accused of plagiarism or doctoring documentation.

The broad history of terrorism, important to the context of current events, has been neglected since September 11. The media have consulted few historians, who might usefully explain that terrorists are not merely demonic individuals who are deeply sick or evil but are dedicated warriors without a state-sponsored power base, large numbers of personnel, or a strong conventional arsenal. Therefore, they must fight a war with what they have, often using unconventional weapons and distasteful strategies. It would surprise many Americans to know that George Washington, heading a weak team of rebels, in 1776 tacitly sanctioned the burning of New York City, base for the much-stronger Crown army. He approved this act of terror out of necessity, and one third of the city burned as a result. He also tried to assassinate Crown generals through such dastardly methods as poison. Historians could explain, also, that not all terrorists have come from Asia or the Middle East. In the 1980s the U.S. officially sponsored Contra terror in Nicaragua, and Americans have informally funded Provisional (IRA) terror in Northern Ireland. When we enjoy watching the life of a Michael Collins on film, we are watching the story of a terrorist.

It is important to understand that the terrorist, in order to weaken a conventional power that is not beatable by formal military means, will fight a psychological battle that involves molding what people think more than it does winning battlefield victories. Conventional military strategies might not work in eliminating terror in the long run because they can backfire in the realm of the mind, of propaganda, where the terrorist can fight on a relatively even playing field. Resisting the temptation to overreact, to appear as the world-class bully slugging the little guy, is crucial for a conventional power. For example, in December 1773 terrorists called the Sons of Liberty dumped an immensely valuable cargo of tea into Boston harbor. Their aim was partly to get the British government to overreact, which it did, closing Boston port and refusing to let the Massachusetts assembly meet. In this way, the terrorists won people's hearts and minds to their cause. Similarly, when Irish rebels rose in Dublin, Easter 1916, leading to the destruction of the central shopping and business district during fierce fighting, public sentiment initially favored the British government. But it then lost the moral high ground by shooting the rebel leaders, precipitating a guerrilla (terrorist) campaign in Ireland that finally led to independence.

We have yet to see whether bombing a weak country like Afghanistan will boomerang and hurt the U.S. in the war of the shadows, the war of the mind, where it counts, in the non-Western world. Because the Taliban excite little world sympathy, the U.S. may win the propaganda as well as the military war this time. But should the war on terror extend to, say, causing more immense suffering to the Iraqi people though a bombing campaign, or should America fail to help secure a fair peace between Israel and Palestine, the U.S. may well begin to lose significant points. The internationally distinguished military historian Michael Howard was quoted in *Harper's,* January 2002, as saying that the war on terror is not like a formal war but a war on crime and drugs and must be fought in a similar way, quietly and carefully, with a minimum of force and a maximum of statecraft. He doubts the effectiveness of a conventional military response and, like all thoughtful authorities on terror, he believes that we must through economic and political channels alleviate the problems that generate terror if we are ever to eradicate it. He is correct and should be given significant media exposure. But his views and those of others who challenge the idea of ending terrorism through conventional military campaigns have not been disseminated widely.

The United States spends a great deal of money on higher education and has one of the finest university systems in the world. It would make sense to see much closer cooperation between academic historians and the media. The fault is by no means on one side. Academic responses to the September 11 events tended to dwell on the responsibility of McWorld for the suffering and consequent anger in the poorer countries, and some campuses saw blanket protests of American military policy lacking focus or intelligent historical analysis. Some left-wing academics can see only a vast selfish conspiracy to dominate world oil supplies in the Bush administration's foreign policy response to September 11. The "town and gown" divide is unfortunate, for historians and the media have much to contribute to each other. Already there are plans to create drama out of the war on terror. Jerry Bruckheimer, producer of *Top Gun*, *Pearl Harbor*, and *Black Hawk Down*, intends to write a television series called "Profiles from the Front Line" to run on ABC in the fall 2002. Can anyone doubt that such a series of dramatic war stories would not gain in authenticity and depth from the input of scholars in the field of military history?

Afterword

Historians with Axes (To Grind)

Certain central themes recur throughout this work. In closing, it might be helpful to suggest some conclusions toward which they appear to be heading.

First, history matters, not only to those born with an innate interest in the past, but to anyone who wishes to better comprehend the world we live in. Today is indelibly shaped by yesterday, and neither can be fully understood without reference to the other. We live in the palm of the hand of history. Military history is of great importance, because wars still play a central role in human activities. When and how we wage war affects our place in the world, as well as the destinies of other peoples. War helps shape the identity of a people and, in turn, national character dictates military organization and activity. War radically changes the human and physical environment, much more than is often appreciated. War elicits nobility, acts of outstanding humanity, comradeship, and excitement, but it is also humanity's costliest endeavor, in financial, human, and environmental, terms. We need to be informed about this ubiquitous, intrusive, and profoundly formative activity.

We should appreciate the Vietnam veterans who have written and spoken about their experiences, because they have raised public awareness of, and interest in, what happens in war. Some criticize the veterans for having turned their demand for attention into a "cottage industry" of lobbying and special pleading. But even if this is partially true, it is a small price to pay for the insights that the public has received.

We are also fortunate for having citizens who study history, not as a profession and for a living, but as an avocation. Many devotees of military history come to this interest after a day's work in a demanding occupation that often has not even the remotest connection to history. Doctors, dentists, lawyers, bankers, computer technicians, chemists, horticul-turalists, store managers, and many more engage with the study of war in their hard-earned leisure time, some turning their interest into an ac-tivity such as reenactment, historical restoration, or volunteer museum staffing. Many university students, too, take courses in military history as electives, not because they are required for their majors in biology or accounting, but because they want to know more about the causes and effects of wars. Such interest on the part of a wide range of people makes a democracy more informed.

The interests of this growing sector of the public are served by a huge output of war books, movies, and television programs. Much is good in quality, but the sheer quantity makes it difficult to digest and organize intellectually for effective understanding. This book has attempted to help by suggesting some important broad patterns for different eras of history, and by demonstrating techniques for analyzing print and visual materials. The more that professional historians engage with the mass of materials on war in popular culture, the better able we will be as a soci-ety to appreciate the relative value of what we read and watch. There should be more cooperation between the great engines of education, academe, and the media. It is to be hoped that more historians will be seen on television, helping talk-show hosts to interpret for viewers events in a historical context. Dare we envisage historians debating issues on *The O'Reilly Factor*?

Many avenues exist for cooperation between professional and lay practitioners of history: advisory boards of museums, state and local history societies, historical preservation groups, and reenactment orga-nizations. Public interest in history is served by the federally-funded National Endowment for the Humanities (NEH) and the State Humani-ties Councils that bring together scholars and community groups. A mi-nority of historians partake in these ventures, but more need to do so. Achieving a higher public profile is in the self-interest of humanists, for they currently face scepticism about their value and utility at both the secondary and higher education levels on the part of those who do not see the importance of history and literature in explicating the world we live in. Greater community involvement means greater appreciation. It is worth noting, too, that military history courses are among the most popu-lar in the discipline today and attract an elective constituency.

A growing number of scholars do address a general audience, and models for cooperation exist. A fine recent example is the work of teachers and community groups to preserve the battlefield of Paoli, Pennsylvania, and make its importance to the history of the Revolutionary War more widely understood. Paoli, fought in 1776 after the better known Battle of Brandywine, was a Patriot defeat and helped to give Philadelphia, the rebel capital, to Lord Howe and the Crown forces. But the ferocity of the redcoats at Paoli also fueled a desire for revenge and helped to keep the spark of rebellion alive. The cooperative work of historians and organizations such as the Pennsylvania Society of the Sons of the Revolution and the Paoli Battlefield Preservation Fund not only upgraded the battlefield but led to the publication of a fine history by Thomas J. McGuire, *Battle of Paoli* (2000). Another excellent potential model is Gettysburg College's annual Civil War Institute, expertly developed by Gabor S. Boritt, which brings hundreds of professional and lay students of history together in caucus. The institute has resulted in a fine series of published anthologies of essays generated as papers for the sessions.

Scholars are increasingly involved in the evaluation of commercial movies. Both *The American Historical Review* and *The Journal of American History,* leading periodicals in the field, post excellent critiques of historical movies on their websites. Also, more books are becoming available that demonstrate through example how to critique movies from a historical viewpoint. An exemplary model is Marc C. Carnes. ed., *Past Imperfect: History According to the Movies* (1995), which offers essays by experts on different historical eras and events as interpreted by the cinema.

The engagement of professional historians in criticism of popular movies is particularly important, because film, the great educator of our time, tends to be less concerned than print media with historical accuracy. The cinema has always been allowed dramatic license in dealing with a historical subject. And it is understood that the film must be entertaining to stay in business, so that interest value must sometimes override authenticity of theme. But some movies claim to hold a mirror to reality while gratuitously and radically distorting. A recent example is *Enslavement: The True Story of Fanny Kemble* (1999).

This film purports to deal with the life of the British actress, Frances Anne Kemble, who married a Sea Islands planter in 1834 and had a brief involvement with slavery. She wrote a good book, attacking the system, called *Journal of a Residence on a Georgian Plantation* (1863), and played a small part during the Civil War in promoting the Union cause in Britain. The film takes off from this historical base to propose that Kemble was a major figure in radical abolitionism who used her house as an Underground Railroad station and submitted to the lash to save a male slave under her protection. These inventions would be fine if the movie claimed to be no more than fiction, but the title bills the piece as accurate history. In such cases, the film must be held to the same standards of veracity and integrity in handling material that govern print history.

A splendid example of a movie that strives for historical authenticity while preserving dramatic appeal is *Mary Silliman's War* (1993), a remarkably nuanced study of one woman's trials in revolutionary Connecticut, made with the help of the NEH and several state humanities councils. The film manages, in ninety-three minutes, to deal with conflicted loyalties, the brutalities of guerrilla war, profiteering, efforts to raise a family and run a farm in a war zone, gender and race issues raised by the revolutionary cry of freedom, and social dislocation in wartime. It has action, too, with kidnaps, night raids, and boat chases. The film is based on Mary Silliman's letters and the fine biography *The Way of Duty* (1985), by Joy Day Buel and Richard Buel Jr. In an accompanying guide the filmmakers note the creative liberties they have taken with the strict record in order to dramatize key points about the wartime experience. What could be more fair?

Overall, there appear to be grounds for optimism about the future place of history, and of military history in particular, in our popular culture. Despite conventional wisdom, Americans are interested in the past, as such organizations as the History Book Club and the Military Book Club suggest. Reenactment, although it cannot fully reproduce the past, gives us a useful visual, practical feel, and certainly performers will continue to work on creating greater realism. Historical movies are enjoying great popularity, and while film cannot achieve the depth of print, it can be a good starting place for gaining the atmosphere of an era, the feel of a subject. Much the same is true of the web, which has an enormous amount of historical material available for browsing. You can, for instance, see every panel of the Bayeux Tapestry in full color, visit colonial battle sites, or explore the interior of the Alamo chapel. You must be discriminating about accepting what you are told on the internet, but that is ultimately simply a matter of knowing something about the subject in hand.

That brings us finally to print. There is no substitute for books in acquiring in-depth knowledge of history. Despite the doomsayers, the computer won't make books obsolete, anymore than did the telegraph and the radio, about which the same predictions were made. Computers and books do not compete, they complement each other. Civil War and World War II publishing currently lead the way in providing military history for the popular audience. We have seen that both of these have to some degree been stuck in a rut. But good original work is also being done, and the success of these fields is a spur to creativity regarding other wars and eras. While history is under assault in some curricula, faculty are well placed to respond to demands for greater community involvement, because the public interest in the field is there, ready to be tapped. The future quality of popular education about the past is in our hands to shape if we choose to embrace the challenge and join the fray.

Exploring Further

The following suggestions for further exploration of themes discussed in the text emphasize both the relevance and readability of the works chosen. It is hoped that they will prove both informative and enjoyable. Not every source consulted during the research and writing of the present book has been included, and works cited in the text are not always referenced here again. Where possible, books and articles have been recommended that can be obtained through a good public or four-year-college library. In a few instances, more difficult to obtain references had to be used.

Works of General Interest

Of the many works available on the historical development of American culture, Carl N. Degler's *Out of Our Past: The Forces That Shaped Modern America* (rev. ed. 1970) is both stimulating and accessible. James W. Loewen, *Lies My Teacher Told Me: Everything Your American History Textbook Got Wrong* (1994), is a recent provocative study of how we view the past. Michael Kammen, *Mystic Chords of Memory: The Transformation of Tradition in American Culture* (1991), suggests how the land of the future acquired a past. On the challenges facing history today, see Harvey J. Kaye, *The Powers of the Past: Reflections on the Crisis and the Promise of History* (1991). James West Davidson and Mark Hamilton Lytle, *After the Fact: The Art of Historical Detection* (2000), gives specific examples of the historian in the role of sleuth. Dennis A. Trinkle, et al., *The History Highway: A Guide to Internet Resources* (1997), is helpful in evaluating the array of materials available on the web. Useful volumes for interpreting movies in an historical context include Mark C. Carnes, ed., *Past Imperfect: History According to the Movies* (1995), Steven Mintz and Randy Roberts, eds., *Hollywood's America: United States History through Its Films* (1993), and Peter Rollins, ed., *Hollywood as Historian: American Film in a Cultural Context* (1983).

The many good general histories of warfare include John Keegan, *A History of Warfare* (1993), Robert L. O'Connell, *Of Arms and Men: A History of War, Weapons, and Aggression* (1989), Bernard and Fawn M. Brodie, *From Crossbow to H-Bomb: The Evolution of the Weapons and Tactics of Warfare* (rev. ed. 1973), and Richard A. Preston, Alex Roland, and Sydney F. Wise, *Men in Arms: A History of Warfare and Its Interrelationships with Western Society* (1991). Michael Howard, *War in European History* (1976), is good but deals only with Europe. Worthwhile studies limited to the modern period include Charles Townshend, ed., *The Oxford History of Modern War* (2000), Jeremy Black, *War and the World: Military Power and the Fate of Continents 1450–2000* (1998), and Brian Bond, *The Pursuit of Victory: From Napoleon to Saddam Hussein* (1996). David D. Perlmutter, *Visions of War: Picturing Warfare from the Stone Age to the Cyber Age* (1999), examines the pictorial representation of war.

Richard Holmes examines the impact of combat on the soldier during different eras in *Acts of War: The Behavior of Men in Battle* (1985). Gwynne Dyer, *War* (1985), Donald Kagan, *On the Origins of War and the Preservation of Peace* (1995), and Robert L. O'Connell, *Ride of the Second Horseman: The Birth and Death of War* (1995), all in some sense try to look at the roots and development of organized aggression.

Maurice Matloff, ed., *American Military History* (1969), although quite old, is exceptionally reliable. Two other good general histories are Allan R. Millet and Peter Maslowski, *For the Common Defense: A Military History of the United States of America* (rev. ed. 1994), and James M. Morris, *America's Armed Forces: A History* (2d ed., 1996). Useful anthologies include David Curtis Skaggs and Robert S. Browning III, eds., *In Defense of the Republic: Readings in American Military History* (1991), and John M. Carroll and Colin F. Baxter, eds., *The American Military Tradition: From Colonial Times to the Present* (1993).

Russell F. Weigley has made fundamental contributions to the interpretation of American military development. His works offer sound research and original theses. I recommend beginning with *The American Way of War: A History of United States Military Strategy and Policy*

(1973). Other issues-oriented histories include John Whiteclay Chambers II and G. Kurt Piehler, eds., *Major Problems in American Military History* (1998), and Robert A. Doughty, et al., *American Military History and the Evolution of Warfare in the Western World* (1996). Geoffrey Peret argues that military conflict was pivotal to U.S. development in *A Country Made by War: From the Revolution to Vietnam* (1989). Works that broadly consider war in an American popular culture context include G. Kurt Piehler, *Remembering War the American Way* (1995), John Limon, *Writing after War: American War Fiction* (1994), Edward Tabor Linenthal, *Changing Images of the Warrior Hero in America: A History of Popular Symbolism* (1982), and *Sacred Ground: Americans and their Battlefields* (1991).

Chapter 1: Knights on Horseback

David Howarth, *1066: The Year of the Conquest* (1977), is a thoughtful analysis of Hastings and the events leading up to the battle. Edwin Tetlow, *The Enigma of Hastings* (1974), is a sound factual account. There have been many studies of the Bayeux Tapestry. Two that contain fine visuals are Charles H. Gibbs-Smith, *The Bayeux Tapestry* (1973), and David J. Bernstein, *The Mystery of the Bayeux Tapestry* (1986). Color representations of the tapestry may be seen on several websites. The incomparable modern rendering of *The Song of Roland* is by Dorothy L. Sayers, published in 1957 and still available in paperback. Readers should not be frightened by the poem because it is now the province of scholars; it was written as popular entertainment and can be approached as such. Christine Fell, Cecily Clark, and Elizabeth Williams give a good view of the Norman Conquest's effect on gender relations in *Women in Anglo-Saxon England and the Impact of 1066* (1984). See also Doris M. Stenton, *The English Woman in History* (1957). R. Allen Brown has a comprehensive view of Norman culture in *The Normans* (1984). Steven Runciman looks at European military culture around the time of Hastings in *The First Crusade* (1980).

On the technological changes that supported the hegemony of the mounted knight, both militarily and economically, see Lynn Townsend White, *Medieval Technology and Social Change* (1962). Frances Gies, *The Knight in History* (1984), is an excellent survey of the heyday of knighthood. Difficult but rewarding examinations of chivalry are Richard Barber, *The Knight and Chivalry* (1974), and Georges Duby, *The Chivalrous Society* (trans. Cynthia Postan, 1977). Jonathan Riley-Smith, ed., *The Oxford Illustrated History of the Crusades* (1997), is an attractive treatment. R.C. Smail, *Crusading Warfare, 1097–1193* (1956) is also a good introduction.

Desmond Seward, *The Hundred Years War* (1978), and Édouard Perrot, *The Hundred Years War* (1965), are good surveys of the long wars between England and France. The classic interpretation of Agincourt is John Keegan, *The Face of Battle* (1976). Jim Bradbury delineates the bowman's importance in *The Medieval Archer* (1985). On the figure of Robin Hood, see Stephen Knight, *Robin Hood: A Complete Study of the English Outlaw* (1994), and Maurice Hugh Keen, *The Outlaws of Medieval Legend* (1961). Anthony Cheetham, *The Life and Times of Richard III* (1972), is an even-handed treatment. Michael Bennett expertly handles Richard's last fight in *The Battle of Bosworth* (1985). The world of the fifteenth-century knightly soldier and politician is captured in Roger Virgoe, ed., *Private Life in the Fifteenth Century: Illustrated Letters of the Paston Family* (1989). Georges Duby, *William Marshal: The Flower of Chivalry* (trans. Richard Howard, 1985), is a good example of the soldier and king's advisor risen from humble beginnings.

The nineteenth-century involvement with chivalry is pursued in Michael C.C. Adams, *The Great Adventure: Male Desire and the Coming of World War I* (1990), T.J. Jackson Lears, *No Place of Grace: Antimodernism and the Transformation of American Culture* (1981), and Mark Girouard, *The Return to Camelot: Chivalry and the English Gentleman* (1981). A good example of the Victorian adventure story set in the Middle Ages is Robert Louis Stevenson's *The Black Arrow: A Tale of the Two Roses* (1888), which includes the bowman as a potent outlaw avenger of wrongs, and a typical portrait of Richard III as "Dick Crookback," brave but cruel and ambitious. The 1984 film version is good, with Oliver Reed playing the villainous traitor knight, Sir Daniel Brackley. Bram Dijkstra, *Idols of Perversity: Fantasies of Feminine Evil in Fin-De-Siècle Literature* (1986), documents the role of the knightly revival in shielding men from women. Dijkstra has excellent examples of art depicting the armored male encountering and dominating the vulnerable female.

Daniel Grotta, *The Biography of J.R.R. Tolkien: Architect of Middle-Earth* (1976), is excellent on Tolkien's retreat from modernity. William

Morris, *The Wood beyond the World* (1894), was an early model for subsequent medieval fantasy literature. In addition to Joseph Campbell's 1988 six-episode television interview with Bill Moyers, titled *The Power of Myth,* the anthropologist's ideas on the hero quest are expounded in his book, *The Hero with a Thousand Faces* (1949), and in John H. Maher and Dennie Briggs, eds., *An Open Life: Joseph Campbell in Conversation with Michael Toms* (1988). Thoughts on the cowboy as a modern knight errant will be found in John Cawelti, *The Six-Gun Mystique* (2d ed., 1984). Simon Lays considers the lasting qualities of knighthood in "The Imitation of Our Lord Don Quixote," *New York Review of Books,* June 11, 1998.

In addition to the Robin Hood movies cited in the text, earlier examples include Errol Flynn's well-reviewed *The Adventurers of Robin Hood* (1938), and Disney's well-crafted *The Story of Robin Hood and His Merrie Men* (1952), starring Richard Todd. The political machinations of the medieval court are delineated in *The Lion in Winter* (1968), starring Peter O'Toole as Henry II of England and Katharine Hepburn as his strong-minded wife, Eleanor of Aquitaine. O'Toole played Henry earlier in *Becket,* the 1964 film adaptation of Jean Anouilh's 1960 play about the murder of Archbishop Thomas à Becket, played by Richard Burton. Although the piece invents a fanciful Norman versus Saxon plot to explain the antagonism between king and prelate, it does suggest the important secular political role of the medieval church.

An early and often overlooked film depiction of medieval warfare is Sergei Eisenstein's *Alexander Nevsky* (1938). Based on Russian prince Alexander Nevsky's 1242 defeat of invading Teutonic Knights, the movie contains one of the most spectacular medieval battle scenes ever filmed, the struggle on the ice of Lake Peipus. During the fight, the Germans form a defensive wedge, perhaps the only screen attempt to recreate this medieval tactical formation, which was probably used by the Earl of Oxford to break up Norfolk's advance at Bosworth in 1485.

Suggesting that interpreters of history have their own agendas in reverting to past events, Eistenstein clearly used the 1242 invasion to warn his fellow Russians of the threat of an attack on the homeland by Adolf Hitler. Making the point absolutely clear, he had the Teutonic foot soldiers wear an adaptation of the modern German steel helmet, the famous "coal scuttle" invented for the trench warfare of World War I. Suggesting that there is not much new under the sun, George Lucas then took the design for the headpiece of Darth Vader, and, of course, called his forces "storm troopers," a term of German derivation from the First World War.

Chapter 2: Brutal Soldiery

Excellent studies of paramilitary groups are Kenneth S. Stern, *A Force upon the Plain: The American Militia Movement and the Politics of Hate* (1997), James William Gibson, *Warrior Dreams: Paramilitary Culture in Post-Vietnam America* (1994), and James Ridgeway, *Blood in the Face: The Ku Klux Klan, Aryan Nations, Nazis, Skinheads and the Rise of a New White Culture* (2d ed., 1995). The Southern Poverty Law Center publishes the quarterly *Intelligence Report* on the activities of radical groups, along with occasional publications such as *False Patriots: The Threat of Anti-Government Extremists* (1996). Excellent material on distrust of government earlier in American history will be found in Richard Hofstadter, *The Paranoid Style in American Politics and Other Essays* (1967), and Carl Bakal, *The Right to Bear Arms* (1966). Bakal is also good on the legal history of the Second Amendment. See also, Robert J. Cottrol, ed., *Gun Control and the Constitution: Sources and Explorations on the Second Amendment* (1994).

The age of the mercenary and the misery of Renaissance warfare are depicted in Elizabeth Hallam, ed., *The Wars of the Roses* (1988), A.L. Rowse, *The Expansion of Elizabethan England* (1972), and C.V. Wedgwood, *The Thirty Years War* (1938). Alden T. Vaughan, *American Genesis: Captain John Smith and the Founding of Virginia* (1975), is a good example of a successful English mercenary captain. The mix of religion, politics, and military force that characterized public policy in the sixteenth and seventeenth centuries is delineated in Richard S. Dunn, *The Age of Religious Wars, 1559–1689* (1970), which includes the parliamentary struggles of the early Stuarts. *The Last Valley* (1970), starring Michael Caine and Omar Sharif, is a stark screen evocation of the destruction caused by mercenary warfare.

C.V. Wedgwood, *The Life of Cromwell* (1966), is an excellent short biography, but Christopher Hill, *God's Englishman: Oliver Cromwell and the English Revolution* (1970), is crucial for understanding Puritan ideology and its impact on military thinking. C.H. Firth, *Cromwell's Army* (1902), although old, is a sound basic study of the Parliamentary military establishment. Ronald Hutton, *The Royalist War Effort, 1642–1646* (1982), sees the war from the other side. A clear account of Naseby is given in Austin Woolrych, *Battles of the English Civil War: Marston Moor, Naseby, Preston* (1961). The movie *Cromwell* (1970), featuring Richard Harris, suggests the atmosphere of the period, but is eulogistic in viewpoint.

Alan Simpson, *Puritanism in Old and New England* (1955), does the important work of bridging the Atlantic. William Bradford, *Of Plymouth Plantation, 1602–1647* (ed. Samuel Eliot Morison, 1952), and Cotton Mather's 1702, *Magnalia Christi Americana, or, The Ecclesiastical History of New England* (ed. Richard J. Cunningham, 1970), give firsthand insight into Puritan attitudes to war and the Native American enemy. Jill Lepore, *The Name of War: King Philip's War and the Origins of American Identity* (1998), is a perceptive if controversial recent analysis. Edmund S. Morgan, *The Puritan Dilemma: The Story of John Winthrop* (1958), gives a sympathetic views of the challenges facing Puritan leadership. Carol F. Karlsen, *The Devil in the Shape of a Woman: Witchcraft in Colonial New England* (1987), emphasizes the repressive nature of the Puritan regime. On the persistence of regionalism, see William R. Taylor, *Cavalier and Yankee: The Old South and American National Character* (1961), and Rollin G. Osterweis, *Romanticism and Nationalism in the Old South* (1949).

Many people are probably most familiar with the Jacobite cause through Robert Louis Stevenson's 1886 adventure novel *Kidnapped,* about young David Balfour and Alan Breck, agent of the Stuart king across the water in France. The story has been filmed four times, notably by Disney in 1960 and in 1995 with Francis Ford Coppola as co-producer. The actual history of the later Stuarts and their military exploits is delineated in Daniel Szechi, *The Jacobites, Britain and Europe, 1688–1788* (1994). Charles is portrayed in Frank McLynn, *Charles Edward Stuart: A Tragedy in Many Acts* (1991), and David Daiches, *The Last Stuart: The Life and Times of Bonnie Prince Charlie* (1973).

The definitive study of Culloden is the 1967 book of that name by John Prebble, part of a trilogy with *Glencoe* and *The Highland Clearances.* In 1964 Peter Watkins made the stark docudrama *Culloden,* which probably contains the most accurate depiction of eighteenth-century warfare ever filmed and brought the battle to an international audience. On the romanticization of the defeated clans see Robert Clyde, *From*

Rebel to Hero: The Image of the Highlander, 1745–1830 (1995). Nice film portraits of the redcoat as rogue appear in *Tom Jones* (1963), with Albert Finney, based on Henry Fielding's 1749 novel; and Stanley Kubrick's *Barry Lyndon* (1975), starring Ryan O'Neal and adapted from William Makepeace Thackeray's 1844 work.

Staughton Lynd, *Intellectual Origins of American Radicalism* (1969), and Kevin Phillips, *The Cousins' Wars: Religion, Politics, and the Triumph of Anglo-America* (1999), examine how the colonists carried on English parliamentary attitudes to central power and the role of the soldiery. Bacon's Rebellion saw the earliest colonial use of redcoats in their police role; see Wilcomb E. Washburn, *The Governor and the Rebel: A History of Bacon's Rebellion in Virginia* (1957). The part played by military affairs in bringing on the Revolution is analyzed in Douglas Edward Leach, *Roots of Conflict: British Armed Forces and Colonial Americans, 1677–1763* (1986), while acts of resistance are described in Hiller B. Zobel, *The Boston Massacre* (1970), and Benjamin Woods Labaree, *The Boston Tea Party* (1966). See also John C. Miller, *Sam Adams: Pioneer in Propaganda* (1936), and Esther Forbes, *Paul Revere and the World He Lived In* (1942).

The events on Lexington Green are carefully reconstructed in David Hackett Fischer, *Paul Revere's Ride* (1994). Robert A. Gross, *The Minutemen and Their World* (1976), is also helpful. The myth that the militia were simply private citizens of a like mind is demolished in John R. Galvin, *The Minute Men: The First Fight* (2d ed., 1989). Continuing American fears of the professional soldier as a potential tyrant are found in James Kirby Martin, *Benedict Arnold, Revolutionary Hero: An American Warrior Reconsidered* (1997). The Revolution as a stimulus for later rhetorical appeals to violence is suggested in Richard Maxwell Brown, "Violence and the American Revolution," in Stephen G. Kurtz and James H. Huston, eds., *Essays on the American Revolution* (1973).

Oscar Handlin notes the Founding Fathers' failure to be clear in writing the Bill of Rights in *The American Scholar* 62:2 (Spring 1993). Walter Millis expertly traces the structural history of the American military, including the militia and the National Guard, in *Arms and Men: A Study in American Military History* (1956). Also good is Russell F. Weigley, *History of the United States Army* (1967). Mark V. Kwasny, *Washington's Partisan War, 1775–1783* (1996), details Washington's views on the military establishment and the proper organization of the militia. Thomas P.

Slaughter, *The Whiskey Rebellion: Frontier Epilogue to the American Rebellion* (1986), is an example of the suppression of a minority claiming the right to bear arms against the central state.

Chapter 3: New Men with Rifles

Good introductory studies of the British regular are A.J. Barker, *Redcoats: The British Soldier in America* (1976), and H.C.B. Rogers, *The British Army of the Eighteenth Century* (1977). The disastrous 1755 campaign is covered in Charles Hamilton, ed. *Braddock's Defeat* (1959), and Paul E. Kopperman, *Braddock at the Monongahela* (1977). John K. Mahon, "Anglo-American Methods of Indian Warfare, 1676–1794," *Mississippi Valley Historical Review* 45:2 (1958), suggests the importance of the bayonet. On the regulars' ability to cope with foreign environments, see Daniel J. Beattie, "The Adaptation of the British Army to Wilderness Warfare, 1755–1763," in Maarten Ultee, ed., *Adapting to Conditions: War and Society in the Eighteenth Century* (1986).

A retired French soldier, St. John de Crèvecoeur, was among the first to talk about the American as a New Man in *Letters From an American Farmer,* published in 1782 and reprinted many times. Also important in studying the myth of the American in an unspoiled natural environment is Henry Nash Smith, *Virgin Land: The American West as Symbol and Myth* (1950). Richard Slotkin considers the attitudes to war and death of the New Man in *Regeneration through Violence: The Mythology of the American Frontier, 1600–1860* (1973).

General studies of colonial Americans at war include John E. Ferling, *A Wilderness of Miseries: War and Warriors in Early America* (1980), and John Morgan Dederer, *War in America to 1775: Before Yankee Doodle* (1990). The character of the provincial soldier is analyzed in Fred Anderson, *A People's Army: Massachusetts Soldiers and Society in the Seven Years' War* (1984). Michael A. Bellesiles, in *Arming America: The Origins of a National Gun Culture* (2000), sides with British regulars in depicting the colonial military as rather inept and very badly armed. Although Bellesiles' makes a persuasive case that America did not have a developed gun culture before the Civil War, he overstates his case regarding the Colonial period. Massachusetts, for example, could put over 20,000 armed men in the field in 1775.

Don Higginbotham, *War and Society in Revolutionary America*

(1988) is a good overview of the war period. The importance of the Continental regular in winning independence is demonstrated in James Kirby Martin and Mark Edward Lender, *A Respectable Army: The Military Origins of the Republic, 1763–1789* (1982). Useful essays will also be found in John Shy, *A People Numerous and Armed: Reflections on the Military Struggle for American Independence* (1976). Recent movies include *The Crossing*, a 2000 Arts and Entertainment presentation, with a teleplay by Howard Fast starring Jeff Daniels as a believable Gen. George Washington. The film gives a good idea of the difficulty Washington faced in fighting with an army made up largely of militia and how he used this to advantage at Trenton. Although the battle scenes are not entirely realistic, the movie achieves historical accuracy and dramatic appeal. *The Patriot,* another 2000 offering, starring Mel Gibson, distorts history liberally. The negative image of the redcoat as an unfeeling brute is taken to an unreasonable level with atrocities like the burning of civilians in a church, and the film purveys the stereotype that only Patriot militia could fight in the American environment.

The disappointing American military situation immediately preceding Andrew Jackson's victory at New Orleans is covered in Anthony S. Pitch, *The Burning of Washington: The British Invasion of 1814* (1998). Paddy Griffith has an excellent analysis of the two armies and their strategies at New Orleans in *Forward into Battle: Fighting Tactics from Waterloo to the Near Future* (2d ed., 1990). The importance of the victory for American myth is deftly demonstrated in John William Ward, *Andrew Jackson, Symbol for an Age* (1955). Robert V. Remini also studies the battle's national implications in *The Battle of New Orleans: Andrew Jackson and America's First Military Victory* (1999). Remini's earlier work, *The Election of Andrew Jackson* (1963), splendidly evokes the changes in public manners and political style brought about by the common man revolution. The French visitor Alexis de Tocqueville was among the first to see the revolutionary nature of the changes wrought in Jackson's era: *Democracy in America* (2 vols., 1835 and 1840), available in various reprints.

The often strained relations between American regulars and amateur soldiers during the early national period are delineated in Marcus Cunliffe, *Soldiers and Civilians: The Martial Spirit in America, 1775–1865* (1968). Stephen E. Ambrose considers attacks on West Point during the Jacksonian era in *Duty, Honor, Country: A History of West Point*

(1966). See also, James L. Morrison Jr., *"The Best School in the World":
West Point, the Pre-Civil War Years, 1833–1866* (1986).

Walter Lord's *A Time to Stand* (1961) is an older but still valuable
study of the Alamo. Good recent histories of the 1835–1836 campaigns
include Jeff Long's provocative *Duel of Eagles: The Mexican and U.S.
Fight for the Alamo* (1990), and Stephen L. Hardin, *Texian Iliad: A
Military History of the Texas Revolution, 1835–1836* (1994). William
C. Davis's biographical study of James Bowie, David Crockett, and William B. Travis, *Three Roads to the Alamo* (1998), is ponderous but worthwhile. James A. Shackford, *David Crockett: The Man and the Legend*
(1956), remains a standard treatment.

Leonard Mosley covers *Disney's World* (1985). Also good on the
1955 Crockett phenomenon is Steven D. Stark, *Glued to the Set: The 60
Television Shows and Events That Made Us Who We Are Today* (1997).
Garry Wills analyzes Wayne's philosophy and goals in *John Wayne's
America* (1998). There is a lot of useful information about the 1960
movie production in Donald Clark and Christopher Anderson, *John
Wayne's The Alamo: The Making of the Epic Film* (1995). The symbol-
ism of the chapel fortress is examined in Susan Schoelwer's *Alamo Im-
ages: Changing Perceptions of a Texas Experience* (1985). The Alamo
Society publishes *The Alamo Journal,* which contains much interesting
Alamo imagery, and the Daughters of the Republic of Texas maintain an
Alamo library and website at the shrine.

Chapter 4: Unlikely Heroes

Entertaining introductions to the British Victorian army are Byron
Farwell's *Mr. Kipling's Army* (1981) and *Eminent Victorian Soldiers:
Seekers of Glory* (1985). A.J. Barker, *The Vainglorious War, 1854–1856*
(1970), and Philip Warner, *The Crimean War: A Reappraisal* (1973), are
useful surveys of the Crimean War. A sound study of the Battle of Balaclava
is John Selby, *The Thin Red Line of Balaclava* (1970). The classic interpretation of why the Charge of the Light Brigade occurred, emphasizing
the personalities involved, is Cecil Woodham-Smith, *The Reason Why*
(1953); the book was the basis for the 1968 movie. John Harris challenged the traditional interpretation of Nolan's action in *The Gallant Six
Hundred: A Tragedy of Obsessions* (1973), arguing that Nolan deliberately pointed to the wrong guns to instigate a charge aimed at proving

his thesis that light cavalry, unsupported by artillery or infantry, could successfully attack a fortified position. *Henry Clifford, V.C.: His Letters and Sketches from the Crimea* (1956) gives an unromanticized picture of the suffering of the soldiers. The war in pictures is shown in Helmut and Alison Gernsheim, *Roger Fenton, Photographer of the Crimean War: His Photographs and Letters from Crimea* (1954). The best biography of Florence Nightingale is Cecil Woodham-Smith, *Florence Nightingale, 1820–1910* (1950).

Jim Cullen, *The Civil War in Popular Culture: A Reusable Past* (1995), has some stimulating observations on the enormous interest in the Civil War. Kent Gramm, *Gettysburg: A Meditation on War and Values* (1994), looks at tourism and American attitudes to the battlefield. Carol Reardon, *Pickett's Charge in History and Memory* (1997), charts the mythic version of Gettysburg. *Gettysburg,* which played at movie theaters in 1993 and was shown on TNT as an expanded, six-hour miniseries in 1994, is generally faithful to Michael Shaara's *The Killer Angels* (1974). Martin Sheen captures the book's version of Robert E. Lee, but Tom Berenger is uncomfortable as James Longstreet, perhaps because of an ill-fitting false beard. The movie's highlights are the defense of Little Round Top by Joshua Chamberlain, played superbly by Jeff Daniels, and the anguish of Gen. Lewis Armistead, played by Richard Jordan, on having to face his old West Point friend, Winfield Scott Hancock, across the lines on Cemetery Ridge. Obviously well-fed reenactors do not convincingly suggest Lee's lean and hungry wolves.

George M. Fredrickson, *The Inner Civil War: Northern Intellectuals and the Crisis of the Union* (1965), looks at the climate of ideas among the Union's leading thinkers. Fredrickson is insightful on both Shaw and Holmes. The tart and perceptive observations of George Templeton Strong are recorded in his *Diary of the Civil War 1850–1865,* ed. Allan Nevins (1962). Also revealing is Mason Wade, ed., *The Journals of Francis Parkman,* 2 vols. (1947). How the public were able to view the conflict through the media is covered in Bob Zeller, *The Civil War in Depth: History in 3-D* (1997), and W. Fletcher Thompson Jr., *The Image of War: The Pictorial Reporting of the American Civil War* (1960). On the reality of fighting, see John Talbott, "Combat Trauma in the American Civil War," *History Today* (March 1996), and Earl J. Hess, *The Union Soldier in Battle: Enduring the Ordeal of Combat* (1997). Stephen W. Sears, *Landscape Turned Red: The Battle of Antietam* (1983), suggests the enormous psychological damage done by just one battle. Peter Svenson, *Battlefield: Farming a Civil War Battleground* (1992), vividly depicts the war as a charnel house. Charles Royster, *The Destructive War: William Tecumseh Sherman, Stonewall Jackson, and the Americans* (1991), looks at the issue of fighting a hard war.

Examples of medical histories include Stewart Brooks, *Civil War Medicine* (1966), and George Worthington Adams, *Doctors in Blue: The Medical History of the Union Army in the Civil War* (1952). Alfred Jay Bollet, *Civil War Medicine: Challenges and Triumphs* (2002), was published too late to be of use, but is a valuable study. The author's thesis is clear from the title. John H. Brinton, *Personal Memoirs of John H. Brinton: Civil War Surgeon, 1861–1865* (1996), and Louisa May Alcott, *Hospital Sketches* (1863; repr. 1993), give individual views. Thomas P. Lowry, *The Story the Soldiers Wouldn't Tell: Sex in the Civil War* (1994), integrates the issues of medicine and sexuality. Catherine Clinton and Nina Silber, eds., consider women's roles in *Divided Houses: Gender and the Civil War* (1992). On the plight of war widows, note Cindy S. Aron, "'To Barter Their Souls for Gold': Female Clerks in Federal Government Offices, 1862–1890," *Journal of American History* 67 (March 1981). The distress of Confederate women is discussed in Bell Irvin Wiley, *Confederate Women* (1975). An individual example is Earl Schenck Miers, ed., *When the World Ended: The Diary of Emma LeConte* (1957; repr. 1987). The perceptive Mary Boykin Chesnut is revealed in C. Vann Woodward and Elisabeth Muhlenfeld, *The Private Mary Chesnut: The Unpublished Civil War Diaries* (1984).

The purpose of John Brown's raid is made clear in Barrie Stavis, *John Brown: The Sword and the Word* (1970). General histories of persons of color in America's wars include Jack D. Foner, *Blacks and the Military in American History: A New Perspective* (1974), along with Jay David and Elaine Crane, eds., *The Black Soldier: From the American Revolution to Vietnam* (1971). A reliable history of the colored regiments is Joseph T. Glatthaar, *Forged in Battle: The Civil War Alliance of Black Soldiers and White Officers* (1990). James W. Geary, *We Need Men: The Union Draft in the Civil War* (1991), deals with the mixed motives behind the raising of the black regiments.

Peter Burchard, *One Gallant Rush: Robert Gould Shaw and His Brave Black Regiment* (1965), is a good short biography. Shaw's letters have been published in Russell Duncan, ed., *Blue-Eyed Child of Fortune*

(1992). An example of the remarkable literacy in the ranks of the Fifty-fourth is Virginia M. Adams, ed., *On the Altar of Freedom: A Black Soldier's Civil War Letters from the Front* (1991), the writings of Cpl. James Henry Gooding. Albert Boime, *The Art of Exclusion: Representing Blacks in the Nineteenth Century* (1990), suggests how unusual was Saint-Gaudens' sculpture in memorializing blacks and thus how the monument helped to keep the Fifty-fourth's story from totally disappearing. On the detailed history of the Shaw monument itself, see Lincoln Kirstein, *Lay This Laurel* (1973).

The colonel of the First South Carolina is ably profiled in Tilden G. Edelstein, *Strange Enthusiasm: A Life of Thomas Wentworth Higginson* (1968). Susie King Taylor was a nurse and teacher in the First; see her *A Black Woman's Civil War Memoirs* (1902; ed. by Patricia W. Romero and repr. 1988). Ray Allen Billington, ed., *The Journal of Charlotte L. Forten* (1953), details one perceptive woman's involvement in the Port Royal Experiment. Clara Barton, the leading nurse, who served in the Sea Islands and knew Shaw well, is biographied by Stephen B. Oates in *A Woman of Valor: Clara Barton and the Civil War* (1994). American fear of communistic experiments during Reconstruction was partly generated by the events in France that are narrated in Alistair Horne, *The Fall of Paris: The Siege and the Commune 1870–71* (1965). On black reenactors see *The True Story of* Glory *Continues,* a 1991 documentary.

Chapter 5: Bearers of Burdens

Charles M. Robinson III, *A Good Year to Die: The Story of the Great Sioux War* (1995), is a balanced account of the 1876 campaigns. Native American views of the Custer battle include Gregory F. Michno, *Lakota Noon: The Indian Narrative of Custer's Defeat* (1997), R.G. Hardorff, ed., *Lakota Recollections of the Custer Fight: New Sources of Indian Military History* (1991), and David Humphreys Miller, *Custer's Fall: The Indian Side of the Story* (1957; repr. 1992). Dee Brown's *Bury My Heart at Wounded Knee: An Indian History of the American West* (1970), while still a good read, clearly mirrors the anti-white bias of much 1960s material. On recent issues regarding the battlefield park, see Robert Paul Jordan, "Ghosts on the Little Bighorn," *National Geographic* 170 (December 1986).

The soldiers of the regular U.S. army are described in Edward M. Coffman, *The Old Army: A Portrait of the American Army in Peacetime, 1784–1898* (1986). Insights into why Crook did not become a public idol will be found in John G. Bourke, *On the Border with Crook* (1891; repr. 1971). There have been many biographies of Custer. An even-handed recent treatment is Jeffry D. Wert, *Custer: The Controversial Life of George Armstrong Custer* (1996). Earlier and provocative interpretations include Evan S. Connell, *Son of the Morning Star* (1984), Charles K. Hofling, *Custer and the Little Big Horn: A Psychobiographical Inquiry* (1981), and W.A. Graham, *The Custer Myth* (1953). The general's symbolic role is explored in Bruce A. Rosenberg, *Custer and the Epic of Defeat* (1974), along with Michael Anglo, *Custer: Man and Myth* (1976). For the representation of the Little Bighorn in art, see Don Russell, *Custer's Last* (1968), and Harrison Lane, "Brush-Palette and the Little Big Horn," *Montana: The Magazine of Western History* 23 (Summer 1973).

Shirley A. Leckie explores Elizabeth's role in building her husband's legend in *Elizabeth Bacon Custer and the Making of a Myth* (1993). Libbie's publications included *Following the Guidon* (1890) as well as her 1885 *Boots and Saddles: or, Life in Dakota with General Custer.* Richard Slotkin examines other promoters of the Custer myth, especially Buffalo Bill Cody, in *Gunfighter Nation: The Myth of the Frontier in Twentieth-Century America* (1992). Important studies of Whitman's social views include Leadie M. Clark, *Walt Whitman's Concept of the American Common Man* (1955), Betsy Erkkila, *Whitman the Political Poet* (1989), and Ed Folsom, *Walt Whitman's Native Representations* (1994). Esther Shephard considered the Whitman persona in *Walt Whitman's Pose* (1938).

The ability to market one's image through the scientific marvel of photography is noted in William C. Darrah, *Cartes de Visite in Nineteenth Century Photography* (1981). Neil Postman, *Amusing Ourselves to Death: Public Discourse in the Age of Show Business* (1985), charts our difficulty in understanding and coping successfully with one important technological advance, television. The British struggle to master the dynamics of the new military technology during their 1879 South African campaign is described in Donald R. Morris, *The Washing of the Spears: The History of the Rise of the Zulu Nation* (1965). Ian Knight, in *Anatomy of the Zulu Army* (1999), reminds us correctly that the Zulus' partial success was due also to their military strategies.

General histories of the Spanish-American War include David F. Trask, *The War with Spain in 1898* (1981), and Walter Millis, *The Martial Spirit* (1931; repr. 1989). Frank Burt Freidel, *The Splendid Little War* (1958), unites a sprightly text with excellent pictures. Naval transition is dealt with in Robert L. O'Connell, *Sacred Vessels: The Cult of the Battleship and the Rise of the U.S. Navy* (1991). Contemporary awe of the steel ships is analyzed in David Axeen "'Heroes of the Engine Room': American Civilization and the War with Spain," *American Quarterly* 36:4 (Fall 1984). The impact of changing military technology on land is charted in John Ellis, *The Social History of the Machine Gun* (1975). George Bernard Shaw's *Arms and the Man,* staged in London in 1894 and published in *Plays Pleasant* in 1898, is an enjoyable parody of heroic antics in the age of the machine gun.

The cultural impetus to war is analyzed in Gerald F. Linderman, *The Mirror of War: American Society and the Spanish-American War* (1974). On war as an invigorating masculine endeavor, see Kristin L. Hoganson, *Fighting for American Manhood: How Gender Politics Provoked the Spanish-American and Philippine-American Wars* (1998). An example of a soldier who believed deeply in the Social Darwinian struggle for survival is Homer Lea, whose ideas were set out in *The Valor of Ignorance* (1909) and *The Day of the Saxon* (1912). The impact of the closing of the frontier and the yearning for continued western-style adventures is covered in Lawrence R. Borne, *Dude Ranching: A Complete History* (1983). In addition to TR's 1899 *The Rough Riders,* his ideas on the life of action will be found in his book *The Strenuous Life: Essays and Addresses* (1902), and Joseph Bucklin Bishop, ed., *Theodore Roosevelt's Letters to His Children* (1964). Dixon Wecter, *The Hero in America* (1963), has an incisive essay on TR as a popular symbol. Early interpreters of the war, in addition to Roosevelt, are covered in Charles H. Brown, *The Correspondents' War: Journalists in the Spanish-American War* (1967). Richard Harding Davis was a leading popular writer, although his work is no longer known. See his *The Cuban and Porto Rican Campaigns* (1898).

Among the relatively few attempts to look in-depth at the more disturbing aspects of the struggle are Leon Wolff, *Little Brown Brother: America's Forgotten Bid for Empire Which Cost 250,00 Lives* (1961), which documents American racial condescension and the appalling loss of Filipino life in the U.S.-Filipino War. Louis A. Pérez Jr., *The War of*

1898: The United States and Cuba in History and Historiography (1998), takes a hard look at the vexed relationship of the two countries arising from the war and finds that the U.S. has made little effort to understand the conflict in anything other than patriotic terms.

There has been little good film dealing with military events in the period. *55 Days at Peking* (1963), starring Charlton Heston as a rugged U.S. major of marines and David Niven as a cool British diplomat, is an action movie set against the background of the Chinese Boxer Rebellion of 1900. The film is ethnocentric and makes little attempt to understand the native resentment of the imperialist presence. TNT's 1997 *Buffalo Soldiers,* starring Danny Glover, is the network's apology for its treatment of the black soldier in *Rough Riders.* The movie is a well-told tale about the campaign to track down the Apache warrior Vittorio, but the movie plays fast and loose with the facts. *Sergeant Rutledge* (1960), an earlier and often-overlooked piece directed by John Ford and starring Woody Strode, is a strong courtroom drama that brings out the continuing prejudice against the black trooper, in this case a sergeant charged with rape and murder. A good history of the black regiments is William H. Leckie, *The Buffalo Soldiers: A Narrative of the Negro Cavalry in the West* (1967).

The British experience in 1898 is detailed in Philip Ziegler, *Omdurman* (1974). The more difficult South African War is covered in Thomas Pakenham, *The Boer War* (1979). *Young Winston,* a 1972 movie by Richard Attenborough and starring Simon Ward, captures the strenuous life of the early Churchill and gives the visual atmosphere of the period, but it stays too close to Churchill's writings, particularly his 1930 *My Early Life: A Roving Commission* (the American edition is titled *A Roving Commission: My Early Life*), to achieve broad insight.

Chapter 6: Innocents at War

The many worthwhile introductions to World War I include A.J.P. Taylor, *The First World War: An Illustrated History* (1972), Cyril Falls, *The Great War* (1959), and Keith Robbins, *The First World War* (1985). On the daily experience of combat, see John Ellis, *Eye-Deep in Hell: Trench Warfare in World War I* (1976). Also, Denis Winter, *Death's Men: Soldiers of the Great War* (1978). On romantic images of war, popular in

Britain and the U.S. during the Great War, see Michael C.C. Adams, *The Great Adventure: Male Desire and the Coming of World War I* (1990). Anita Leslie examines reactions by British civilians, in particular the class that produced the officer corps, to the killing in *The Marlborough House Set* (1972). The key 1916 British offensive is recreated in Martin Middlebrook, *The First Day on the Somme: 1 July 1916* (1972). James D. Atwater has interesting eyewitness accounts in "Survivors of the Somme," *Smithsonian* 18:8 (November 1987).

American participation in the war is covered in Edward M. Coffman, *The War to End All Wars: The American Military Experience of World War I* (1968; repr. 1998), and Meirion and Susie Harries, *The Last Days of Innocence: America at War 1917–1918* (1997). David M. Kennedy looks at the war in relation to American culture in *Over Here: The First World War and American Society* (1980). Eddie V. Rickenbacker, *Fighting the Flying Circus* (1967), is a revealing American memoir. See also Bert Hall and John Jacob Niles, *One Man's War* (1980), and James Norman Hall, *High Adventure* (1980). Kenneth S. Lynn critiques Ernest Hemingway's war experience in *Hemingway: The Life and the Work* (1987).

On retrospective attitudes to the war, see Stanley Weintraub, *A Stillness Heard round the World: The End of the Great War, November 1918* (1985). The indispensable guide to the literary history of the war is Paul Fussell, *The Great War and Modern Memory* (1975). In addition to the Lost Generation authors mentioned in the text, note C. Day Lewis, ed., *The Collected Poems of Wilfred Owen* (1963), and Candace Ward, *World War One British Poets: Brooke, Owen, Sassoon, Rosenberg, and Others* (1997). To see how close in theme and tone the Great War writers are to Vietnam War veterans, compare with Lynda Van Devanter and Joan A. Furey, eds., *Visions of War, Dreams of Peace: Writings of Women in the Vietnam War* (1991).

On Irish attitudes, see Margery Forester, *Michael Collins: The Lost Leader* (1971), and Michael O'Suilleabhain, *Where Mountainy Men Have Sown* (1965). In addition to Vera Brittain's 1933 memoir, *Testament of Youth* (repr. 1994), her original war diary has been published as *Chronicle of Youth* (1982). Hilary Bailey, *Vera Brittain* (1987), is a good short account of her life. Patty Lou Floyd analyzes audience reaction to the successful television series in *Backstairs with "Upstairs, Downstairs"* (1988).

On American 1960s disillusion, see Tom Engelhardt, *The End of Victory Culture: Cold War America and the Disillusioning of a Generation* (1995).

For more detail on the making of the "Good War" myth of World War II, see Michael C.C. Adams, *The Best War Ever: America and World War II* (1994), and Paul Fussell, *Wartime: Understanding and Behavior in the Second World War* (1989). Studs Terkel's interviews demonstrate the complex reality of the World War II experience in *"The Good War": An Oral History of World War Two* (1985). The grinding nature of combat is the theme of John Ellis, *Brute Force: Allied Strategy and Tactics in the Second World War* (1990). The movie *The Bridge at Remagen* (1969) captures this aspect of the fighting. Gerald F. Linderman, *The World within War: America's Combat Experience in World War II* (1997), contains good eyewitness material. On-the-spot analysis of men in combat was provided by U.S. Army investigative teams whose conclusions were published in Samuel A. Stouffer, et al., *The American Soldier* (2 vols, 1949; repr. 1965).

The lingering emotional trauma caused by combat was analyzed in Robert J. Havighurst, et al., *The American Veteran Back Home: A Study of Veteran Readjustment* (1951), and Eli Ginzberg, et al., *The Ineffective Soldier: Lessons for Management and the Nation* (3 vols., 1959). *Maria's Lovers* (1984) is one of the few commercial movies to deal with lingering combat trauma after the war. *The Execution of Private Slovik* (1974), starring Martin Sheen as a young soldier shot for cowardice, looks at one case of emotional breakdown in war.

Allan M. Winkler has a good domestic survey, *Home Front U.S.A.: America during World War II* (2d ed. 2000). Also insightful are John Morton Blum, *V Was for Victory: Politics and American Culture During World War II* (1976), and Richard R. Lingeman, *Don't You Know There's a War On? The American Home Front 1941–1945* (1968). Specific educational deficiencies were examined in Edward A. Strecker, *Their Mothers' Sons: The Psychiatrist Examines an American Problem* (1946), and David L. Cohn, "Should Fighting Men Think?" *The Saturday Review of Literature*, January 18, 1947. Racial problems are discussed in Neil A. Wynn, *The Afro-American and the Second World War* (1976). A specific violent incident is described in Domenic J. Capeci and Martha Wilkerson, *Layered Violence: The Detroit Rioters of 1943* (1991). Graham Smith looks at the segregation of U.S. forces overseas in *When Jim*

Crow Met John Bull: Black American Soldiers in World War II Britain (1987). Although it deals with Japanese American rather than African American issues, *Come See the Paradise* (1990) is a perceptive cinema view of race in the era.

On the making of the acclaimed movie, see Linda Sunshine, ed., *Saving Private Ryan: The Men, The Mission, The Movie* (1998). Epic forerunners to the movie include *The Longest Day* (1962) about D-Day, and *Patton* (1970) about the famous tank general. *A Bridge Too Far* (1977), about Gen. Bernard Montgomery's failed post D-Day operation, Market Garden, straddles the distance between the epic and a more critical genre of war films, such as Carl Foreman's bleakly ironic 1963 offering, *The Victors*. The context of patriotic rhetoric within which the discussion of World War II often takes place is analyzed in Edward T. Linenthal and Tom Engelhardt, eds., *History Wars: The Enola Gay and Other Battles for the American Past* (1996). Good examples of the complex analysis that took place between the world wars, in the aftermath of a so-called bad war, as opposed to the celebratory tone of "Good War" pieces, are Edith Abbott, "The Civil War and the Crime Wave of 1865–70," *Social Science Review* 1 (1927), and Betty Rosenbaum, "The Relationship Between War and Crime in the U.S.," *Journal of Criminal Law and Criminality* 30 (1940). *Citizen Soldiers: The U.S. Army from the Normandy Beaches . . . to the Surrender of Germany* (1997) and *Americans at War* (1997) are good examples of Stephen E. Ambrose's recent work.

War psychosis or rage against the enemy, which troubled writers and participants like Kurt Vonnegut, is the basis for the charge by Canadian author James Bacque that German POWs were abused by the Allies: *Other Losses: An Investigation into the Mass Deaths of German Prisoners at the Hands of the French and Americans after World War II* (1989). Peter Schrijvers, *The Crash of Ruin: American Combat Soldiers in Europe during World War II* (1998), looks at how GIs became calloused to civilian suffering in Europe. John Dower, *War without Mercy: Race and Power in the Pacific War* (1986), charts mutual rage and atrocity in the Pacific Theater.

The growing importance of American air power in World War II and its destructive capacity are examined in Ronald Schaffer, *Wings of Judgment: American Bombing in World War II* (1985), and Michael S. Sherry, *The Rise of American Air Power: The Creation of Armageddon* (1987).

Martin J. Sherwin, *A World Destroyed* (1975), discusses the history and meaning of the atom bombs. Robert A. Pape brings the story of strategic bombing to the eve of the twenty-first century in *Bombing to Win: Air Power and Coercion in War* (1996). Pape is excellent on why bombing strategies alone usually fail to produce lasting solutions to international conflicts. The error in believing that we can rely on technology alone for military solutions, particularly via the air, is also pointed out in H. Bruce Franklin, *War Stars: The Superweapon and the American Imagination* (1988). The distinct American aversion to long wars and overseas ground involvement is pointed out in Eric V. Larson, *Casualties and Consensus: The Historical Role of Casualties in Domestic Support for U.S. Military Operations* (1996). John Tirman, ed., *The Fallacy of Star Wars* (1984), punctures the dream of achieving ultimate invulnerability through control of the heavens using current technology.

Dave Grossman, *On Killing: The Psychological Cost of Learning to Kill in War and Society* (1995), describes Cold War military changes in arms training. George C. Herring, *America's Longest War: The United States and Vietnam, 1950–1975* (4th ed. 2000), is a readable and insightful introduction to the conflict. Edward Doyle, Stephen Weiss, et al., *A Collision of Cultures* (1984), deals with the problem of mutual incomprehension. *Go Tell the Spartans* (1978), one of the best movies about the war, stars Burt Lancaster as an early-war officer with doubts about the viability of America's mission. Michael J. Arlen, *Living-Room War* (1969), refutes the myth that the war was lost through negative media publicity and consequent loss of the will to fight.

The reimaging of the war is analyzed in John Hellmann, *American Myth and the Legacy of Vietnam* (1986), as well as Bill McCloud, *What Should We Tell Our Children about Vietnam?* (1989). Albert Auster and Leonard Quart, *How the War Was Remembered: Hollywood and Vietnam* (1988), deals with cinema interpretations. See also Kenneth J. Bindas and Craig Houston, "'Takin' Care of Business': Rock Music, Vietnam and the Protest Myth," *The Historian* 52 (November 1989). The enormous sense of emotional loss evoked by the war is charted in H. Bruce Franklin, *M.I.A.: Or Mythmaking in America* (1992). The movie *In Country* (1989), based on the 1985 novel by Bobbie Ann Mason, is a moving story of one girl's struggle to understand her missing father and reconcile to his loss.

S.L.A. Marshall, *Men against Fire: The Problem of Battle Command in Future War* (1947), revealed publicly the failure of GIs in World War II to fire their weapons, which led to changes in basic weapons training. Al Santoli, *Everything We Had: An Oral History of the Vietnam War* (1982), gives excellent candid interviews with veterans. Ron Kovic's searing memoir, *Born On the Fourth of July* (1976), was filmed by Oliver Stone in 1989 and starred Tom Cruise. The emotional problems encountered by Vietnam era soldiers are detailed in Jonathan Shay, *Achilles in Vietnam: Combat Trauma and the Undoing of Character* (1995). *Coming Home* (1978) is a good movie look at the war's lasting emotional impact. Eric T. Dean Jr., *Shook over Hell: Post-Traumatic Stress, Vietnam, and the Civil War* (1997), shows clearly that PTSD is not a new phenomenon. Not everyone will agree with Dean's argument that Civil War veterans showed more character than recent soldiers by not talking about their trauma.

Seymour M. Hersh, *My Lai 4: A Report on the Massacre and Its Aftermath* (1970), was one of the first comprehensive studies of the massacre. James S. Olsen and Randy Roberts, *My Lai: A Brief History with Documents* (1998), is a more recent study that follows much the same approach. Both tend to place heavy responsibility on individuals. Films that stress individual psychoses in portraying the ultra-violence of Vietnam include Francis Ford Coppola's *Apocalypse Now* (1979) and Stanley Kubrick's *Full Metal Jacket* (1987), both of which are heavily stylized in their presentation of the grunts at war. The man held most responsible for My Lai explains his actions in John Sack, *Lieutenant Calley: His Own Story* (1971). Philip Caputo testifies to the pressure brought on the ground soldiers from above to produce evidence that the war was being won, even by questionable means, in *A Rumor of War* (1977). The book was filmed nicely in 1980 with Brad Davis in the starring role.

Lawrence H. Keeley, *War before Civilization* (1996), and Susan Niditch, *War in the Hebrew Bible: A Study in the Ethics of Violence* (1993), deal with the problem of massacre and total war early in human history. See also Peter Marsh and Anne Campbell, eds., *Aggression and Violence* (1982).

On Washington's unorthodox activities in the Revolution, see Thomas Fleming, "George Washington, Spymaster," *American Heritage,*

February/March 2000. Robert Taber, *The War of the Flea: A Study of Guerilla Warfare Theory and Practice* (1970), is an excellent introduction to unconventional warfare. Note also Robert B. Asprey, *War in the Shadows: The Guerilla in History,* 2 vols, 1975. On Ireland, see William Irwin Thompson, *The Imagination of an Insurrection: Dublin, Easter 1916* (1967).

Index